# Entrepreneurship in Context

# Routledge Studies in Entrepreneurship

EDITED BY JAY MITRA *(Essex University, UK)* & ZOLTAN ACS
*(George Mason University, USA)*

This series extends the meaning and scope of entrepreneurship by capturing new research
and enquiry on economic, social, cultural and personal value creation. Entrepreneurship
as value creation represents the endeavours of innovative people and organisations
in creative environments that open up opportunities for developing new products,
new services, new firms and new forms of policy making in different environments
seeking sustainable economic growth and social development. In setting this objective
the series includes books which cover a diverse range of conceptual, empirical and
scholarly topics that both inform the field and push the boundaries of entrepreneurship.

# Entrepreneurship in Context

**Edited by Marco van Gelderen
and Enno Masurel**

Routledge
Taylor & Francis Group

NEW YORK AND LONDON

First published 2012
by Routledge
711 Third Avenue, New York, NY 10017

Simultaneously published in the UK
by Routledge
2 Park Square, Milton Park, Abingdon, Oxfordshire OX14 4RN

First issued in paperback 2016

*Routledge is an imprint of the Taylor & Francis Group,
an informa business*

Typeset in Sabon by IBT Global.
Printed and bound in the United States of America on acid-free paper by
IBT Global.

*Library of Congress Cataloging-in-Publication Data*
    Entrepreneurship in context / edited by Marco van Gelderen and Enno
Masurel. — 1st ed.
        p. cm. — (Routledge studies in entrepreneurship ; 3)
    Includes bibliographical references and index.
    1.    Entrepreneurship—Case studies.    I. Gelderen, Marco van.
    II. Masurel, Enno, 1959–
    HB615.E6236 2011
    338'.04—dc22
    2011014620

ISBN 13: 978-1-138-21271-8 (pbk)
ISBN 13: 978-0-415-89092-2 (hbk)

# Contents

## PART I
## Introduction

## PART II
## Micro-Context

## PART III
## Engaging with Context

## PART IV
## Entrepreneurship as Context

## PART V
## Wider Contextual Influences

# Figures

# Tables

# Foreword

Entrepreneurship is a fascinating phenomenon and is increasingly becoming relevant in a world in which top-down policy approaches fail. New developments are often emerging from the initiatives of entrepreneurs pursuing opportunities. One entrepreneur perhaps does not make much of a difference, but series of such entrepreneurial initiatives could drive change in particular contexts. Take for example the rise of Silicon Valley, which has been developed by high-tech entrepreneurs. These entrepreneurs did not operate in isolation; they were part of a context: the Silicon Valley business environment. This environment, or 'habitat,' is geared towards the creation of entrepreneurial ventures (Lee et al., 2000). Many have tried to copy the Silicon Valley success and many have failed to do so, largely because of a lack of understanding of the contextual dynamics. Somehow, these dynamics play a crucial role in nascent entrepreneurs' decisions to start and subsequently build a successful company.

The case of the Silicon Valley business context is only one example showing the relevance of studying entrepreneurship in context. This book offers a much broader perspective on the role of context in the study of entrepreneurship. The authors address a gap in the field as much of the entrepreneurship literature is concerned with the individual entrepreneur and his/her particular personality, ability, and background. The interrelations between entrepreneurs and contexts is the focus of this book. These contexts refer not only to the industrial-geographical nexus, as is the case with Silicon Valley, but also to personal and situational contexts and broader social, cultural, and institutional contexts. The common denominator in the book is the way entrepreneurs involve, engage with, and influence their contexts and as a result are able to discover, create, and exploit opportunities.

As head of the Department of Management and Organization of VU University Amsterdam, I am proud that the Amsterdam Center of Entrepreneurship at VU has taken the initiative to develop the idea for this book and to realize and publish it. It is a unique edited volume as it has been able to bring together different disciplines such as anthropology, psychology, economics, technology, and sociology into a common perspective to contribute to the debate on the relation between the agency of the entrepreneur and the contexts in which the entrepreneur is embedded. The result of this collective interdisciplinary journey will enrich the ambition of our university to put entrepreneurship higher on the agenda of scholars, students, and our partners in Amsterdam.

Tom Elfring
Professor of Strategic Management
Head of Department of Management and Organization
Faculty of Economics and Business Administration
VU University Amsterdam

## BIBLIOGRAPHY

Lee, C., Miller, W. F., Hancock, M. G., & H. S. Rowen (Eds.). (2000). The Silicon Valley edge; A habitat for innovation and entrepreneurship. Palo Alto, CA: Stanford University Press.

# Part I
# Introduction

# 1 Introduction to 'Entrepreneurship in Context'

*Marco van Gelderen, Karen Verduyn, and Enno Masurel*

## INTRODUCTION

This volume aims to provide insight into the role of context in the world of entrepreneurship. Even though context is a widely used and often mentioned aspect in studies of organizational and entrepreneurial life, its precise meaning and role often remain unspecified. In the current volume, we draw attention to the various meanings and roles, as well as the importance of context in entrepreneurship studies. In recent decades, a wide variety of scientific disciplines have started to pay increased attention to context. These include anthropology, archaeology, art history, geography, intellectual history, law, linguistics, literary criticism, philosophy, politics, psychology, sociology, and theology (Burke, 2002). Entrepreneurship research is no exception and, like so many other fields of science, has increasingly included the topic of context. For entrepreneurship, the importance of context goes beyond gaining understanding and avoiding mistakes. The reciprocal influence exercised by the entrepreneurial venture and its corresponding context is at the very heart of the entrepreneur as an agent of change.

This volume addresses context in a narrow sense, namely, a person's life situation and local, situational characteristics. It also deals with wider contexts such as social, industry, cultural, ethnic, sustainability-related, institutional, and historical contexts. The volume studies the interconnectedness of all these various subcontexts. It zooms in on the actions that entrepreneurs take to involve, engage, and influence their context and shows the changing and dynamic nature of context. It also provides lessons for entrepreneurs about which contextual elements should be prioritized, engaged, and sought out. For entrepreneurship, the importance of context goes beyond gaining understanding and avoiding mistakes. The reciprocal influence exercised by the entrepreneurial venture and its corresponding context is at the very heart of the entrepreneur as an agent of change.

A focus on context is the common denominator of the chapters in this volume. Each chapter looks into entrepreneurship as a context-bound phenomenon. No study presents ideas or research results as universally and timelessly valid. In addition, there are other common factors. The contributors all have some form of association with the VU University Amsterdam. Entrepreneurship research at this university takes context as a unifying theme. Another feature is that all of the authors were urged to produce texts that are transparent and accessible, without compromising academic standards.

The book has a common theme, yet at the same time it is highly heterogeneous. Context comes in many shapes and forms—as does entrepreneurship. In order to allow for diversity and demonstrate the multifaceted nature of entrepreneurship in context, the editors did not impose a unifying definition of the key terms. With respect to the term 'entrepreneurship,' the various definitions that are in circulation each imply their own context, for example, the context for high-growth or high-tech entrepreneurship differs in many respects from the context for a low-growth, low-tech business. Of all the various possible meanings of the term entrepreneurship (e.g., running a business, starting a business, growth, innovation, opportunity discovery and exploitation), the first two are most frequently used throughout the volume.

As with entrepreneurship, the editors did not impose a particular definition of the term context. Context, as mentioned previously, has various dimensions. The word 'context' is derived from the Latin word *contexere*, which means 'to weave together,' where 'con' comes from *com* (together) and 'text' from *texere* (to weave). The original meaning of the word thus emphasizes the relationship between individual parts and the whole and the corresponding holistic nature. Other dimensions refer to the narrow and the wider setting.

This introduction is organized as follows. The next section will give a brief overview of the increasing attention paid to context within entrepreneurship research. The third section will add a number of observations about the various meanings and attributes of context. Then a few of the limitations and dangers of studying entrepreneurship in context are pointed out. Finally, an overview of the volume will be provided and the various chapters will be introduced.

## THE INCREASING ATTENTION PAID TO CONTEXT

In recent decades, a wide variety of scientific disciplines have started to pay increased attention to context. Some have labeled this as a 'contextual turn,' however, Burke (2002) doubts whether this is truly the case because scholars have always paid attention to context. For example, the classical Greeks taught that conduct and rhetoric should be adjusted to the time, place, and type of audience in order to be effective (O'Keefe, 2002).

The increased focus on context may be better understood in relation to the traditions following the Enlightenment and the Scientific Revolution (Shapin, 1996), positivism in particular, which were anticontextual in the sense that participants were concerned with formulating laws of nature and society, generalizations that would be valid whatever the circumstances of time, place, or persons.

In response to these developments, the term 'context' expanded in meaning (Burke, 2002). Initially referring to the immediate setting, the term then shifted from the micro context of local circumstances to the macro context of an entire culture, society, or age, including reference to the historical context. In a number of disciplines, in the 1920s and 1930s the term 'situation' came to play a central role. These disciplines included sociology, psychology, history, and anthropology. For instance, Karl Mannheim, one of the pioneers of the sociology of knowledge, treated ideas as being socially situated (literally 'tied to the situation,' *situationsgebunden*). In psychology, a 'field theory' was put forward by Kurt Lewin. Without studying the field, he argued, the behavior of individuals and groups cannot be understood (Lewin, 1943).

Likewise, during the last few decades there have been several calls for the study of context in entrepreneurship research. Low and MacMillan (1988) defended their early call for including context in the study of entrepreneurship by stating that when mere direct influences on business performance were investigated, it might be overlooked that a factor could function as a 'success factor' in one context, but be a 'fail factor' in another (see Hmieleski & Ensley (2007) for an example of a contextual examination of new venture performance). Low and MacMillan (1988) also suggested that two factors could combine to be a success factor when studied separately, but that the same two success factors could become a fail factor when joined by a third factor. A configurational approach would therefore be more suitable, an approach that had long been advocated by Miller (1987; 1996).

Aldrich and collaborators (Aldrich & Fiol, 1994; Aldrich & Martinez, 2001; Aldrich & Zimmer, 1986) were also early pioneers of context studies, who focused on the social and institutional contexts of new ventures and new industries. Their work highlighted that these contexts present entrepreneurs with constraints as well as opportunities. In their view, entrepreneurship is embedded in a social context, channeled and facilitated, or constrained and inhibited by people's position in a social network. Only collective action by entrepreneurs and other stakeholders, such as investors, can help them overcome the 'liability of newness' and produce the legitimacy that is needed for the creation of a viable new enterprise. Their work sheds light on the actions that entrepreneurs and their stakeholders should take to develop their firms and industries.

Schoonhoven and Romanelli's (2001) report on the 2000 *Balboa Conference* was dedicated to the study of entrepreneurship in context. The epilogue of this edited volume framed the contributions as a response to two broad perspectives. The first, perhaps inspired by Schumpeter, is the so-called 'lonely wolf myth,' that entrepreneurs just venture out on their own, combat difficulties, and emerge successful (or not). The second they label as the 'demand side myth,' which purports that when the right conditions are set, entrepreneurship is bound to emerge, in other words, that entrepreneurial activity will arise as a function of economic, cultural, technological, and political conditions. Schoonhoven and Romanelli (2001) critique both perspectives and draw attention to the importance of the local and the individual context in determining success. Entrepreneurs cocreate their ventures together with their environments. Neither an innate psychological disposition nor attractive external conditions are sufficient conditions for successful venturing. Both critiqued perspectives disregard the importance of the situational context and, even more important, the necessity for entrepreneurs to work together in a community of stakeholders to achieve success.

The importance of locality is also taken up by studies that explore embeddedness (Dacin, Ventresca, & Beal, 1999). For example, Jack and Anderson (2002) study rural entrepreneurs' local embeddedness, defined as the nature, depth, and extent of an individual's ties into the environment. They discovered that the information and resources gathered through being embedded compensated for environmental constraints and facilitated the entrepreneurial process. The authors also concluded that being embedded actually creates opportunities that are unlikely to be available to others who are not embedded.

The streams of literature on effectuation and bricolage study *how* entrepreneurial actors actually engage with their immediate context. A core theme of the effectuation literature (Sarasvathy, 2001) is that the entrepreneurial process is not a linear one in which a preconceived plan is executed. Rather, entrepreneurship is an iterative process of trial and error in which the entrepreneur improvises with whatever means at hand to achieve his or her goals. The bricolage literature ("making do with what is at hand"; Baker &Nelson, 2005, p. 329) picks up on the same theme. The direct environment is a constantly changing resource with which improvised exchange takes place. Sarasvathy (2004) suggests that it is exactly this interface between the inner and outer environment that is really interesting about entrepreneurship.

The notion of entrepreneurial opportunities as *created*, and not something 'out there,' waiting to be discovered, has also been taken up by social constructionist studies of entrepreneurship. Such studies aim to understand how entrepreneurship is enacted, a social, situated practice (cf. Bruni, Gherardi, & Poggio, 2004), hence taking a microperspective on context. They help gain insight into the complex and social-dynamic processes connected with the creation of legitimacy for a new initiative (cf. De Clercq & Voronov, 2009; Lounsbury & Glynn, 2001), or the processes of entrepreneurial identity formation (cf. Hytti, 2003; Essers, 2008). Their aim is to understand opportunity as a process, rather than a 'thing', or sticking to an understanding of opportunity as an endresult of something that is not further specified or scrutinized (see also Korsgaard & Neergaard, 2010). From this point of view, opportunities change as the process evolves, taking other shapes (as well as *being* shaped by entrepreneurial agents) and thus being different at different times and in different places. By doing so, these studies also add *time* and *space* as contextual dimensions of the entrepreneurial process and help provide a more nuanced portrayal of entrepreneurship. This does not portray a merely heroic picture of entrepreneurs as 'saviors' of economies.

This brief review shows that the study of entrepreneurship in context can build on previous work within and outside the realm of entrepreneurship research. The next section presents a number of observations about context that are aimed towards contributing to this literature.

## SOME OBSERVATIONS ABOUT CONTEXT

### Dimensions of Context

Context runs in ever-widening circles because every context has its own context. There is the microcontext of each individual, and that individual lives in a wider context that itself has a wider context, and so forth. Hence the anthropologist Mitchell (1987) speaks of "nested contexts." A similar idea has been expressed by Lonegan (qtd. in Burke, 2002, p. 175): "The context of the word is the sentence. The context of the sentence is the paragraph. The context of the paragraph is the chapter. The context of the chapter is the book. The context of the book is the author's *opera omnia*, his life and times, the state of the question in his day, his problems, prospective readers, scope and aim." The message is clear: context can be studied at many levels. However, the nature of these levels and their linkages may not always be that clear as in Lonegan's example. At one extreme, context can be seen as a separable outside entity, whereas at the other extreme, context can be seen as being continuously created by individuals and organizations, and thus being inseparable from the actor involved. Perspectives of context differ depending on one's philosophical leanings. It also depends on the dimension of context observed.

One common distinction is between the narrow (or micro) context, and the wider setting. The wide and narrow dimensions of context correspond to different focuses. Kurt Lewin (1936) employed the term *field* as a synonym for an individual or group's 'life-space' or environment. Investigations of the narrow setting (for example, that of locality, the immediate social setting, individual circumstances and conditions), will often reveal how each case is different and unique, and is a required context to analyze extreme cases. At the same time, the study of the microcontext may also uncover principles that apply to a variety of cases (as research on effectuation and bricolage has shown). An investigation of the wider setting (e.g., the historical, institutional, cultural, global context) may reveal communalities between cases that were previously not in focus. At the same time, comparative approaches may reveal differences as well as similarities.

The wider the context, the more difficult it is to influence, at least in the shortterm. Issues that are directly controlled by an individual will not usually be regarded as context, at least not from the individual's perspective. The immediate social environment will be viewed as something to engage and deal with. When moving to wider contexts (such as the institutional context) it becomes ever harder to perceive this context as changeable. Nevertheless, some entrepreneurs have managed to successfully transform institutions in their role as change agents (cf. Dacin et al., 2002; Munir & Phillips, 2005).

For outside observers, but not for the actors themselves, the microcontext may also include the individual's preferences, aims, and intentions. Entrepreneurship can take many shapes and forms, and it may fulfill many different motives. For instance, whether a hunter intentionally shot a fellow hunter in the head, or whether he or she thought the friend to be a wild animal, is vital in the courtroom. Similarly, the intention of the entrepreneurial actor, whether an individual entrepreneur, a team, or a business, makes a big difference to the picture. This relates back to the discussion of the definition of entrepreneurship in the first part of this introduction. It is not only researchers who choose from various forms of entrepreneurship; lay people do the same. This point was made by Sarasvathy (2004) when delineating entrepreneurship as a 'science of design' that focuses on how individuals and firms 'design' adaptive and negotiated goals and strategies that shape both themselves and their environments over time.

In addition to microcontext and the wider setting, context has a third important meaning. This is what the Germans call *Zusammenhang*, the way things 'hang together.' Context in this sense refers to how the parts relate to a whole and to each other, thus describing a holistic quality to context that may make it difficult to transfer one best practice to another setting. For example, features that apparently allow Silicon Valley to function as a hotbed for entrepreneurial ventures have been widely copied but often with limited success (Rosenberg, 2001). Perhaps one or more contextual elements were missing from the new context that made it different from the actual Silicon Valley situation.

Different contexts simultaneously affect the venture. There are so many that it is not possible to talk about *the* context of the venture: Context is better used in the plural because more than one context invariably is at play. From a research point of view, however, it is challenging to study multiple contexts and how they interact. A successful example of such a study is provided by Essers and Benschop (Chapter 8 in this volume) who study how Muslim businesswomen manage ethnicity, gender, and religion in their pursuit of business ventures.

Context is easily missed or misinterpreted, both by 'insiders' and 'outsiders.' Insiders may be so entrenched that it is difficult for them to capture any influences that are only narrowly within the scope of attention. Outsiders, on the other hand, may lack the intimate knowledge needed to assess the venturing situation correctly. For example, a local business may have a great knowledge of local context but lack knowledge about wider dynamics (e.g., developments in overseas markets). The foreign firm that plans to enter the local market, however, may miss out on certain local contextual cues because they lack the capability to pick up and decipher these localized signals. Yet even when context is missed and knowledge of context may be lacking, context cannot be escaped. Various contexts affect the business venture, whether or not the actors want it to be so.

## Agency and Context

*Zusammenhang* and the relationships between the levels and types of context are of clear interest to entrepreneurs as well as those who aim to understand or stimulate entrepreneurial activity. The ability to 'recontextualize' may be crucial here. In many cases a particular practice or knowledge cannot be readily transferred, but rather needs adaptation in order to fit the micro setting (both in terms of local conditions and individual aims and circumstances) and the wider setting. In fact, the notions of bricolage (Nelson & Baker, 2001) and effectuation (Sarasvathy, 2001) imply the ability to recontextualize: to reframe social and material resources in order to create new value. The participants in these studies creatively adapt, rather than invent from scratch.

This idea is being picked up by more and more entrepreneurship researchers who have started to see entrepreneurialism as "an emancipatory process with broad change potential" (Rindova, Barry, & Ketchen 2009, p. 477). Value creation is viewed as not only pertaining to the economic sphere, but also encompasses entrepreneurs as active (change) agents initiating a broad variety of change-oriented activities, thus bringing about not only economic value but also social, institutional, and cultural value. This type of entrepreneur *engages* with context, (co)creating new ones and changing existing ones. There is also another sense in which contexts can be changed. For example, a business can switch to another industry or move to another (part of the) country. This will reveal another context, however, in return.

## The Dynamic Nature of Context

Whether studied at the micro, meso, or macro level, contexts are always changing, which adds 'time' as context. This opens up the opportunity to study context in a dynamic perspective—to show how the context itself evolves, how that impacts on the actors involved, and how actors cocreate their context. In this volume, an example of a dynamic microlevel study is provided by Karen Verduyn, and an investigation of changes in the meso and macro levels is offered by Karel Davids. Even at the widest levels, contexts cannot be taken as static. For example, in recent years the global economic context has changed with the increasing importance of China and worsening debt levels of Western countries, and the institutional context has changed with banks being put under a different regime. In fact, contexts seem to change increasingly faster. There is a general feeling that the pace of change is increasing; social, cultural, institutional, demographic, technological changes abound, with industries changing at an ever faster pace in terms of business practices, processes, products, and services (cf. Rosa, 2003).

With contexts changing, whether at the individual, industry, or macro levels, it becomes ever more imperative to study and to be aware of context, including its nonstatic nature. Contexts of the past can still impact current practices, even though the justification for those practices has gone. Here, we also see the legacy of tradition, history, and culture, which continues to impact even though the fit with current instances may not be optimal. Without being alert to all of the changes taking place, a business or even a whole industry runs the risk of becoming outdated. For example, the rise of outsourcing and of low-wage countries such as China have meant many industries have disappeared from the economic landscape in Western countries (Fishman, 2006; Kynge 2006). Having good general knowledge, a broad and diverse network, and relevant information sources is becoming ever more important for ventures in order to keep up with developments. Entrepreneurs will need to decide which contextual elements have to be prioritized as the capacity for attention and action is limited.

For researchers, the consequence of the dynamism of context is that research may become outmoded ever more quickly. This may particularly apply to research that abstracts from context and that seemingly claims validity regardless of time, place, and the actor(s) involved. If the idiosyncratic features of the study are not made apparent, it is, ironically, even more difficult to assess a study's validity. Knowing about the context of the studied objects makes it possible to generalize knowledge to other settings and time frames, whereas a study that does not show this information offers less opportunity for generalization, rather than the other way round (Johns, 2006; Rousseau and Fried, 2001).

## The Societal Context

The context of entrepreneurship is not just about contextual influences affecting ventures and entrepreneurial agents engaging with context. The effects of entrepreneurial actions on the wider societal context are also relevant. This point is especially relevant given the role of entrepreneurs as change agents. Schipper in Chapter 2 in this volume, addresses this point when juxtaposing entrepreneurial ethos and entrepreneurial ethics. In his opinion, the ethos of entrepreneurship is about creating change, innovation, and taking risks. However, practicing this ethos will have wider implications for the society of which the entrepreneur is part. The ethics of entrepreneurship may conflict with the ethos as change, innovation, and risks may have wider negative implications for the society of which the entrepreneur is part.

## Entrepreneurship as Context

The different meanings of context, its dynamic nature, their *zusammenhang*, and their interrelations (between types of context as well as between micro and wider levels) are core elements to consider when discussing context, as is the relationship between the entrepreneurial venture and its context. Nevertheless, one type of context study has been missing from this discussion, namely, entrepreneurship itself as a context for studying other phenomena. Baum, Frese, and Baron (2007) recommend exactly this type of context study; they argue that entrepreneurship offers a microenvironment context that allows for the study of a great variety of phenomena. The microsetting allows control or exclusion of many of the features that would have had an impact if these studies had taken place in a wider setting. Such topics might be of interest to organizational behavior scholars and also to scholars from other disciplines, including anthropology and sociology. This volume contains two studies that employ entrepreneurship as a research setting (the contributions by Essers & Benschop, chapter 8; and by Peverelli & Song, chapter 9).

## STUDYING ENTREPRENEURSHIP IN CONTEXT: GAINS AND DIFFICULTIES

There are various benefits to studying entrepreneurship in context. It provides a better understanding of individual cases, issues, and problems, both in terms of the microcontext involved and the wider setting. It draws attention to *zusammenhang*, the holistic nature of entrepreneurial actions and conditions. It brings in focus how different levels or units of analysis affect one another, and may provide more comprehensive explanations of research outcomes. According to Johns (2006), explanations for anomalous or inconsistent research can often be found in contextual influences. Moreover, attention to context may lead to a process perspective when this entails an analysis of how the entrepreneurial agent engages and influences context. Studies of context using a process perspective have the advantage of unveiling not only how the entrepreneurial venture evolves but also how the context coevolves with it.

## Generalization and Applicability

According to Zahra, many articles appear to avoid mentioning contextual information:

> Reading recent entrepreneurship papers, however, one rarely gets a sense of the substance, magnitude or dynamics of the research context. These variables are often described in terms of summary statistics that are easy to understand but leave the reader wanting more information about the context of the research. Readers have no sense of what the researchers have observed, felt or thought. Alternative arguments or explanations are often omitted. Thus, theories are applied to sterile and highly sanitized settings, leaving a major gap in our understanding. As in silent movies, there is action, but readers have to watch carefully to infer what actors say and do. They need to read the actors' lips in order to decipher what is happening. (Zahra, 2007, p. 445)

The preceding quotation suggests that some of those who submit to and review for entrepreneurship journals prefer context to be hidden, perhaps in order to promote external validity (Johns, 2006; Rousseau and Fried, 2001). Obviously, there are huge gains to 'generalizability.' Science aims to further understanding by capturing the essence, by reducing to a core. Parsimony and generalizability are great attributes for a research project; however, the perceived prominence of generalizability may itself become a context that causes authors to hide context. After all, features that make the sample or other aspects of the research unique may be interpreted as a threat to external validity. It may seem prudent for submitters to stress in their presentation how similar their sample and research settings are to those commonly encountered in the population, rather than stress the unique aspects. If any particular circumstances or idiosyncrasies were present, it might seem wise to render these unimportant because, if the research is particular to certain samples or settings, it could be argued by the reviewers that it is therefore not of interest to a wider audience.

A downside of these practices, paradoxically, is a lack of applicability. Simple, generic rules that apply to all settings may be hard to find for a field such as entrepreneurship, where heterogeneity is the norm (Davidsson, 2008; Gartner, 1985). The lack of contextual information may be a reason why practitioners show relatively little interest in entrepreneurial studies, as in other fields of business research (Johns, 2006; Shapiro, Kirkman, & Courtney, 2007; Van de Ven & Johnson, 2006). Practitioners may feel that the research is too generic, that theory and research do not apply to their particular circumstances (e.g., those reflecting their industry). Specifying the context incurs the opposite risk, that is, practitioners again feel that the research is not about them as it now seems too specific. But perhaps practitioners relate better to contexts that are specifically described than to a lack of context (Johns, 2006).

Explicating the research context not only benefits practitioners, but also fellow researchers. As Rousseau and Fried (2001) argue, there is a difference between simplicity and parsimony. Leaving contextual information out does not make a research generalizable by itself, and endangers validity if underlying complexity is not represented. Various journal editors have made calls for the explicit 'contextualization' of research (Bamberger, 2008; Johns, 2006; Rousseau and Fried, 2001). According to Rousseau and Fried, "contextualization entails linking observations to a set of relevant facts, events, or points of view that make possible research and theory that form part of a larger whole" (p. 1). This contextualization of research can occur in any stage of the research process: question formulation, site selection, data measurement and analysis, interpretation, and reporting. A first step in contextualization involves a detailed, thick description of the role of context (Rousseau and Fried, 2001). One great advantage of thick description is that it makes the restriction of range of any research explicit (Johns, 2006). A second step is the direct observation and analysis of contextual effects. Bamberger (2008) goes a step further, and states management research should move beyond contextualization to the generation and testing of context theories, which are "theories that specify how surrounding phenomena or temporal conditions directly influence lower-level phenomena, condition relations between one or more variables at different levels of analysis, or are influenced by the phenomena nested within them" (p. 841).

## Methodological Concerns

Studying context has many benefits but is methodologically challenging. A generic feature of investigations of context is that a particular phenomenon is not studied in isolation, but on multiple levels, involving one or more forms of context, whether on the micro, meso, or macro level. Simultaneously, the dynamic and changing nature of context, as well as the interaction of entrepreneurial agents with their context, calls for process studies. Comparative methods are highly useful, as they allow the comparison of a phenomenon in various settings (Rousseau and Fried, 2001). Replication research fulfills the same purpose, when original research is replicated in a different context.

The variety of meanings and types of context and their dynamic nature make it impossible to specify *the* method for studying context (one that could be applied regardless of context). Singling out particular methods as appropriate for the study of context is troublesome as the choice of method depends on context. Nonetheless, some general suggestions may be given.

Quantitative studies of context will typically involve the study of moderators (will a particular relationship between two variables hold in a different context?), multi-level models (Davidsson and Wiklund, 2001; Hitt et al., 2007), or configurational approaches, in which not only interaction effects are studied but also the relationships between various independent variables (Harms, Kraus, & Schwarz, 2009). As Miller (1996, p. 509) states: "Since configurations are about organizational wholes, more should be done to . . . probe into just why and how their elements interrelate and complement each other to produce the driving character of an enterprise." The notion of the *fit* between various entrepreneurial attributes and their contexts (Davidsson, 2008; Miller 1992) is equally relevant. Explicit attention to context may result in the careful use of a number of control variables representing various contextual influences. However, Johns (2001) warns against context being "controlled away" (p. 39). Bamberger (2008) and Johns (2001, 2006) argue that context should whenever possible be incorporated into the theory and the research design.

Traditionally, qualitative studies have already tended to include process-based and contextual elements in their efforts to understand the entrepreneurship phenomenon (cf. Gartner & Birley, 2002; Steyaert, 1997). Such studies tend to aim to zoom in on specific entrepreneurial situations to reach multiperspective and detailed understanding. In particular ethnographic entrepreneurship research does not usually aim for generalizability (cf. Reveley, Down, & Taylor, 2004). In qualitative studies "there is typically an immersion into the muddled circumstances of an entrepreneurial phenomenon that is cluttered and confusing" (Gartner & Birley, 2002, p. 394). Making sense of complex, messy data is a qualitative researcher's daily work. Generally speaking, these studies tend to take contextual elements in their stride, but they do not tend to be studies of context per se. This could be a challenge for qualitative studies of context in the light of entrepreneurial initiatives: to not only take along the contextual dimensions but to make the contextual dynamics the actual focus of their investigations.

## Some Remaining Issues

The study of context will never be complete. When studying some contexts, there will always be others that are not studied. This does not need to be a problem in itself, but it lays context studies wide open to the easy criticism that the study is not comprehensive. As Schegloff (1992, p. 215) observes: "Context is something I noticed about your work that you didn't write about."

The influence of context, especially when studying the wider context, can easily fall into the trap of becoming acontextual itself, of pointing out generalities with deterministic influences. History, tradition, institutions, and culture do have impact, but entrepreneurs and their ventures each have their microcontext and take action to negotiate the various contexts of which they are part. The opposite danger is also everpresent. If the strong claim is made that entrepreneurial action varies crucially from context to context, then generalization is undermined altogether and we once again have contextual determinism, which renders context as a prison from which escape is impossible (Burke, 2002).

By bringing together the contributions as presented in this volume, we have tried to achieve a situation in which we can no longer speak of 'context' without specifying what is actually meant. With this extensive and rich (and we hope, refreshing) exploration of the various dimensions, meanings, and roles of context, we invite entrepreneurship researchers to no longer speak of 'the context' and leave it at that but rather to make it specific: What context, whose context, what 'level,' what moment-in-time is being examined? With this agenda in mind, we provide our readers with an overview of the contributions as presented in this volume.

## OVERVIEW OF VOLUME CHAPTERS

As the previous sections have shown, it is not possible to comprehensively cover all contexts and types of context study. Instead, a bottom-up approach was taken. A wide variety of scholars connected to the VU University Amsterdam are involved in the study of entrepreneurship, and although not working within a formal, united research program, their research has in common that it explicitly involves the study of context. All contributors were asked to make explicit how and why their contribution is a study of context.

As a result, this book is highly diverse. Among the disciplines represented are business administration, health and life sciences, philosophy, history, sociology, psychology, and anthropology. Table 1.1 presents the chapters and classifies them according to a number of characteristics. The table shows that a wide variety of contexts are taken into consideration. Nearly all contributions study multiple contexts. Seven chapters refer to the Dutch situation, five chapters investigate non-Dutch settings, and four chapters present reviews or conceptual developments. Seven chapters present empirical data, four are reviews, and five are conceptual. In terms of level of analysis, five chapters concern the individual, three the interaction between firm and context, three the industry, two the ethnic group, one the community, and two the nation.

Entrepreneurship takes place in a wider societal context, and the embedding of entrepreneurial actions within ethical bounds is so fundamental that we have included chapter 2, by Frits Schipper in the introductory part of this book. This chapter focuses on normative, moral issues in connection with entrepreneurship. It elaborates upon the notion of entrepreneurial ethos and explores several issues involved in an ethics related to it, including integrity risks and the creation and destruction of value. Schipper argues that the ethics of entrepreneurship refers to general views about 'good life' and 'good society'; however, more specific, normative elements may also be involved, depending on the context. A stakeholder approach is proposed for both.

The next two chapters are concerned with microcontext. Chapter 3, by Karen Verduyn, analyzes the process of the emergence and creation of the Republic of Tea (TRoT) as an ongoing, dynamic process. In this chapter the notion of rhythm, as conceptualized and proposed by French

Table 1.1  Overview of Chapters

| Ch. | | Level of analysis | Institutions | Ethnic | Social | Region/Location | Culture | Religious |
|---|---|---|---|---|---|---|---|---|
| 2 | | Schipper | Individual/firm | x | | x | | | x |
| 3 | Microcontext | Verduyn | Individual | | | x | | | |
| 4 | | Van Gelderen | Individual | | | | | | |
| 5 | Engaging with context | Stam-Hulsink & Hulsink | Firm/context interaction | x | | x | | | |
| 6 | | Bossink | Firm/context interaction | x | | x | | | |
| 7 | | Kouwenhoven, Bulterman, & Reddy | Industry | | | | | x | |
| 8 | entrepreneurship as context | Essers & Benschop | Individual | | x | x | | x | x |
| 9 | | Peverelli & Song | Individual | x | | x | | x | x |
| 10 | Contextual influences | Davids | Industry | x | | x | x | x | x |
| 11 | | Koning | Ethnic group | x | x | x | x | x | x |
| 12 | | Dahles | Nation | x | | x | | x | |
| 13 | | Roessingh | Community | x | | | | x | |
| 14 | | Thurik & Dejardin | Nation | | x | | | x | |
| 15 | | Kourtit & Nijkamp | Ethnic group | | x | | | x | x |
| 16 | | Masurel & Grunberg | Industry | | | | x | x | |
| 17 | | Pronker, Osterhaus, Claassen, & Hulsink | Firm/context interaction | x | | x | | | |

| Ch. | | Time perspective: Historical/dynamic | Gender | Environment | Industry | Situated: Dutch/foreign | Method: Comparative | Type of paper |
|---|---|---|---|---|---|---|---|---|
| 2 | Schipper | | | | | | x | Conceptual |
| 3 | Verduyn — Microcontext | x | | | x | Foreign | x | Empirical |
| 4 | Van Gelderen | | | | | | x | Conceptual |
| 5 | Stam & Hulsink — Engaging with context | | | | | NL | | Empirical |
| 6 | Bossink | | x | | | NL | | Conceptual |
| 7 | Kouwenhoven et al. | | x | | x | NL | | Conceptual |
| 8 | Essers & Benschop — entrepreneurship as context | | | x | | NL | x | Empirical |
| 9 | Peverelli & Song | | | | x | Foreign | | Empirical |
| 10 | Davids — Contextual influences | x | | | | NL | | Review |
| 11 | Koning | x | | | | Foreign | | Review |
| 12 | Dahles | | | | | Foreign | | Review |
| 13 | Roessingh | | | | x | Foreign | x | Empirical |
| 14 | Thurik & Dejardin | | | | | | | Review |
| 15 | Kourtit & Nijkamp — Descriptive studies | | | | x | NL | | Empirical |
| 16 | Masurel & Grunberg | | | x | | NL | | Empirical |
| 17 | Pronker et al. | | | | x | | | Conceptual |

philosopher Henri Lefebvre, is adopted for understanding the actions and events associated with the process of emergence and creation of TRoT in the temporalities in which they unfold, hence adding *time* as context. This 'rhythmanalysis' is based on the sequence of events and actions as described in the faxes, letters, and reflections of the founders of a company called *The Republic of Tea*. Their book relates a sequence of events and actions over a period of around 20 months. Verduyn shows that the creation of an organization occurs in ways that are compatible with the natural rhythms of its founders.

In chapter 4, Marco van Gelderen presents a vision of entrepreneurship education that has as its ultimate objective the student's capacity for autonomous action. The chapter aims to convince the reader of the timeliness and relevance of such an approach. The view of enterprising behavior as actions to realize personal goals implies that each student presents a unique individual context. Teachers, schools, and institutions that wish to adapt this approach need to adopt individualized, empowering approaches. Various implementation-related issues are discussed, including trade-offs between guidance and freedom, information and pressure, the self and others, and choice and relevance; the effects of student behavior on autonomy support by faculty; and the suitability of autonomy-supportive entrepreneurship education for different kinds of students and educational settings.

Part 3 of this volume contains chapters that study the engagement with context on the business and the industry level. How can this context be engaged in bringing an entrepreneurial venture to existence and success? What can be done to involve stakeholders? And how is the changing context a source of new venture opportunities? Such questions are taken up in this part of the volume. Chapter 5, by Eveline Stam-Hulsink and Willem Hulsink, addresses the process of pioneering entrepreneurs actively developing relationships with stakeholders within the institutionalized context in order to generate legitimacy—social acceptance—for the introduction of novel healthcare products and services. These ventures take place within administered contexts—which shows the importance of networks and networking. The findings demonstrate how different entrepreneurial networking strategies of innovative ventures turn into different stakeholder mobilization processes.

Bart Bossink authored chapter 6, which substantiates the idea that several distinct professionals share the entrepreneurial role in the development of environmentally sustainable designs. This chapter proposes that it is not just the designer's capability to create environmentally sustainable designs that is important; equally significant is the designer's capability to contextualize the design. The designer's ability to gain access to, become a member of, and cooperate with members of entrepreneurial networks of environmentally aware governmental, institutional, and commercial organizations appears to be just as important as the design and design process itself.

In chapter 7, Gerry Kouwenhoven, Sergej Bulterman, and Vijayender Reddy study the food-service industry (hotel, catering, and restaurants) and suggest a framework that conveys that people, planet, and profit (as well as pleasure) can be addressed in this sector by means of client service, food preparation, stock control, and purchasing. It then discusses the increased importance of the reduction of food waste and the opportunities this implies. Opportunities are often thought to derive from change (Kirzner, 2009; Shane, 2003), and this study provides an example of engaging with a change in context (increasing food prices, increased need for sustainable practices) to arrive at ideas for entrepreneurial action.

The fourth part of the book presents studies wherein entrepreneurship itself serves as context. In chapter 8, Caroline Essers and Yvonne Benschop show how female entrepreneurs of Moroccan and Turkish origin in the Netherlands construct their ethnic, gender, and entrepreneurial identities in relation to their Muslim identity. The paper draws on four narratives to illustrate how the women interviewed perform creative boundary work at these hitherto underresearched intersections. Islam is employed as a boundary to let religious norms and values prevail over cultural ones and make space for individualism, honor, and entrepreneurship. Moreover, different individual religious identities are crafted to stretch the boundaries of what is allowed for female entrepreneurs in order to resist traditional, dogmatic interpretations of Islam. The study shows how these female entrepreneurs gain agency at the crossroads of gender, ethnicity, and religion.

Chapter 9 is written by Peter Peverelli and Lynda Jiwen Song. An important current debate in entrepreneurship research concerns the social embeddedness of entrepreneurs. This topic is inextricably related to social network analysis as *the* tool to analyze embeddedness. This chapter intends to enrich current social network theory with a module that links networks on the basis of multiple inclusions of actors in several groups (networks). Human actors tend to form relationships on the basis of institutional affiliation and inclusion in social groups. The expanded model is applied to the analysis of the social capital of a Chinese entrepreneur.

The fifth part of the book details influences of context. A wide range of contexts are studied: A non-exhaustive list includes the institutional, historical, cultural, religious, ethnicity, social, gender, environmental, and local contexts. Chapter 10, by Karel Davids, discusses social contexts of entrepreneurship in the 19th and 20th centuries. During this period, Western societies went through a series of major economic changes: a revolutionary transition from a preindustrial to an industrial (and partly postindustrial) economy, several ups and downs in terms of globalization, and a number of violent fluctuations in business cycles. The key question addressed in this chapter is how and to what extent entrepreneurship continued to be shaped by regional, familial, and religious networks and values. Empirical evidence from the Netherlands is combined with a broader comparative framework.

18    *Marco van Gelderen, Karen Verduyn, and Enno Masurel*

In chapter 11, Juliette Koning discusses the role and meaning of 'Chineseness' in business conduct among different generations of Chinese-Indonesian entrepreneurs active in small- and medium-sized enterprises. These Chinese Indonesians form an ethnic minority that has a strong representation in the business sectors of the Indonesian economy. Since the 1980s scholars have been debating the successful business activities of ethnic Chinese groups in Southeast Asia. Based on ethnographic fieldwork, this paper argues that the business conduct of Chinese-Indonesian entrepreneurs is better understood if we pay attention to context and embeddedness: historical developments, national ethnic policies, local cultural circumstances, and generational differences.

Chapter 12 is written by Heidi Dahles, and it analyzes returnee entrepreneurship in various countries. In many countries that have experienced major migration-based movements, returnees may have a role to play in processes of economic development and social change, in particular through entrepreneurial activities. As returnees are embedded to varying degrees in their home and host countries, this comparative analysis reveals that context plays a large role in the way returnee entrepreneurship emerges, develops, and impacts on home-country economies. The aim of the chapter is pursued via a comparative review of current literature on returnee capital investments and entrepreneurship in Western and non-Western countries.

In chapter 13, Carel Roessingh studies community entrepreneurship practices of Belizian Mennonites. Several groups of Mennonites in Belize, Central America, are notably present in the entrepreneurial arena of the country. The Mennonites are, both in their culture and religion, largely inwardlooking. They have their own schools and speak a language called 'Low German.' Despite the fact that most Mennonites live on the 'edges' of society, they have been able to establish a strong and stable economic position inside Belize. The focus of this chapter is the way in which a Mennonite settlement organizes its community-based enterprises against the backdrop of their religious and social context.

In chapter 14, Roy Thurik and Marcus Dejardin provide an overview of the conceptual as well as empirical relationships between entrepreneurship and culture. The chapter offers a survey of recent work about the determinants of entrepreneurial activities that tests the influence of cultural variables as a subset of contextual variables. The relative stability of differences in entrepreneurial activities across countries suggests that factors other than economic factors are at play. The results show that variables related to postmaterialism, dissatisfaction, and uncertainty avoidance seem to explain differences in entrepreneurial activities across countries.

The final part of the volume is made up of chapters that contribute descriptive studies. Chapter 15, by Karima Kourtit and Peter Nijkamp, concerns recent Dutch immigrants' activities in the creative sector. Entrepreneurship offers opportunities for immigrants with a business-oriented attitude. Many foreign migrants appear to possess excellent entrepreneurial skills, are responsible for a flourishing SME sector in cities, and have a great impact on urban socioeconomic vitality. Against this background, the chapter aims to provide an overview of this new Dutch entrepreneurship, and describes the results of a case study on higher-educated young Moroccan entrepreneurs in the creative industries concentrated in the four largest cities in the Netherlands.

In chapter 16, Enno Masurel and Sentini Grunberg investigate the relevance of a generic list of entrepreneurial skills in the context of a particular industry, the dance sector. The validity and importance of six entrepreneurial competences—need for achievement, self-efficacy, creativity, opportunity identification, risk-taking propensity, and proper management—is established in a survey of Dutch dance teachers. Surprisingly, creativity is considered least important. One explanation is that creativity is so common for dance teachers that they do not regard it as vital. Instead, self-efficacy is seen as the most essential competence, perhaps because the environment in which the dance teachers operate is constantly changing.

The final chapter, by Esther Pronker, Ab Osterhaus, Eric Claassen, and Willem Hulsink, discusses the context of science-based venturing. It specifies the distinctive roles of the researcher, the entrepreneur, large firms, and public laboratories and their interactions in developing vaccines and introducing them to the market and society. Product development in the pharmaceutical industry has become increasingly complex with R&D costs rising exponentially and long timeperiods required for drug development and product launch. Effective coordination of the activities of all the stakeholders in the value chain is needed in order to produce an ethical, safe, and efficacious medical product.

## ACKNOWLEDGMENTS

Ralph Bathurst, Bart Bossink, Rene Brohm, Wendelin Kupers, Donna Ladkin, and Ida Sabelis provided valuable comments on this introduction. The usual disclaimer applies.

## REFERENCES

Aldrich, H.E., & Martinez, M.A. (2001). Many are called but few are chosen. *Entrepreneurship Theory and Practice, 25*(4), 41–56.

Aldrich, H. E., & Fiol, M. C. (1994). Fools rush in? The institutional context of industry creation. *Academy of Management Review, 19*(4), 645–670.

Aldrich, H.E., & Zimmer, C. (1986). Entrepreneurship through social networks. In D. Sexton & R. Smilor (Eds.), *The art and science of entrepreneurship* (pp. 3–23). New York:Ballinger.

Baker, T., & Nelson, R.E. (2005). Creating something from nothing: Resource construction through entrepreneurial bricolage. *Administrative Science Quarterly, 50*, 329–366.

Baum, J.R., Frese, M., & Baron, R.A. (2007). *The psychology of entrepreneurship.* Mahwah, NJ: Lawrence Erlbaum.

Bruni, A., Gherardi, S., & Poggio,B. (2004). Doing gender, doing entrepreneurship: An ethnographic account of intertwined practices. *Gender, Work and Organization, 11*(4), 406–429.

Burke, P. (2002). Context in context. *Common Knowledge, 8*(1), 152–177.

De Clercq, D., & Voronov, M. (2009). Toward a practice perspective of entrepreneurship: Entrepreneurial legitimacy as habitus. *International Small Business Journal, 27*(4), 395–419.

Dacin, M.T., Ventresca, M.J., & Beal, B.D. (1999). The embeddedness of organizations: Dialogue and directions. *Journal of Management, 25*(3), 317–356.

Dacin, M.T., Goodstein, J., & Scott, W.R. (2002). Institutional theory and institutional change: Introduction to the special research forum. *Academy of Management Journal, 45*(1), 45–57.

Davidsson, P. (2001). Levels of analysis in entrepeneurship research: Current research practice and suggestions for the future. *Entrepreneurship Theory and Practice, 25*(4), 81–100.

Davidsson, P. (2008). *The entrepreneurship research challenge.* Cheltenham: Edward Elgar.

Essers, C. (2008). *Enterprising identities: Female entrepreneurs of Moroccan and Turkish origin in the Netherlands.* PhD thesis, Radboud University, Nijmegen.

Fishman, T. (2006). *China Inc.* New York: Scribner.

Gartner, W.B. (1989). "Who is an entrepreneur" is the wrong question. *Entrepreneurship Theory and Practice, 13*(4), 47–68.

Gartner, W.B. (1985). A conceptual framework for describing the phenomenon of new venture creation. *Academy of Management Journal, 10*(4), 696–706.

Gartner, W.B., & Birley, S. (2002). Introduction to the special issue on qualitative research methods in entrepreneurship research. *Journal of Business Venturing, 17,* 387–395

Harms, R., Kraus, S., & Schwarz, E. (2009). The suitability of the configuration approach in entrepreneurship research. *Entrepreneurship & Regional Development, 21*(1), 25–49.

Hitt, M.A., Beamish, P.W., Jackson, S.E., & Mathieu, J.E. (2007). Building theoretical and empirical bridges across levels: Multilevel research in management. *Academy of Management Journal, 50*(6), 1385–1399.

Hmieleski, K.M., & Ensley, M. (2007). A contextual examination of new venture performance: Entrepreneur leadership behavior, top management team heterogeneity, and environmental dynamism. *Journal of Organizational Behavior, 28,* 865–889.

Hytti, U. (2003). *Stories of entrepreneurs: Narrative construction of identity.* Turku: Turku School of Economics and Business Administration.

Jack, S.L., & Anderson, A.R. (2002). The effects of embeddedness on the entrepreneurial process. *Journal of Business Venturing, 17,* 467–487.

Johns, G. (2001). In praise of context. *Journal of Organizational Behavior, 22*(1), 31–42.

Johns, G. (2006). The essential impact of context on organizational behavior. *Academy of Management Review, 31*(2), 386–408.

Kirzner, I. (2009). The alert and creative entrepreneur: A clarification. *Small Business Economics, 32,* 145–152.

Korsgaard, S.T., & Neergaard, H. (2010).Sites and enactments: A nominalist approach to opportunities. *ENTER: Entrepreneurial Narrative Theory Ethnomethodology and Reflexivity; An IssueaboutThe Republic of Tea,* 137–152.

Kynge, J. (2006). *China shakes the world.* New York: Houghton Mifflin.

Lewin, K. (1936). *Principles of topological psychology*. New York: McGraw-Hill.

Lewin, K. (1943). Defining the 'field at a given time.' *Psychological Review, 50*, 292–310.

Lounsbury, M.,& Glynn, M. A. (2001). Cultural entrepreneurship: Stories, legitimacy, and the acquisition of resources. *Strategic Management Journal, 22*, 545–564.

Low, M.B. (2001). The adolescence of entrepreneurship: Specification of purpose. *Entrepreneurship Theory and Practice, 25*, 17–25.

Low, M.B., & MacMillan, I. (1988). Entrepreneurship: Past research and future challenges. *Journal of Management, 14*(2), 139–161.

Miller, D. (1987). The genesis of configuration. *Academy of Management Journal, 12*, 686–701.

Miller, D. (1992). Environmental fit versus internal fit. *Organization Science, 3*, 159–178.

Miller, D. (1996). Configurations revisited. *Strategic Management Journal, 17*, 505–512.

Mitchell, J.C. (1987). The Situational Perspective. In J.C. Mitchel (Ed.), *Cities, society and social perception: A Central African perspective* (pp. 1–33). Oxford: Clarendon.

Munir, K.A., & Phillips, N. (2005). The birth of the 'Kodak moment': Institutional entrepreneurship and the birth of new technologies. *Organization Studies, 26*(11), 1665–1687.

O'Keefe, D. (2002). *Persuasion: Theory and research*. Thousand Oaks, CA: Sage.

Reveley, J., Down, S., & Taylor, S. (2004). Beyond the boundaries: An ethnographic analysis of spatially diffuse control in a small firm. *International Small Business Journal, 22*(4), 349–367.

Rindova, V., Barry, D., & Ketchen D.,Jr. (2009). Entrepreneuring as emancipation. *Academy of Management Review, 343*, 477–491.

Rosa, H. (2003). Social acceleration: Ethical and political consequences of a desynchronized high speed society. *Constellations, 10*(1), 3–33.

Rosenberg, D. (2001). *Cloning Silicon Valley: The next generation high-tech hotspots*. Upper Saddle River, NJ: FT/Prentice Hall.

Rousseau, D.M., & Fried, Y. (2001). Location, location, location: Contextualizing organizational research. *Journal of Organizational Behavior, 22*, 1–13.

Sarasvathy, S.D. (2001). Causation and effectuation: Toward a theoretical shift from economic inevitability to entrepreneurial contingency. *Academy of Management Review, 26*(2), 243–263.

Sarasvathy, S.D. (2004). The questions we ask and the questions we care about: Reformulating some problems in entrepreneurship research. *Journal of Business Venturing, 19*, 707–717.

Schoonhoven, C.B., & Romanelli, E. (2001). Emergent themes and the next wave of entrepreneurship research. In C.B. Schoonhoven & E. Romanelli (Eds.), *The Entrepreneurship Dynamic* (pp. 383–408). Stanford, CA: Stanford University Press.

Schegloff, E.A. (1992). In another context. In A. Duranti & C. Goodwin (Eds.), *Rethinking context: Language as an interactive phenomenon* (pp. 193–227). Cambridge, MA: Cambridge University Press.

Shane, S. (2003). *A general theory of entrepreneurship: The individual-opportunity nexus*. Cheltenham: Edward Elgar

Shapin, S. (1996). *The Scientific Revolution*. Chicago: University of Chicago Press.

Steyaert, C. (1997). A qualitative methodology for process studies of entrepreneurship: Creating local knowledge through stories. *International Studies of Management & Organization, 27*(3), 13–33.

Shapiro, D.L., Kirkman, B.L., & Courtney, H.G. (2007). Perceived causes and solutions of the translation problem in management research. *Academy of Management Journal,50*(2), 249–266.
Van de Ven, A.H., & Johnson, P.E. (2006). Knowledge for theory and practice. *Academy of Management Review, 31*(4), 902–931.
Zahra, S. (2007). Contextualizing theory building in entrepreneurship research. *Journal of Business Venturing, 22*, 443–452.

# 2 Some Reflections Concerning the Ethos and Ethics of Entrepreneurship

*Frits Schipper*

## INTRODUCTION

While using Heathrow airport as a stepping-stone on my way to the *Philosophy of Management Conference* in July 2010 in Oxford, I received the July 22 issue of the *Financial Times*. Its front page carried news about President Obama signing the bill to overhaul Wall Street, considered the most sweeping rules shake-up since the 1930s. After reading this, something else drew my attention: an article presenting the image of the Scout Association's new entrepreneur badge, a medium blue square with light brown edging. The square showed the word 'entrepreneur' at the bottom and, above this, a rising bar chart and an upswing shaped arrow, with the international scout's lilylike symbol at the top. The new badge was launched to mark an addition to the list of approved activities, that is, businesslike start-ups of new ventures, such as mobile barbeques to attract attention to the organization and raise of funds. Scouts can now be awarded the badge for organizing these kinds of activities.

The fact that a traditional organization such as the Scouts embraces entrepreneurship might be seen as an indication that it is 'hot.' Its significance can also be felt as a result of many other references to entrepreneurship, especially those outside the world of business. Entrepreneurship is promoted within the arts, scientific research, education, health care, and government, to name but a few. Furthermore, the current linguistic trend of describing difficulties, problems, and the like as 'challenges' suggests that people would do well to take an entrepreneurial approach to their own lives. So it seems that the entrepreneur is one of the major characters of our time. The philosopher MacIntyre in his 1981 book *After Virtue* speaks of the manager, the therapist, and the aestheticist as major characters at the time. Now, however, things seem to have changed, and the entrepreneur has been turned into a favorite icon. The expression 'entrepreneurial ethos' is also often used in today's culture, giving it a normative flavor (Du Gay, 2000, p. 79; see also many websites found while using this phrase as a search term). From a wider cultural perspective, this transformation into an icon also relates to the retreat of the welfare state as well as to globalization

trends. The overall assessment is that entrepreneurship should be stimulated in various societal areas because it represents something good.

Stimulating entrepreneurship induces attempts to discern, through
empirical research, conditional, favoring factors. The studies involved can
be conducted within the context of different disciplines: economics, sociology, law, and history, to name but a few. Sociology, for instance, can investigate the role of culture. In economics, regional diversity may be constitute
subject matter. The critique of rational equilibrium models of the economy,
based on the role of entrepreneurs, is also well known. From the perspective of law, the role of the firm, that is, a legal person having limited liability, disconnecting entrepreneur and firm, often is considered a favorable
factor. Perspectives sometimes can mingle, for instance, if the influence of a
particular change of bankruptcy law on entrepreneurial efforts is studied.
If adequate knowledge results, the suggestion is that this can be used to
implement facilitating factors. In line with this, Peter Drucker speaks of
"organized, systematic, rational work" (Drucker, 1986, p. 65). So going
beyond rationality—see the critique of equilibrium models—as well as
exercising it both seem important. However, without further explanatory
rationale, this is paradoxical and barely comprehensible. The stimulation
of entrepreneurship is also behind the widespread introduction of teaching
it as a subject in higher education, with curricula consisting of different
modules. Doing this presupposes the idea that there is something to be
learned, that knowledge and skills must be gained in order to be successful.
This is analogous to health care, for example. In the same way that teaching medicine concerns the transfer of knowledge based on the empirical
research of relevant phenomena, teaching entrepreneurship is supposed to
involve the results of this type of study too.

All this involves ideas concerning the 'goodness' of entrepreneurship and
the meaning of success, and questions such as 'is entrepreneurship good as
such?' will have to be asked. If entrepreneurship is considered to be related
to (a) resource mobilization and (b) innovative engagement, it may also be
involved in activities we usually consider as being criminal (Brenkert, 2002).
Or does the *entrepreneurial ethos* perhaps go beyond this? So, what do we
then mean by 'good' and 'successful'? As soon as notions such as these are
employed, we are transcending the level of empirical studies, touching upon
normative matters, and introducing philosophical questions: What content
*should* be ascribed to the notion of entrepreneurial success? What *should*
the 'goodness' of entrepreneurship be? What is essential for the entrepreneurial ethos? Is there an 'ethics of entrepreneurship' that has to be part of
the aforementioned curricula?[1]

In the following text, I will further elaborate the theme of an ethics of
entrepreneurship. I will argue that such ethics relates to the entrepreneurial
ethos, analogous to what in philosophy is considered in relation to the connection of ethics and ethos in general. I will start by examining this theme
and, thereafter, will provide an explication of the entrepreneurial ethos,
followed by a proposal regarding possible ethics of entrepreneurship, of

which some aspects will be discussed. It will be argued that these ethics, on the one hand, refer to general views about the 'good life' and the 'good society,' and on the other—depending on the context—involve more specific, normative elements as well. However, it is beyond the scope of this contribution to elaborate on the notions of the 'good life' and the 'good society' at length.[2] I also will not go into terminological matters about who is to be considered to be an entrepreneur and who is not.[3]

## ETHOS

When reference is made to some kind of ethos, what is indicated is ascribed a normative flavor[4] differentiating it from, for instance, the 'style' of doing things. Style can be an individual matter; ethos, however, points beyond this to something more communal. The word 'ethos' originates from the classical Greek terms *éthos* (habit, custom) and *ēthos* (morality). What is meant by the latter can become manifest in the meaning of the former but cannot be reduced to it.

In current parlance, 'ethos' refers to a coherent whole of (a) values, norms, and rules; and (b) virtues, dispositions, and attitudes. Within this, values—justice, well-being, and sustainability are important examples— are general critical standards for judging thinking and acting to which people can mutually refer, and virtues are basic traits of character that are perceived as good. It is also noteworthy that (b) is informed by and aligned to (a). Hence, ethos becomes manifest in human thinking and action. In connection with the latter one can also point to habits and customs. Both can be various, not overly interrelated, and active on an unconscious rather than conscious level. Ethos, on the contrary, requires coherence and a level of attentive intentionality involving an overall purpose. As such, ethos is characterized by a basic 'sense of direction,' and people talk of the 'ethos of the Enlightenment,' for instance, which can be found in Immanuel Kant's 'Sapere Aude,' which means 'daring to discern,' 'daring to think for yourselves.'

An ethos can be examined without having to identify with it. It is, for example, possible to descriptively speak of ethos in the context of both closed societies and open ones. If this is the case and open societies are more differentiated, it could be said that this also applies to ethos. This therefore means that closed societies have only narrow differentiation whereas, in the others, ethos is more varied. Open societies, in particular, include different cultural fields, all of which have their own sense of direction. This implies that ethos allows distinctions too. In connection with this we may consider, for instance, the ethos of health care, of teaching, of engineering, and so on. However, such a descriptive analysis does not detract from the fact that in open societies, the persons active in these fields are supposed to identify with the ethos of the work they are involved in, to regard it as something to be 'put into practice.'

The previous proposition introduces the issue of the validity and justification of all ethoses. When philosophers such as Plato began to talk about 'ethos,' it was meant not just descriptively but also in terms of a reflection on the proper foundation and content of human ethos being essential for seeking the right one. Since the start of ancient philosophy this has, indeed, become an important line of thinking. Hence, it became inevitable to pose reflective questions. This also means the introduction of reflexivity as an element of ethos itself. In all this, defining values and virtues became (and still is) important, as is relating them to ideas about the good life and the good society. It may also be suggested that this issue at hand here is actually seeking appropriate ethics. The themes discussed include:

1. Is ethics to be considered as a mere explanation of the content of the current ideas of the good life, good society, and aligned ethos?

Or, the other way around:

2. Should ethics be seen as independent, that is, independent from what is in use already, that being the search for defining the good life as well as the good society and an aligned ethos?

Both questions seem to address opposing points of view, implying that we have to decide in favor of one or the other. This short chapter, however, is not the appropriate place to investigate this subject matter in any depth. Nevertheless, if asked, I would argue for a position between the two. Passing by this issue now, it is important to notice that reflexivity is also unavoidable when it comes to professional ethos. Hence, all such ethos points, in some way or another, to related ethics and vice versa. Examples include the ethos of health care and medical ethics, and the ethos of business and business ethics. Eventually, each of the aforementioned ethoses and ethics involve a particular focus on both the good life and the good society, specifically locating it in connection with the kind of practice involved. The previous questions are also relevant to this context, and we may also opt for a stance between the two.

## ENTREPRENEURIAL ETHOS

From a historical point of view, it can be said that attention for entrepreneurs in the works of the French thinkers Cantillon and Say was very much related to economics. When 'entrepreneurship' became a buzzword, releasing subject matters from the field of economy, the same happened to the notion of 'entrepreneurial ethos.' There is, however, no longer an exclusive relationship with economy. In the following section, therefore, I will propose an explication of this ethos without confining it to economics. It should be clear, however, that defining and clarifying the 'entrepreneurial ethos' is not the same as trying to grasp a common personality of entrepreneurs;[5] it is something very much more abstract.

When talking about ethos in general, I have suggested that it refers to a coherent whole of (a) values, norms, and rules; as well as (b) aligned virtues, dispositions, and attitudes. This is no different when discussing entrepreneurial ethos. I will start with a few remarks concerning the values involved in entrepreneurial ethos.

## Values

As far as values are concerned, a basic requirement for the entrepreneurial ethos is a kind of metavalue or seeking to create value that did not exist before. This created value is always context dependent. Sometimes people speak of social, economical, and ecological value (see Masurel and Grunberg's chapter in this volume), implying that the value created can be more dimensional. The notion of 'existence' has different meanings too. It may refer to local existence in place and time, but it might also imply a much wider context. The degree of 'newness' may also differ in relation to the value created. It may involve something that is deemed to be new in a particular place and time setting but that is not new when considered in a wider cultural context. When someone starts baking and selling traditional artisan bread in a new city area, value is created where value did not exist before. Hence, it is locally new, but not novel when considered from a general cultural perspective. In this example, the created value refers to a value that was already present and that related to a preexisting need for fresh and tasty bread. It may also be, however, that the value created really does go beyond what was already there. If indeed this is the case, 'value' itself becomes 'novel,' as was the case with the invention of air traffic. Here, as in all cases of creativity, imagination—that is, going beyond existing possibilities of travelling that are—was active; see the next section about virtues.

When new local value is created, the entrepreneurial ethos involved has to deal with norms and rules. This can mean two things, (a) taking them into account or (b) improving them in connection with the value created. However, in the case of novel items, existing norms and rules will probably need to be replaced by others, in accordance with the created value. For example, the entrepreneurial efforts that made air traffic possible created novel value in connection to human mobility. It also had to draw up aligned norms and rules, namely, in connection to safety. Such things do not happen overnight, of course, but it goes without saying that all this is a matter of entrepreneurial ethos.

## Virtues

As suggested earlier, virtues are basic traits of character that are beneficial for a person. Over the last 20 years or so, virtues have been on the philosophical agenda once again. I say once again because there was already a focus on virtues in ancient times (Aristotle, for instance). Examples of classical virtues include temperance, prudence, fortitude, and justice. The Christian tradition added virtues such as faith, hope, and love. Other traditions, such as Chinese philosophy, Islam, and the rest all have something to say about virtues. The more recent attention paid to virtues in connection with ethics is a reaction to a deontological approach based on general, more or less abstract principles that run the risk of remaining isolated from practice. Within the context of ethics, virtues as character traits that are beneficial to a moral person are thus supposed to fill the gap between the indicated generality and abstractness of moral principles on the one hand and the particularities of real practice on the other.[6]

The question, therefore, is which virtues are central to the entrepreneurial ethos, that is, which basic traits of character are beneficial for an entrepreneurial person. It is no surprise to find out that creativity and a well-developed sense of imagination are crucial. Imaginativeness is the ability to see beyond existing realities, and creativity is the capacity to bring the unreal into existence. However, it is not just imaginativeness and creativity as such. What counts in connection with the entrepreneurial ethos is that both are oriented toward value creation. In case of new local realities, imaginativeness and creativity are less demanding than the requirements when novelty is what matters. Another virtue involved in the entrepreneurial ethos is independence from certain existing interests and control by other people. Independence, however, is not the same as 'unrelatedness.' The value to be created is not idiosyncratic, only recognizable by the 'entrepreneur' involved. On the contrary, only when a connection is made with other people can this new creation be of value. It is also clear that independence does not exclude cooperation.[7] So relatedness, or connectedness, is another important virtue included within the entrepreneurial ethos. Whereas Drucker speaks of 'creating a customer' (Drucker, 1986, p. 271), nowadays it is preferable to focus on stakeholder networks (Dew & Sarasvathy, 2007; Venkataraman, 2002; Werhane & Freeman, 2003). In case of the latter, this relatedness becomes more complex as it takes into account the interests of various stakeholders such as customers, clients, workers, or shareholders, and so on.

In terms of entrepreneurial ethos, the four virtues referred to earlier are to be taken in concert. This is quite easy to say, but actually doing so is rather more difficult and requires other virtues to play a role as well. Courage (carrying on while facing difficulties and setbacks), prudence (in relation to risk-taking, for instance), and above all, integrity are worthy of mention here. The latter virtue also arouses much attention in connection to business ethics. Integrity is sometimes considered to be a 'super virtue' that brings it all together (Solomon, 1993). As such, integrity is relevant to all walks of life (Schipper & Bojé, 2008). We also have to recognize that it is part of the entrepreneurial ethos. In terms of dispositions and attitudes, I shall only suggest that the entrepreneurial ethos involves a disposition that allows one to see opportunities and an attitude that enables one to take the initiative and not be afraid of failure.

## Ethics and Entrepreneurial Ethos

Analogous to the relationship between ethos and ethics in general, the entrepreneurial ethos can also be the subject of normative, reflective questioning. Hence, just as there are ethics in connection to ethos, also required is an ethics of entrepreneurship, that is, founding and seeking proper content for the entrepreneurial ethos. Reflexivity is involved here too, ensuring this effort is eventually to be considered as an aspect of the ethos itself. I will now discuss various issues involved in such ethics. First, I shall set out some general ideas, and then I shall add more specific remarks concerning entrepreneurship as it might appear in different contexts and fields of human activity involving integrity risks. Second, attention will be paid to the creation and destruction of value.

## General and Specific Ethics

From a philosophical point of view it is clear that, although distinctions can be made, the entrepreneurial ethos cannot be separated from ethos in general. This also means the ethics of entrepreneurship cannot be seen as disconnected from ethics of a more general nature. Moreover, the aforementioned reflexivity eventually implies that living the entrepreneurial ethos requires an understanding of both the good life and the good society. When Sarasvathy states that the task of entrepreneurship "is to move us from the world we have to live in to the world we want to live in," it demonstrates that this indeed requires an articulated view concerning both the good life and society (2002, p. 96). However, whether it is possible to have a definitive understanding of both is an important philosophical question. I would like to argue that it is not very likely. About 100 years ago, for example, ecological sustainability was not a generally recognized item, but now we consider it to be a basic aspect of the world in which we want to live. Moreover, because we are historical creatures, it would be very presumptuous to say that we have now reached a final view. As I see it, the good life and the good society functions as a regulative idea, which requires continuous creative understanding.

It may be argued that seeking this understanding and the possibility of living the entrepreneurial ethos could be considered aspects of the good life and the good society, which are already present. Another way of expressing this is to say that this 'living' is an important manifestation of human freedom. Moreover, searching for the creative understanding indicated is a particular 'entrepreneurial' effort. However, taking up these arguments does not automatically imply that entrepreneurship must have the status of a societal icon (see introduction).

Besides what is discussed generally, it is important to note that living the entrepreneurial ethos always requires a context, that is, a field of human activity, be it business, education, science, health care, or the arts. If this is the case, the entrepreneurial ethos and related ethics also have to be linked with what is essential therein. Depending on the situation involved, business ethics, the ethics of healthcare, or the ethics of science will have to be co-guiding, which adds a field-specific content to the ethics of entrepreneurship. This content, however, does not have to be at odds with what was suggested in the previous paragraph because—as discussed later—all specific ethics are supposed to relate to more specific ideas concerning the good life and the good society.

By implication, the entrepreneurial ethos also has to take account of both general and specific ethical concerns. Concrete situations can be rather complicated, however. Take, for example, an entrepreneurial venture in which business and scientific research are involved. In these circumstances, the entrepreneurial ethos has to take into account both business ethics and the ethics of science. Economic conditions have to be met when doing business, and these may intermingle with scientific research, thereby putting pressure on knowledge and the scientific quality of what is done (see Radder, 2010). If this is the case, the entrepreneurial ethos involved has to cope with (at least) double-focused value creation, and this can easily lead to integrity risks. In such situations, upholding a situated, contextual ethics of entrepreneurship—as indicated in the previous paragraph—will not be an easy job. However, carrying on as if everything is running smoothly is also unwise, as the integrity risks may cause underlying damage that may go unnoticed for some time.[8] Virtues mentioned in connection with the entrepreneurial ethos, such as independence and relatedness, are also involved herein. Putting too much emphasis on either one of them also creates integrity risks. It is difficult, however, to define 'too much' in general; it all depends on the particular circumstances. This notwithstanding, it is required that the ethics of entrepreneurship is relied upon to point out potential integrity risks. Simultaneously, this ethics is not external. Only when the people who identify with the entrepreneurial ethos also start asking themselves reflective questions can the ethics of entrepreneurship become meaningful for practice.

## Creation and Loss of Value

A complicating factor that the ethics of entrepreneurship has to deal with is the decline and disappearance of value. In relation to this phenomenon, Schumpeter coined the famous expression "creative destruction":

> The opening up of new markets, foreign or domestic, and the organizational development from the craft shop and the factory to such concerns as U.S. Steel illustrate the same process of industrial mutation—if

I may use that biological term—that incessantly revolutionizes the economic structure *from within*, incessantly destroying the old one, incessantly creating a new one. This process of Creative Destruction is the essential fact about capitalism. (Schumpeter, 1975, p. 83)

According to Schumpeter, creative destruction is due to imposition of "new combinations" that can be attributed to a particular type of "economic agent" called the "entrepreneur" (Schumpeter, 2003, p. 64). Although writing about economics, Schumpeter suggests that something analogous can also be discerned in other "areas of social life," such as art and science (ibid., p. 105). This would indicate that it is not only within economics that 'living the entrepreneurial ethos' would involve the creation as well as the destruction of value. Of course, we could ask whether it is the same in all areas. The answer is not provided by Schumpeter, and it may not be the same everywhere. People still enjoy the beauty of Renaissance music and use Newtonian physics, for instance.

Schumpeter principally discusses development within economics. A simple example of this is an individual entrepreneur who starts to use new machinery, replacing the still-functional older equipment that is sold as scrap iron. He certainly incurs a loss, which then has to be accounted for in his books. However, expected gains in economic value must (at least) outweigh these. In this example, there is just one common and simple measure that illustrates the net creation of value. When we look at the approach of Drucker, who suggests that entrepreneurship is about creating customers, matters may appear rather more smooth. Loss of value can be said to exist when customers opt for new/novel products in favor of the old. This is done on the basis of an expected net gain in value. This picture changes, however, if we take a wider perspective on economic development. At a particular point during his argument, Schumpeter remarks that the prosperity or despair of economic agents is often inextricably linked to a certain type of management or production method. When these are in decline, the agents too will be in decline. So:

> By development, entire layers of society lose ground under their feet. . . .
> Through generations, the people in question live a poorer life and ever poorer life with even more bleak hopelessness. Slowly they lose moral and intellectual level, the more so the darker the economic prospects around them are becoming. (Schumpeter, 2003, p. 85)

It may be possible to neglect this from an external position, judging the losses to be the flip side of development. Schumpeter, however, adds:

> People who participate in the drama themselves, and those who are close to them, have a different point of view. They would still be of a different opinion, even if they thoroughly grasped the nature of the process. . . .

They cannot close their ears to the cries of those about to be crushed when the wheels of the new era roll over them. (Schumpeter, 2003, p. 85)

I have extensively quoted Schumpeter because more than half a century ago, he was already expressing the concept of value destruction very vividly. Economists may try, as Schumpeter did, to look at the overall economic gain in terms of efficiency as the main value. Nonetheless, the quoted argument points to what development means in terms of what we now like to call stakeholders in the economic venture. From this perspective, grasping the balance of loss and gain in value cannot be a matter of using just one measurement method. This also applies to sustainability, a value to which this chapter refers several times. At first sight, a loss of value might seem to oppose the quest for sustainability. However, the question 'sustainability of what?' may lead to various answers that concretize the issues involved, providing space for a multivaried view of gain and loss.

What if we are seeking the ethics of entrepreneurship regarding gain and loss of value in connection to a particular innovation? It follows from the argument given so far that at least two issues are important, issues that can be indicated by the following questions:

1. What or which 'areas of social life' is/are involved? This may include, for instance, art, education, health care, business, and science.
2. Who are the potentially relevant stakeholders?

Of course, the character of the particular innovation influences the answers to these questions. Answers will differ depending on the kind of innovation (technical product, service, performance, organizational practice, management, etc.), and this also applies to the potential variety of value, the gain and loss of which will have to be assessed. Hence, the actual circumstances can be rather complicated. Another aspect of this complexity is that win-win situations are not easy to come by.[9] A responsible entrepreneurial ethos requires people to be conscious of this, and the concept sometimes referred to as 'social entrepreneurship' can be seen as a positive step in this direction. Venkataraman (2002) discusses aligned subject matters in the context of business, opting to equilibrate the very likely possibility of conflicts between stakeholders, whereas Freeman seeks to elaborate the view that "stakeholder interests are joint" (Freeman, 2009, p. 106). These issues, of course, can also be dealt with at a rather abstract level. We have to realize, however, that stakeholders are real people with concrete experiences or expectations about gain and loss. Comprehensive ethics of entrepreneurship have to take these into account as far as possible.

I will now conclude this section by discussing a theme very much related to what has been presented thus far: our limited capability to forecast the future. This creates much uncertainty, particularly when true novelty is involved, and means that it might not always be easy even to identify stake-holders, let alone gauge the prospective (positive and negative) impact an innovation will have on them. This creates a significant problem because the ethics of entrepreneurship has to be relevant both before and after the event. Moreover, it must also be noted that the indicated epistemic situation concerning the future implies the difficulty of determining what is important in advance and knowing when this knowledge is sufficient. This issue concerns metaknowledge and is sometimes referred to within philosophy as 'the frame problem.' Measures can be taken to deal with this situation and to gain knowledge (for example, by testing products); however, this does not solve the frame problem. Being at the 'ethical frontier' (Wicks, Freeman, Werhane, & Martin, 2010), therefore, involves many uncertainties, and the ethics of entrepreneurship has to find ways of coping with this. If our focus is on innovation within a (potentially) global setting with wide time-horizons, the uncertainties may well have a paralyzing effect on entrepreneurship because the required knowledge seems to be *impossible*. In order to prevent this, Dew and Sarasvathy have put forward the interesting proposal of looking at entrepreneurship in terms of an "entrepreneurial venture . . . thought of as a *network of stakeholders* engaged in an ongoing process of (re)negotiating the design of innovations, a process which continually shapes and alters the consequences of innovations" (2007, p. 275). In their view, this means looking at a local setting, with self-selected and committed stakeholders who are actively engaged and not just passively waiting "to be impacted by events outside their control" (ibid., p. 281). Commitment is particularly vital to prevent encountering a confusing cacophony of voices. When this approach is taken, the entrepreneurial ethos and ethics become linked to entrepreneurial ventures. If this is so, balancing gains and losses becomes a *process* and, as such, part of the venture itself. The ideas proposed earlier, however, in relation to values, virtues, the good life, and the good society still remain relevant. Of course, Dew and Sarasvathy's proposal is not a panacea to solve all problems. On the contrary, it potentially includes new ones, for instance, relating to power relations among stakeholders. Apart from this though, it can be regarded as doing something possible in the direction of the impossible. Besides, potential community building that results from stakeholder interaction might be a positive side effect. And might this side effect itself not be considered an aspect of the good life and the good society, which nevertheless still remains a regulative idea?

## CONCLUSION

In the introduction of this chapter, normative issues concerning entrepreneurial success and the benefit of entrepreneurship were raised. I also posed the question of whether an 'ethics of entrepreneurship' should be included in entrepreneurial curricula. In light of the preceding argument, this question can be answered positively. Of course, such ethics can never be set in stone. Hence, the intention is to present ideas and views that might be helpful in keeping the subject matter open and responsive while at the same time providing it with contextual content. Besides, several areas that have thus far not been mentioned also must included, namely, 'trust' and how to deal with 'secrecy' and 'power.' A lack of transparency sometimes seems to be necessary within entrepreneurial efforts too; but when it is justifiable and when is it not, and how is trust to be involved in this? Power can work internally as well as being involved in stakeholder relationships. All entrepreneurial ventures require power, otherwise nothing can be achieved. This power, however, can be misused; but when is this the case and when is it not? These questions cannot be avoided, and the ethics of entrepreneurship must deal with them too.

## NOTES

1. It is striking that Duening (2010), although he values ethics as part of Gardner's 'minds' approach, does not mention entrepreneurial ethics as being among the intellectual foundations of entrepreneurship curricula.
2. For an introduction to ethics, see Blackburn (2001). Authors such as Martha Nussbaum, Amartya Sen, and John Rawls are important for contemporary ideas concerning the good, just society.
3. The broad view of entrepreneurship taken in Masurel and Grunberg's chapter in this volume is suitable enough. Various disciplines dealing with entrepreneurship all have their own, sometimes nominal, definitions of what it is. From a philosophical perspective, these are not particularly relevant. An example can be found in Dutch tax law, in which debtor risk is a crucial factor.
4. The same remark was made in the introduction concerning the entrepreneurial ethos.
5. From literature we can see that empirical attempts to grasp this seem to have failed so far. This has no implications, however, for trying to explicate the entrepreneurial ethos.
6. As I see it, virtue ethics cannot stand on their own, but always needs a basis to which they can be related. This paper, however, is not the appropriate place to discuss this issue.
7. For information on cooperative entrepreneurship see, for instance, Rocha and Miles (2009). Moreover, ethos being more communal than style, it is also possible that a particular entrepreneurial ethos has industry-wide backing.
8. See for instance chapter 17 of the present volume. The authors mention important issues such as 'secrecy requirements', 'risk of pressure' and 'rules to prevent fraud'. At the end of their chapter they also refer to 'international ethical [ . . . ] standards'. All of these are relevant for reflecting on integrity risks in the context of academic/business joint ventures.
9. Bossink's chapter in this volume on entrepreneurship for environmentally sustainable design seems to present a positive example. He takes a stakeholder approach to make an inventory of factors that help to create a win-win situation. He considers cooperation important.

# REFERENCES

Blackburn, S. (2001). *Being good: A short introduction to ethics*. Oxford: Oxford University Press.

Brenkert, G. G. (2002). Entrepreneurship ethics and the good society. In *Ethics and entrepreneurship*. Ruffin Series of the Society for Business Ethics, Vol. 3 (pp. 5–43). Charlottesville, VA: Philosophy Documentation Center.

Dew, N., & Sarasvathy, S. D. (2007). Innovations, stakeholders and entrepreneurship. *Journal of Business Ethics, 74,* 267–283.

Duening, T. N. (2010). Five minds for the entrepreneurial future: Cognitive skills as the intellectual foundation for the next generation of entrepreneurship curricula. *The Journal of Entrepreneurship, 19*(1), 1–22.

Drucker, P. (1986). *Innovation and entrepreneurship*. London: Pan.

Freeman, R. E. (2009). Stakeholder theory: 25 years later. *Philosophy of Management, 8*(3), 97–107.

Du Gay, P. (2000). *In praise of bureaucracy*. London: Sage.

MacIntyre, A. (1981). *After virtue: A study in moral theory*. London: Duckworth.

Radder, H. (2010). *The commodification of academic research: Science and the modern university*. Pittsburgh: University of Pittsburgh Press.

Rocha, H., & Miles, R. (2009). A model of collaborative entrepreneurship for a more humanistic management. *Journal of Business Ethics, 88,* 445–467.

Sarasvathy, S. D. (2002). Entrepreneurship as economics with imagination. In *Ethics and entrepreneurship*. Ruffin Series of the Society for Business Ethics, Vol. 3 (pp. 95–112). Charlottesville, VA: Philosophy Documentation Center.

Schipper, F., & Bojé, D. (2008). Transparency, integrity and openness: The Nike example. In G. Scherer & G. Palazzo (Eds.), *A handbook of research on corporate citizenship* (pp. 501–527). Cheltenham, UK: Edward Elgar.

Schumpeter, J. A. (1975). *Capitalism, socialism and democracy*. New York: Harper.

Schumpeter, J. A. (2003). The theory of economic development. In J. Brockhaus (Ed.), *Joseph Alois Schumpeter: Entrepreneurship, style and vision* (pp. 61–116). Boston: Kluwer Academic.

Solomon, R. C. (1993). *Ethics and excellence: Cooperation and integrity in business*. Oxford: Oxford University Press.

Venkataraman, S. (2002). Stakeholder value equilibration and the entrepreneurial process. In *Ethics and entrepreneurship*. Ruffin Series of the Society for Business Ethics, Vol. 3 (pp. 45–57). Charlottesville, VA: Philosophy Documentation Center.

Werhane, P.H., & Freeman, R. E. (2003). Corporate responsibility. In H. LaFolette (Ed.), *The Oxford handbook of practical ethics* (pp. 514–539). Oxford: Oxford University Press.

Wicks, A.C., Freeman, R. E., Werhane, P. H., & Martin, K. E. (2010). *Business ethics: A managerial approach*. Boston: Prentice Hall.

## Part II

# Micro-Context

## 3 Rhythmanalyzing the Emergence of the Republic of Tea

### *Karen Verduyn*

### INTRODUCTION

The book *The Republic of Tea: The Story of the Creation of a Business, As Told Through the Personal Letters of Its Founders* relates a sequence of events and actions over a duration of around 20 months. These events eventually result in the foundation of the Republic of Tea (TRoT), a company exclusively devoted to tea. The narrative begins when the 'idea is born,' in April 1990. The book mainly consists of faxes and letters that Mel Ziegler and Bill Rosenzweig (mostly) and Patricia Ziegler (to a lesser extent) sent to each other during this period. The first fax is one sent by Bill Rosenzweig to Mel Ziegler dated April 7, 1990. The last one—also sent by Bill Rosenzweig to Mel Ziegler—is dated December 17, 1991. The company was eventually created on January 22, 1992.

In the book, numerous mention is made of time and tempo: "fleeing the race-to-nowhere that had been my life, I tasted the joys of existence in a new way—sip by sip rather than gulp by gulp" (p. 3); "we were in a highly charged no-man's-land, outside space and time, where The Source of an Idea was revealing itself to us in its as yet unborn state" (p. 7); and "the life of tea is the life of the moment. We have only Now" (p. 16). The idea that manifested itself to Mel and Bill during their flight to San Francisco is in fact larded with references to time and pace. What's more, the initial idea is all about slowing down, escaping from a life that 'moved very rapidly' and was more of a 'race-to-nowhere.' Whereas the fast life is compared to coffee, the slower life—the life of moments—is the life of tea.

Given that this is the philosophy behind their idea, it is perhaps somewhat striking that Mel gets impatient with Bill at some points: "I found myself yearning for Bill to stop typing faxes and start starting the company. . . . Taking action, not talk about taking action, is the one absolute requirement to start a business" (pp. 165–166). From the book, we learn that the emergence and creation of TRoT got off to a 'flying start,' slowed down in June and July of 1990, even came to a complete stop after July 16, 1990, only to start again one year later, on July 16, 1991. Previous research in the area of time and timing in relation to setting up new ventures indicates, among other things, that if it takes longer than a year for a venture to emerge, it is unlikely that it ever will (Carter, Gartner, & Reynolds,

1996). Likewise, entrepreneurship research has emphasized the importance of speed in venture creation (cf. Carter et al., 1996; Capelleras & Greene, 2008). This chapter aims to contribute to a richer and deeper understanding of the temporal events (Capelleras & Greene, 2008, p. 318) associated with the emergence of a new venture. The book gives us a glimpse into what could very well have been the 'everyday events' (Steyaert, 2004) associated with the creation of TRoT—an ongoing and dynamic process. "Rhythmanalysis" (Lefebvre, 2004) is proposed in this chapter as a means to analyze the daily efforts—as portrayed through the book—connected with the setting up of TRoT. Lefebvre's rhythmanalysis will be introduced in the third section. But first, the extant literature on speed and time in relation to entrepreneurship will be presented and discussed. The next to final section illustrates how the ideas of rhythm interact within the book. Last, these illustrations will be related to the extant knowledge on speed and timing in relation to entrepreneurship.

## SPEED, TIME, AND ENTREPRENEURSHIP

Time is deemed crucial in understanding entrepreneurial behavior (Jaques, 1997): "temporal dynamics are at the very heart of entrepreneurship" (Bird & West, 1997, p. 6). Time is "a valuable, if scarce, resource" in setting up a new venture (Capelleras & Greene, 2008, p. 317). And "prior research has emphasized the practical importance of speed in venture creation" (ibid.). However, "little is known about what factors influence the speed of venture creation" (ibid.). Venture creation speed is defined as "the time taken from the inception of the idea to the beginning of actual trading" (ibid., p. 318). In their study, Capelleras and Greene show that there is a positive relationship between prior entrepreneurial experience and speed but that "business planning retards venture creation" (ibid., p. 317).

Because matters of time and timing are very much a matter of an (implicit) perspective on time (cf. Bird & West, 1997), it is important to see what time perspective is in use. Capelleras and Greene (2008) affirm that their approach to time is a social constructionist one. According to Bird and West, there is a 'traditional' perspective on the one hand, one that is "grounded in western logic; where time is linear and scarce, faster is better, and the future is held to be more important than the past" (1997, p. 5), whereas on the other hand, we also find "alternative conceptualizations of time that offer compelling ways of understanding entrepreneurship" (ibid., p. 5), such as the social constructionist approach that Capelleras and Greene (2008) claim has been used in their investigation of factors that influence the speed of venture creation.

There seem to be two dominant views of time when it comes to the entrepreneurship phenomenon: (a) time as enacted, as socially constructed (and therefore controllable; cf. Capelleras & Greene, 2008; and Fischer,

Reuber, Hababou, Johnson, & Lee, 1997); and (b) time as an (individual) orientation toward (or outlook on, or sense of) time (cf. Bluedorn & Martin, 2008; and Das & Teng, 1997)—an *individual* temporal perspective. What these studies seem to have in common is an (implicit) assumption that acceleration (speed) is a good thing, important even (also see Slevin & Covin, 1997). The book, however, invites an 'approach' to time and timing that does not assume that speed (or even growth) is necessarily a good thing; indeed, the book is all about 'slowing down.' Furthermore, as stated previously, I aim to develop an understanding of the process of creation and emergence of TRoT at the level of the everyday acts and events portrayed through the book. This is why I propose adopting Lefebvre's rhythmanalysis. His approach will be introduced and explained in the next section.

## RHYTHMANALYSIS

French philosopher Henri Lefebvre (1901–1991) has 'rethought' several themes through the concept of rhythm: "Lefebvre uses rhythm as a mode of analysis . . . to examine and re-examine a range of topics" (Elden, 2004, p. xii). Lefebvre's rhythmanalysis is useful in two ways as far as understanding something 'in its everydayness' is concerned: "*Le quotidian* means the mundane, the everyday, but also the repetitive, what happens every day" (Elden, 2004, p. ix; italics in original). Rhythm as conceptualized and proposed by Lefebvre is about understanding actions and events *in the temporalities in which they unfold.* Lefebvre's rhythmanalysis is not, however, about analyzing flows of events as they happen chronologically (first this event, then the next) and not as them being a sequence of events having some preconceived or retrospective goal as a result (a teleological progression). An analysis such as Lefebvre proposes means that events should not even necessarily be understood as connected, as 'one event leads up to the next' and not as a unitary, cohesive stream of events. Rather, there are always multiple rhythms to be discerned, each moving at their own pace, and 'time' (as well as 'history') should sooner be understood in terms of 'moments' or 'instants' (Lefebvre has also referred to 'rhythmanalysis' as the 'theory of moments') rather than *durée* ('duration').[1] According to Lefebvre, it is in moments (a 'niche in time') that the course of things (the rhythm) changes: "For Lefebvre, moments are significant times when existing orthodoxies are open to challenge, when things have the potential to be overturned or radically altered, moments of crisis in the original sense of the term" (Elden, 2004, p. x).

Lefebvre discerns two types of repetition: linear and cyclical. These are in fact inseparable, or intertwined, but they should nevertheless be distinguished and separated when analyzing rhythm. Cyclical repetition is about cyclic *returns*, about rotation, so to speak. An example is the day, forever starting with dawn. Or a monthly cycle, or a year etc. The linear type of repetition is consecutive; it is about the reproduction of the same (kind of) phenomenon, the same (kind of) activity. It is the repetition of time in the everyday that creates the repetitive organization of a daily routine.

Lefebvre's preferred mode of rhythm is a nonlinear one. However, as has also been contended by Bird and West (1997; see previous section), it is the linear rhythm that has become dominant in Western societies because here "everyday life is modeled on abstract, quantitative time, the time of watches and clocks" (Lefebvre, 2004, p. 73). In association with clocks and time-tables, time is visualized, spatialized and bounded, linear and sequential (Hosking, 2007). The time of the clock "was introduced bit by bit in the West after the invention of watches, in the course of their entry into social practice. This homogeneous . . . time has emerged victorious since it supplied *the measure of the time of work*" (Lefebvre, p. 73; italics in original).

The time of work, according to Lefebvre, is "subordinating to the organization of work in space other aspects of the everyday: the hours of sleep and waking, meal-times and the hours of private life" (2004, p. 73). The time of work is an imposed time, creating (hourly, daily) demands, such as schedules, resulting in the repetitive organization of daily routine. Linear work rhythms are about progress (Burrell, 1994), where what is 'new' is better than what is 'old,' making progress goal oriented, or *purposeful*. In work time, there is a high rate of activity, schedules are fixed, calendars are dominant, and time has exchange value ('if you give me a little time,' in other words, 'if you do this for me,' 'then I will do that for you,' perhaps by means of another currency—for instance, money).

Contrasting with the imposed time of work, we have appropriated time (or differential time), which is about temporalities that allow for different rhythms—rhythms that break free from abstract repetition (Ivanchikova, 2006) and which make appropriated time about time 'emancipation' (emancipated from the dominant—mechanical—time). The differentiated rhythm is actually a more natural one, where the everyday rhythmic structure comes closer to the body's needs and the cosmic cycles. The natural rhythm is a flexible one. It is not about productivity and 'busyness' but involves 'idleness' and 'futile' actions; it is a relatively slow rhythm. Rather than being an imposed rhythm, this rhythm is about spontaneity, about creativity, about pleasure (Ivanchikova, 2006).

Differentiated, natural time is the time of the individual, not imposed by societal demands, where time is something to be used at free will. Natural time is slower because things take the time they take and just happen as they do. Efficiency or schedules do not determine the end of the moment. Natural rhythm involves a far lower rate of activity. Therefore, from the point of view of linear rhythm, natural rhythm would be immature, irresponsible even (Ivanchikova, 2006). However, it is in natural rhythm that time becomes "the locus of possibility for the emergence of the new" (ibid., p. 157).

The difference between work time and natural time is illustrated by means of table 3.1.

*Table 3.1*　Work Time Versus Natural Time

| Work time | Natural time |
|---|---|
| Imposed rhythm. | Differentiated (emancipated) rhythm. |
| Societal demands determine rhythmic structure. | Time and rhythm are individual. |
| Abstract, homogeneous time. | Lived time. |
| Schedules. | Flexibility. |
| Repetitive (routine). | Cyclical. |
| 'Progress,' every movement has an aim or purpose. | 'Idleness,' (seemingly) futile actions. |
| Fast. | Slow. |
| The 'fixed.' | The 'possible.' |
| Time has exchange value. | Time is a resource. |
| Separate from 'leisure' or private time. | Work time and private time are integrated. |

In the next section I will illustrate how these ideas apply to the daily efforts associated with the emergence of TRoT, in relation to *The Republic of Tea*.

## RHYTHMANALYZING THE EMERGENCE OF THE REPUBLIC OF TEA

The first fax is one sent by Bill (Rosenzweig) to Mell (Ziegler), on April 7, 1990. What follows immediately thereafter is a frantic transaction of (new) ideas, musings, thoughts, and plans. After June 9, however, we see that the "interaction quieted and cooled" (p. 216), until "several weeks later [Billis] family . . . moved to Mill Valley, California, and [he] began [his] new job in San Francisco as president of Clement Mok Designs" (Bill, p. 22). There is one more fax exchange, on July 16, 1990. One year later, on July 16, 1991, Bill sends Mel another fax. And then another on July 30, 1991. A period of renewed activity has commenced.

Although the book narrates the creation of the Republic of Tea as a *mutual* process instigated for the largest part by Bill Rosenzweig and Mel Ziegler, evidently there is simultaneous, or synchronic, recounting going on. First, Bill and Mel apparently have their own flows of action, which are partially illustrated via their faxes and reflections. One could say that Bill and Mel's rhythms connect—or interact—*from time to time*, mostly through their fax machines. There is more rhythm to Bill and to Mel than we learn about in the book. In addition, notwithstanding the fact that the interaction of Bill and Mel's rhythms is most prominent in the book, there are other rhythms as well. First, this concerns the other persons involved and mentioned in the book, such as Patricia Ziegler, Sam Rosenzweig, Zio Ziegler, and Bruce Katz, although the book demonstrates that their rhythms seem to interact less frequently than Bill and Mel's do. TRoT also has its own rhythm: "Let's get things in the biggest perspective. There's you, there's me, there's Patricia, and there's TroT. We are *not* TRoT, TRoT is not us. TRoT has come to life, and it is its own entity, a living energy separate from us. It speaks for itself. It knows what it needs to realize itself. Our job here is to get out of the way and allow 'it' to be. If we can learn to listen to it, it will make perfectly clear what we are to do" (Mel's fax to Bill, May 6, 1990, p. 124).

Numerous other flows are not explicitly narrated in the book, such as the somewhat ephemeral stream that has 'brought' the idea to Bill and Mel (and provided them with 'an inexplicable energy'). All these flows, or rhythms, move at their own pace. There is a difference in the number of faxes sent by either one (Bill sends 87 faxes during the entire process, Mel 53), for example, and this implies there is more action (and thus a higher rate of activity) from Bill's side. But is this so? Why then does Mel complain about Bill's lack of tempo? And why is there a gap of one whole year, arrhythm in Lefebvre's terms? Given that Bill is all about 'progress' (Bill's self-assigned title is 'Minister of Progress'), why is no progress actually made? It seems that the book allows us to clearly discern at least three rhythms: Mel's, Bill's and TRoT's.

Mel seems to live a natural, emancipated, slow rhythm and has no wish to set up a new business: "It was not in my then Tea Mind to actively involve myself getting another business started. I had stashed enough money in the bank. . . . As much as I liked Bill and loved the idea of being in the tea business, I could see no reason to torture myself by going round and round in the mind-thick unreality maze necessitated by lawyers, accountants, and investors" (p. 51). Mel is free; his actions are his own choice. Mel explains that 'idleness' (or 'not-doing' as he calls it) is important for him and elaborates on how it can be accomplished: "Observing your odyssey brings me back to that 'moment' when I myself became, truly, The Minister of Leaves. Many years before, I had been reading Lao Tzu, when suddenly he ambushed me with this stunning thought: 'Practice not-doing and everything will fall into place.' I hadn't the slightest idea what it was, but something about those words rang deeply true. Imagine: Doing nothing. And everything falling into place. . . . And so I set out with great determination to 'do nothing'" (Mel to Bill, October 13, 1991, p. 239). According to Mel, not-doing, or idleness, makes things fall into place.

For Mel, work time and private time are (or should be) integrated. According to Mel, there is a 'socially condoned hypocrisy' associated with being in business (p. 270). This socially condoned hypocrisy, according to Mel, invokes a hierarchy, namely, that 'being in business' is elevated to "a station higher than being human" (ibid.). By this Mel means that "in our culture" (ibid.) a dichotomy exists between being and acting as a businessman and being and acting as 'just a man.' In terms of Lefebvre, this is similar to the dichotomy between work time and leisure time. Being human is associated with being 'decent,' being warm, loving, and generous, whereas being a businessperson is compared to being "a wolf so I can get the better of you" (ibid.) and the "logic mind" (p. 271). For Mel, there is no difference between one or the other: "In being a businessman, I find no license to do or be things I could not do or be as a man" (ibid.).

Bill, on the other hand, badly wants TRoT to materialize. Something, however, seems to be holding Bill back, making it appear as if he is not achieving any *real* progress. Bill's contemplations about whether to take a job or go on working on the concept for the Republic of Tea are recurrent. Finally, in June 1990, Bill decides to start working for Clement Mok Designs. And while Bill is working here, no progress is made with TRoT. Through Lefebvre's rhythmanalysis we could make an attempt at understanding why this was the case. The rhythm associated with labor is a mechanical, linear rhythm, and this type of rhythm is all about repetition, the reproduction of the same kind of activity and the "busyness of a goal-oriented movement" (Ivanchikova, 2006, p. 161). It is goal oriented, but it is the rhythm of repetition and imposition, not of the emergence of the new.

Furthermore, associated with Bill's need for an income is a reluctance to be idle, a fear of his actions being futile. More than once, Bill makes a reference to being afraid that his efforts may end up being in some way pointless. For Bill, progress simply *has* to be made. And that is why Bill concocts plan after plan, scheme after scheme.

In addition, according to Lefebvre, experience, or background, is a 'dangerous thing'; it helps form the daily routine, creating a dichotomy between the security of the old versus the unknown of the new. The security of the old favors routine events, that is, things just 'going as they go.' Maintaining a daily routine means going along with the flow of things and allowing them to happen. Breaking with the daily routine means intervening and creating something different, something new. The book also mentions a dichotomy between 'the plan' and 'the flow' (Bill, July 16, 1991, p. 227), where the plan represents intervention in the flow. The security of the old and the unknown of the new can, however, actually produce a third dimension: the joy of the opportunity and possibility, and this is what seems to happen to Bill. Nevertheless, Bill still requires a little assistance at the point at which he decides to 'jump in': "Fate has given me a healthy shove off the board and into the pool" (Bill, October 13, 1991, p. 238).

Analogous to table 3.1, the differences between and Bill's (initial) and Mel's rhythms can be summarized as in table 3.2.

Mel's rhythm is, therefore, the emancipated one; Mel is 'free,' living a natural and slow rhythm. Bill, on the other hand, is not free; he seems to live an imposed rhythm. 'Something' is holding Bill back; (perceived)

*Table 3.2* Bill's Rhythm Versus Mel's Rhythm

| Bill ('Minister of Progress') | Mel ('Minister of Leaves') |
| --- | --- |
| *Imposed rhythm* | *Emancipated rhythm* |
| Abstract, homogeneous time ("Dear Leaves, when is the right time to start a business?" October 22, 1991, p. 253).[2] | Lived time ("I wanted a direct experience of life," p. 174). |
| Writes plans and 'progress reports.' | Literally leaves ("I decided to take off for a week at a meditation retreat to clear my mind," p. 170). |
| Every act, every movement seems to have to have an aim or purpose ('progress *has* to be made'). | Loves 'idleness,' (seemingly) futile actions. |
| *Make* things happen. | *Let* things happen. |
| Higher rate of activity. | Slower rhythm. |
| Time has exchange value: Bill exchanges his time for money to provide an income. | Time is a resource to be used at free will. |
| For Bill, TRoT time is private (leisure) time, separate from work time, which provides monetary funding. | Work time and private time are integrated. |

demands determine Bill's rhythmic structure. Whether these are Bill's monetary concerns, hesitations, or his constant quest for the approval and commitment of others, they call for an emancipatory move, for breaking with the ongoing flow of his routine. But where does this leave the Republic of Tea?

The very idea of TRoT just 'happens.' It comes to Bill and Mel *in a moment* (indeed, a 'niche in time'; Lefebvre, 2004): "We were in a highly charged no-man's-land, outside space and time, where The Source of an Idea was revealing itself to us in its as yet unborn state. Time and space reappeared seven hours later, when we looked up and saw that the plane, on the ground in San Francisco, was empty" (Mel, p. 7). From then on, TRoT's rhythm seems to manifest from time to time, and it keeps doing so through moments: "After an hour of nonstop, sweat-provoking cycling we reached West Point Inn. . . . We almost fell off our bikes from exhaustion. . . . Soon a man appeared. . . . He approached us and kindly offered us not a glass of water, not a Coke, but a CUP of TEA! . . . I was stunned. I can't explain much more except to say that I took this mini tea ceremony on the mountaintop as some kind of confirmation that we were on the right track" (Bill, in an afterthought, p. 144).

These moments intervene in the interactive flow between Mel and Bill. As stated previously, these interactions also show repetition, a repetition in the exchange of (new) ideas, musings, thoughts, and plans (the latter come predominantly from Bill's side). This repetition, these exchanges are

Mel and Bill's, and TRoT 'itself' seems to just pop up from time to time. Throughout the book it becomes clear that TRoT seems to have to 'ride' on Bill's rhythm. And although Bill is obviously enthralled by TRoT, he is also held back by the demands that make his rhythm an imposed one, as has been argued previously. According to Mel, "a business creates itself when the circumstances are ready for it. And if the people it needs to create it are not ready, or up to the task, it will wait" (p. 51). And so TRoT waits. As asserted by Ivanchikova, it is in natural rhythm that time becomes "the locus of possibility for the emergence of the new" (Ivanchikova, 2006, p. 157). This particular idea seems to have, indeed, needed an emancipatory move to turn into an actual venture. This move concerns the emancipation of Bill's rhythm but also emancipation from the repetition of the exchanges between Bill and Mel. TRoT was only "ready to be born" (Mel, p. 291) when Bill started allowing things to happen, as with natural rhythm. In the next section these observations will be related to the extant knowledge on speed and timing in relation to entrepreneurship.

## DISCUSSION

Extant knowledge on time and timing in relation to entrepreneurship emphasizes the importance of understanding the temporal dynamics of entrepreneurial action (Bird & West, 1997; Capelleras & Greene, 2008; Jaques, 1997). Likewise, extant knowledge stipulates the importance of speed in new venture creation (Capelleras & Greene, 2008; Carter et al., 1996). Apart from conceptualizations of time as linear and 'given' (clock time; cf. Bird & West, 1997), there are other conceptualizations of time, such as time that is socially constructed. In this view, time is not pre-given but enacted, created during human interaction, and is thus seen as (co) created and multiple. This is also the case with Lefebvre. When applying rhythmanalysis to the emergence of TRoT, we indeed see *multiple* rhythms, each moving at its own pace. But what's more, when we look closely and carefully, we see that the new venture also has its own rhythm. So, whereas Capelleras and Greene (2008) state that "very many entrepreneurial opportunities are time-sensitive, so that faster decision speeds may enable entrepreneurs to exploit opportunities before they vanish or become considerably less attractive" (pp. 317–318), with TRoT, we see that "the Republic of Tea came to life when it was ready to be born" (p. 291). Conceiving of a new firm as having its own rhythm sheds a totally different light on the opportunity-creation versus opportunity-discovery debate in entrepreneurship literature (as in Alvarez & Barney, 2007). With Lefebvre's rhythmanalysis, opportunities are not to be seen as waiting impatiently to be 'discovered' or as required to be created within the time frame of one year (as has been asserted by Carter et al., 1996). Rather, opportunities are to be seen as creating themselves, albeit only when they get the chance to interact with other rhythms. And these should be rhythms that give them the space to grow. Until that happens, Mel asserts, opportunities patiently wait: "A business creates itself when the circumstances are ready for it. And if the people it needs to create it are not yet ready, or up to the task, it will wait" (Mel, in an afterthought, p. 51). So, speed is important in venture creation. Or is it?

## CONCLUSION

In this chapter, attempts have been made to analyze the daily efforts (actual acts and events) associated with the creation of the Republic of Tea, as relayed through the book *The Republic of Tea: The Story of the Creation of a Business, As Told Through the Personal Letters of Its Founders* in a contextual manner. When looking at these acts and events through Lefebvre's rhythmanalysis we can 'see' activities as they occur, as they are happening (or, in this case, have been happening), without presupposing that they should lead to something or would have been better off if they had been conceived in another manner (such as presupposing that they should have happened sooner or faster). Rhythmanalysis analyzes events just as they are. This is the way in which I wanted to add to existing knowledge on time, speed, and entrepreneurship. With Lefebvre's rhythmanalysis we can see that the foundation of a new venture is not one homogeneous flow of action; we can discern multiple rhythms (i.e., contextualizing them) and can see that the incumbent company also has its own rhythm. When it comes to the temporal context and the aspect of timing specifically, the TRoT story seems to teach us that emancipation of the rhythm of routine is important, that a business is not created but creates itself by interacting with other rhythms, and that it does so in its own good time.

## NOTES

1. In this respect, Lefebvre challenges Bergson (Elden qtd. in Lefebvre, 2004, p. x).
2. Mel's answer: "Dear Progress, never and always" (p. 253).

## REFERENCES

Alvarez, S. A., & Barney, J. B. (2007). Discovery and creation: Alternative theories of entrepreneurial action. *Strategic Entrepreneurship Journal, 1*, 11–26.
Bird, B. J., & West, G. P., III. (1997). Time and entrepreneurship. *Entrepreneurship Theory and Practice, 22*(2), 5–9.
Bluedorn, A. C., & Martin, G. (2008). The time frames of entrepreneurs. *Journal of Business Venturing, 23*(1), 1–20.

Burrell, G. (1994). Back to the future: Time and organisation. In M. Reed & M. Hughes (Eds.), *Rethinking organisation: New directions in organisation theory and analysis*. London: Sage, 165–183.

Capelleras, J., & Greene, F. J. (2008). The determinants and growth implications of venture creation speed. *Entrepreneurship & Regional Development, 20*(4), 317–343.

Carter, N., Gartner, W., & Reynolds, P. (1996). Exploring startup event sequences. *Journal of Business Venturing, 11*, 151–166.

Das, T. K., & Teng, B.-S. (1997). Time and entrepreneurial risk behavior. *Entrepreneurship Theory and Practice, 22*(2), 69–88.

Fischer, E., Reuber, A. R., Hababou, M., Johnson, W., & Lee, S. (1997). The role of socially constructed temporal perspectives in the emergence of rapid-growth firms. *Entrepreneurship Theory and Practice, 22*(2), 13–30.

Hosking, D. (2007). Can constructionism be critical? In J. Holstein & J. Gubrium (Eds.), *Handbook of constructionist research*. New York: Guilford, 669–686.

Ivanchikova, A. (2006). On Henri Lefebvre, queer temporality, and rhythm. *Journal for Politics, Gender and Culture, 5*, 151–170.

Jaques, E. (1997). Introduction to special issue on time and entrepreneurship. *Entrepreneurship Theory and Practice, 22*(2), 11–12.

Lefebvre, H.(2004). *Rhythmanalysis: Space, time and everyday life*. New York: Continuum.

Slevin, D. P., & Covin, J. G. (1997). Time, growth, complexity and transitions: Entrepreneurial challenges for the future. *Entrepreneurship Theory and Practice, 22*(2), 53–68.

Steyaert, C. (2004). The prosaics of entrepreneurship. In D. Hjorth & C. Steyaert (Eds.), *Narrative and discursive approaches in entrepreneurship: A second movements in entrepreneurship book*. Cheltenham: Edward Elgar, 8–21.

Ziegler, M., Ziegler, P., & Rosenzweig, B. (1994). *The Republic of Tea: The story of the creation of a business, as told through the personal letters of its founders*. New York: Currency Doubleday.

# 4  Individualizing Entrepreneurship Education
## Putting Each Student Into Context

*Marco van Gelderen*

Autonomy represents an inner endorsement of one's actions—the sense that one's actions emanate from oneself and are one's own (Deci & Ryan, 2000). Autonomy pertains to striving toward the development and realization of personal goals, values, and interests (Assor, Kaplan, & Roth, 2002). Autonomy extends beyond having decisional freedoms to self-awareness, knowing what one's dreams and aims are, and acting on those dreams and aims. This chapter's central argument is that autonomy can be a guiding aim in entrepreneurship education. There are three purposes to this chapter: first, to present a vision of entrepreneurship education that has the student's capacity for autonomous action as its ultimate aim; second, to convince the reader of the timeliness and relevance of such an approach; and finally, to outline how this can be implemented. It starts out by presenting several arguments to support the view that student autonomy can be an ultimate aim of entrepreneurship education.

## THE RELEVANCE OF PERSONAL AUTONOMY
## FOR ENTREPRENEURSHIP EDUCATION

Both entrepreneurship research and entrepreneurship education are oriented toward explaining and furthering the financial performance of firms. Yet, research of entrepreneurial motivation shows that it is not financial gain but autonomy that is most often mentioned or rated as the most important motive for starting a business (Shane, Locke, & Collins, 2003; Van Gelderen & Jansen, 2006). Recent research on work satisfaction shows that this finding cannot be taken for granted, however. Studies show that the self-employed (and entrepreneurs, as a subgroup of the self-employed) have higher work satisfaction than the employed (Benz & Frey, 2008a, 2008b; Hundley, 2001; Lange, in press; Prottas, 2008; Schjoedt, 2009). This relationship persists, irrespective of income earned or hours worked (Benz & Frey, 2008a), the level of the employee in the organization (Schjoedt, 2009), differences in culture (Benz & Frey, 2008b), or the type of business owned (both owners of businesses employing others and independent contractors have higher satisfaction scores;[1] Prottas, 2008). Even more interesting, the difference in satisfaction can to a large extent be explained by the level of autonomy enjoyed (Benz & Frey, 2008a, 2008b; Hundley, 2001; Lange, in press; Prottas, 2008; Schjoedt, 2009). Prottas (2008) shows that when employees have comparable levels of autonomy, they also have similar satisfaction scores. Overall, the research shows that autonomy is not only a dominant entrepreneurial motivation but also a dominant source of entrepreneurial satisfaction.

There are yet more reasons to put autonomy center stage. According to Gibb (2002a, 2002b), we live in a society in which we increasingly need the capacity to cope with, and enjoy, an enterprising way of life. This way of life is characterized by uncertainty, change, and complexity on the one hand and freedom, individual responsibility, and the opportunity to reap the fruits of one's own labor on the other. Gibb claims that more and more people are taking part in this enterprising way of life as a result of several powerful trends in the ways in which individuals relate to the state, organizations, and to other individuals.

All these trends strongly favor self-reliance. First, some changes increase the attractiveness of the enterprising way of life, for example, as a result of individualization processes (Gibb 2002a, 2002b). Being capable of autonomous action is crucial in light of these 'preference' trends. Entrepreneurship students can be expected to have elevated needs for autonomy and to call for independent action. It is important to stimulate this spirit of autonomy, not to temper it. Second, there are enabling trends, such as the democratization of production and distribution (Anderson, 2006), and the increased importance of services and knowledge-based business (Gibb, 2002a, 2002b). Autonomy is essential in light of the trends that enable the enterprising way of life; in order to make full use of the possibilities, people must have the capacity for autonomous action. Finally, there are trends that force us into an enterprising way of life, for example, globalization, governmental budget cuts, reduced welfare spending, reduced opportunities for lifelong employment, and the increased use of short-term contracts (Gibb, 2002a, 2002b). Autonomy is also crucial for the trends that 'force' the enterprising way of life; the capacity for autonomous action is essential to respond effectively to the demands of the world of work.

Autonomy is strongly associated with entrepreneurship because of the decisional freedoms it entails: One can decide what, how, and when work will be done (Lange, in press; Prottas, 2008; Schjoedt, 2009). These freedoms arise irrespective of whether the entrepreneurship takes the form of an independent contractor or a business employing others. However, the need for autonomy can also be a prerequisite for the fulfillment of other motives (Van Gelderen & Jansen, 2006). Van Gelderen and Jansen (2006) asked business starters why they wanted autonomy. Many wanted autonomy in order to have the freedom to make their own decisions. However, people also need autonomy because it is instrumental to the fulfillment of other motives. Some were motivated by 'negative' freedom, that is to say that they generally disliked, or had recently experienced, a difficult boss or stifling organizational rules. Others emphasized that they wanted to do 'their own thing': In their view, entrepreneurship offered the opportunity to work according to their own goals, values, tastes, and beliefs. Still others emphasized the opportunities offered by entrepreneurship in terms of being in charge, directing, and for leading instead of being led.

When these motives are unfulfilled, some may not persist in their entrepreneurial ventures, and conversely, autonomy may spur others to carry on in spite of financial underperformance (Gimeno, Folta, Cooper, & Woo, 1997). The attainment of autonomy cannot be taken for granted or assumed as each underlying motive is paradoxical. Instead of working for a boss, one has to deal with clients, suppliers, and other stakeholders; one may like to do one's own thing, but customers may want the entrepreneur to work according to their specifications; one may be in control within one's company, but uncertainty with regard to stakeholders outside the company can be severe. If autonomy is lacking, entrepreneurs may give up in spite of financial success. Given that autonomy is a dominant motivation and source of satisfaction, far more attention should be paid in entrepreneurship research and education to whether and how autonomy is realized.

Neither can it be automatically assumed that entrepreneurship education furthers autonomy. With the ever-increasing inevitability of the enterprising way of life, business education should not aim to produce graduates who look to others to take responsibility, who are other directed or who have an employee attitude. Yet, if students do their coursework only because they feel obliged, pressured, or merely because they just want the degree; or if students' coursework only consists of finding out what the teacher expects and subsequently jumping over the required hurdles, then students are not strengthened in their ability to behave autonomously. On the contrary, all this conditions people to become docile followers who look to others to be told what and how to do things. Even worse, there is the risk of alienation, and it may be difficult for people to regain their capacity for autonomous action, as autonomy seems to work in a 'use it or lose it' type of fashion (Baumann & Kuhl, 2005).

Entrepreneurship education should aim to prepare people to take a leading role in the enterprising way of life, rather than a supporting one. This chapter argues that autonomy can be a guiding aim for entrepreneurship education. How can this be achieved? What practices are conducive? Which trade-offs and issues are encountered? These are the questions this chapter will address.

The remainder of this chapter proceeds as follows: Presented first are two perspectives in educational psychology that give central emphasis to autonomy, self-determination theory and self-directed learning. Then, empirical studies of autonomy-supportive teacher behaviors and their consequences are reported. Finally, a range of potential implementation issues that can arise when applying this knowledge to entrepreneurship education are discussed.

## AUTONOMY IN EDUCATIONAL PSYCHOLOGY

Students' motivation reflects both intrapersonal and interpersonal processes (Reeve & Jang, 2006). In general, psychological research has focused on individual intrapsychic influences on motivation. In contrast, educational research has focused on teacher behaviors that should be effective in promoting student motivation (Skinner & Belmont, 1993). At their intersection are theories that proceed deductively from the intrapsychic influences on student motivation in order to analyze the variety of classroom practices that affect these student attitudes and beliefs (Skinner & Belmont, 1993). Two such positions, self-determination theory and self-directed learning, will now be discussed.

### Self-Determination Theory

Self-determination theory (SDT) views humans as innately motivated to learn and develop, as long as the social environment provides for their basic psychological needs (Deci & Ryan, 2000; Ryan & Deci, 2000). SDT postulates three of those needs: autonomy, competence, and relatedness. The need for autonomy refers to the need to feel a sense of full volition and 'choicefulness' regarding one's activities and goals, a feeling that emerges when actions and goals are experienced as emanating from one's authentic self. The need for relatedness refers to the need to feel closely related to other people. The need for competence is the need to be effective in one's interactions with the environment and to feel that one is capable of mastering challenges (Deci & Ryan, 2000; Ryan & Deci, 2000). The theory is mainly concerned with the conditions that support or thwart the innate propensity to be autonomous, related, and competent. SDT emphasizes that students' motivation to learn can vary in its relative autonomy, ranging from behaviors stimulated by external reward and punishment (controlled motivation) to those that are energized by interests and values (autonomous motivation).

SDT distinguishes four types of extrinsic motivation. Externally regulated behaviors are performed to satisfy an external demand or to obtain an externally imposed reward contingency. A second type of extrinsic motivation is introjected regulation. Introjection describes a type of internal regulation that is controlling because people perform such actions with a feeling of pressure in order to avoid guilt or anxiety, or to attain ego enhancements or pride. A more autonomous, or self-determined, form of extrinsic motivation is regulation through identification. Here, the person has identified with the personal importance of a behavior and has thus accepted its regulation as his or her own. Finally, the most autonomous form of extrinsic motivation is integrated regulation. Integration occurs when identified regulations have been fully brought into congruence with one's values and needs. Integrated motivation shares many qualities with intrinsic motivation. However, in intrinsic motivation, behavior is undertaken for its own sake, whereas in integrated regulation, behavior is performed for its presumed instrumental value with respect to some outcome that is separate from the behavior, even though it is volitional and valued by the self (Deci & Ryan, 2000; Ryan & Deci, 2000). Both evidence and theory suggest that the more one's motivation is autonomous, the more the quality of learning, persistence, and affective experience are enhanced (Niemiec & Ryan, 2009).

The achievement of enterprising goals typically requires a mixture of both intrinsic and extrinsic motivation: Some aspects are intrinsically motivating, but it is not all fun and games. Enterprising goals are typically midrange goals that require effort to enact and often involve obstacles, competing temptations, or just plain inertia being overcome (Sheldon & Elliott, 1998). Sometimes the goals may be intrinsically motivating, but the means to get there may require internalization and identification. Understanding how to facilitate autonomous motivation is a critical educational agenda in SDT (Niemiec & Ryan, 2009).

## Self-Directed Learning

Whereas SDT is concerned with how autonomous motivation can be promoted through identification and integration processes, in contrast, self-directed learning (SDL) takes autonomous motivation as its starting point. It claims that the student has decision rights in the setting of learning goals, activities, and outcome evaluations (Knowles, 1975). Individuals select, manage, and assess their own learning activities, which can be pursued at any time, in any place, through any means, at any age. SDL involves, perhaps counterintuitively, extensive collaboration with teachers and peers (Brookfield, 1985). Learning environments that foster SDL are believed to promote deep-level processing because learners have the freedom to choose what they learn and how they learn it (Knowles, 1975). SDL has been applied to entrepreneurship education by Bird (2002), who asked her students to design and execute a learning contract in which they identify the competencies that they want to develop and the activities that are necessary for them to undertake.

In SDL, the teacher seems to have a merely facilitating role. However, SDL proponents have also made it clear that, without teacher support, students may stagnate in their learning (Brookfield, 1985), and that students need their teachers to help them become self-directed. A later section will go more deeply into the tension between guidance and freedom. SDT and

SDL have inspired a wide range of autonomy-supportive practices. These will now be discussed.

## Autonomy-Supportive Practices and Their Effects

Autonomy-supportive teachers seek to proceed from the aims, abilities, and preferences of the student. They ask, inquire into, and acknowledge what their students want and need and what their goals, values, and interests are to proceed from there (Reeve & Jang, 2006). Learning activities are then tied to each person's individual context. Whenever possible, the educator takes actions that help students to understand their work as contributing to the realization of their personal goals, interests, and values. Thus, the personal relevance of learning activities is made explicit (Assor & Kaplan, 2001; Assor, Kaplan, & Roth, 2002; Katz & Assor, 2007; Skinner & Belmont, 1993). Autonomy-supportive teachers are also open to feedback and critique from their students as this allows them to link educational activities to individual circumstances, interests, and aims (Assor et al., 2002; Reeve, Jang, Carrell, Jeon, & Barch, 2004).

Sometimes educational activities cannot be integrated with a student's aims, ambitions, or needs because these have not yet been developed by the student. In this situation, autonomy-supportive teachers aim at identification, the next type of autonomous motivation according to SDT. Rationales are offered to explain why the activity is important (Reeve et al., 2004; Reeve & Jang, 2006) without referring to the student's unique personal situation (Stefanou, Perencevich, DiCintio, & Turner, 2004).

The provision of choice is also an important autonomy-supportive practice, especially if it allows the student to choose activities that are personally relevant (Assor et al., 2002; Katz & Assor, 2007). Stimulating the self-initiation of learning activities, encouraging independent thinking (Assor & Kaplan, 2001) and allowing students to find their own solutions to puzzles or problems (Stefanou et al., 2004) are other examples of autonomy-supporting practices that provide students with leeway. Choice can also refer to organizational or procedural aspects, such as seating arrangements in the classroom, deadlines, working methods, and sequencing (Ames, 1992; Katz & Assor, 2007; Reeve & Jang, 2006; Skinner & Belmont, 1993; Stefanou et al., 2004). Research has repeatedly shown that choice by itself is not enough to support student autonomy and is of lesser importance to the provision of (personal) relevance (Assor & Kaplan, 2001; Assor et al., 2002; Stefanou et al., 2004). A later section will delve deeper into this issue.

Autonomy-supportive teachers minimize the use of controls (Katz & Assor, 2007; Reeve & Jang, 2006; Skinner & Belmont, 1993). This applies to controls aimed at both extrinsic motivation (punishments, bonuses) and introjected controlled motivation (inducing guilt, shame, or public comparisons with peers). They refrain from close surveillance and frequent intrusions (Assor & Kaplan, 2001; Assor et al., 2002). In contrast, controlling teachers influence students' ways of thinking, feeling, and behaving in ways consistent with behavior modification programs. For them, the idea is to establish an agenda of what students should and should not do, then shape students toward that agenda by using external contingencies and pressuring language (Reeve & Jang, 2006).

In terms of evaluation practices, autonomy-supportive teachers emphasize individual improvement and development (rather than generic norms) and, to this end, provide informational (rather than controlling) feedback (Ames, 1992; Reeve et al., 2004; Reeve & Jang, 2006). They recognize effort and allow errors to be made, as mistakes are seen as part of the learning process (Ames, 1992). Self-monitoring is strongly encouraged. Evaluations are kept private rather than ranking classmates in terms of percentile scores. Finally, autonomy-supportive teachers typically do not practice all the aforementioned in isolation; they also create a warm, safe climate (in response to relational needs) and make sure that challenges are optimal for each person (in response to competence needs). Learning is seen as a social activity, and students are encouraged to share and learn from each other.

The primary aim of autonomy-supportive practices is to allow students to work from their own inner motivational resource base. Contradicting the expectancy-valence approach to achievement behavior that does not distinguish between autonomous and controlled motivation, research finds that autonomous motivation is related to increased levels of engagement (Niemiec & Ryan, 2009; Reeve & Jang, 2006); effort (Ryan & Brown, 2005); persistence (Reeve & Jang, 2006; Sheldon & Elliott, 1998); self-directedness, flexibility, and creativeness (Sheldon & Elliott, 1998); deep-level learning (Ryan & Deci, 2000; Niemiec & Ryan, 2009); personal goal attainment (Sheldon & Elliott, 1998); and well-being (Reeve & Jang, 2006). These outcomes are directly relevant for enterprising behaviors as these behaviors tend to be risky, require effort to enact, and encounter obstacles along the way; are self-starting, require flexibility, creative approaches, and continuous learning; and are tied to personal goals and beliefs (Gibb, 1993).

## IMPLEMENTATION TRADE-OFFS AND ISSUES

### Guidance and Freedom

Autonomy as the guiding principle of entrepreneurship education may appear to suggest that students are best left alone to pursue their own learning processes. However, autonomy support is not about undirected, unguided learning (Loyens, Magda, & Rikers, 2008). In fact, students, paradoxically perhaps, want their teachers to help them become more self-directed (Loyens et al., 2008). As Assor et al. (2002) state, autonomy support is not about the minimization of guidance and consultation by educators so as to leave sufficient space for the emergence of the student's true self, but rather about taking an active emphatic role in helping them to develop and realize personal goals. Individuation and identity-formation processes do not require detachment from supportive others (Assor & Kaplan, 2001). Teachers can offer new vistas, alternative ways to view the world (Brookfield, 1985). Students may be caught in narrowly defined frameworks of thought and action (Brookfield, 1985). Moreover, their goals may be emergent rather than known. Without teacher guidance, learning may stagnate (Mezirow, 1985).

The question, therefore, is how to balance guidance and freedom: to optimize individual autonomy whenever possible without excluding guidance. Solutions to the tension between instruction and autonomy can be found in course design features that individualize entrepreneurship education. One solution, paradoxically, is to require students to develop goals and tasks that they are motivated to do. Another is to assign a right to students to replace assignments and readings with ones that they feel to fit better. The opposite problem may also arise, namely, when the teacher intends to support autonomy but the student demands teacher-directed learning. This will be further discussed later.

## Information Versus Pressure

Autonomy-supportive teachers aim to provide feedback that relates to each person's circumstances and psychology. However, there is a thin line between informational and controlling feedback. Two examples are the use of praise and hints. Praise can be used as a controlling extrinsic reward in which social approval and positive evaluation act as contingent rewards for right answers and acceptable behaviors. Teachers also use praise as positive informational feedback to affirm the student's progress, improvement, or task mastery (Reeve & Jang, 2006). Similarly, hints represent a teacher's instructional effort to provide students with information when they reach an impasse. Hints can support the student's own learning processes. However, they can also be taken as directives and as indications of 'the right answer.' The difficulty is that praise or hints act in support of autonomy or become controlling depending on the perception of the student. Praise and hints may be intended as supporting autonomy but can be interpreted as controlling, perhaps especially by independence-driven entrepreneurship students. Autonomy-supportive teachers stress the informational value of their feedback.

## The Self and Others

Autonomy may carry an association with singular, soloist behavior. Both SDT and SDL emphasize that this is not the case. SDT posits three basic needs: autonomy, competence, and relatedness. Ryan and Deci (2000) argue that autonomy without relatedness is problematic, just as the following section will discuss the suggestion that autonomy without competence is problematic. SDL research shows that successful self-directed learners place their learning within a social context, and other people are cited as the most important learning resource (Brookfield, 1985). A personalized approach makes it interesting to engage with other students. Peers and fellow learners provide information, serve as skill models, act as reinforcers of learning, and serve as counselors at times of crisis (Brookfield, 1985). A community of learning thus emerges.

This focus on social embeddedness fits well with the enterprising way of life. Being enterprising is about creating value for others, especially in the case of social entrepreneurship. Moreover, the enterprising way of life strongly requires networking and influence competencies. A community of learners can practice these competencies and itself becomes a vital and important network of enterprising individuals.

## Choice and Relevance

Research has shown that organizational or procedural choice by itself is not enough to support student autonomy and is of lesser importance than the provision of (personal) relevance (Assor & Kaplan, 2001; Assor et al., 2002). Teachers who provide choice create a space that allows students to exercise their autonomy. However, it is possible that many students do not know what to do in this open space. Encouraging independent thinking (Assor & Kaplan, 2001) and allowing students to find their own solutions to puzzles or problems (Stefanou et al., 2004) also presupposes a certain level of competence.

Choice must thus support not only autonomy but also competence. Just as Ryan and Deci (2000) argue that autonomy without relatedness is problematic, so too is autonomy without competence. Competence can be enhanced by creating challenges that are neither too easy nor too difficult. An individualized approach helps to match choices to each person's capability, circumstances, and zone of proximal development.

## Reciprocal Effects: Influences of Students on Faculty

Thus far, this analysis has reported autonomy-supportive practices that have been found to influence students. The question also arises whether student behavior influences the autonomy support of faculty. If a student does not respond well to autonomy support, will the teacher increase his or her efforts or instead resort to more controlling methods? Skinner and Belmont (1993) found evidence for the latter pattern. Students who show higher initial levels of behavioral engagement receive even more subsequent autonomy support, and students who show lower initial levels of behavioral engagement subsequently receive less. Skinner and Belmont acknowledge that passivity can be interpreted as lack of internal motivation, which leads teachers to apply increased coercion to get the student to participate in classroom activities. Although understandable, this suggests that students who are behaviorally disengaged receive teacher responses that will undermine their motivation even further. This raises the question whether each and every entrepreneurship student is ready for autonomy support.

## Is Autonomy Support Suitable for Every Student?

A lack of readiness for autonomy support may arise out of preference or out of inability. First, as noted by Bird (2002), students often prefer teacher-directed learning, having had a long history of passive learning. Many want to know exactly where the bar is set to get an *A*, *B*, or *C* and follow the most efficient pathway to that goal. Just like other students, entrepreneurship students want to graduate, and they want to know how they can achieve this. However, an entrepreneurship student without the drive for autonomous action is somewhat of a contradiction. It is difficult to see why someone who is guided mainly by external standards, as opposed to their own, would want to graduate as an entrepreneurship student. If students are not ready for autonomy support because they prefer to be teacher led, then it is not unreasonable to ask them to reflect on their suitability as entrepreneurship students.

A second issue is that students may feel unable to cope with entrepreneurship education aimed at furthering the ability to take autonomous action (Stefanou et al., 2004). As discussed earlier, course activities must be tied to individual levels of academic competence. Moreover, students are asked to develop a strong sense of self as autonomy pertains to striving to develop and realize personal goals, values, and interests (Assor et al., 2002). Students may not yet sufficiently know themselves. But this is exactly an area where autonomy-supportive teaching can explore and experiment. Students may have a number of possible selves (Markus & Nurius, 1986), which they might like to explore in the context of entrepreneurship. Depending on their outlook, they may design the type of entrepreneurship that is right for them (Sarasvathy, 2004).

## Is Autonomy-Support Suitable for Every Type and Level of Entrepreneurship Education?

Gibb (1999) distinguishes three aims of entrepreneurship education. The first is to learn to understand entrepreneurship: what it is, what entrepreneurs do, why they are needed, and the like. The second aim is to become entrepreneurial as a person: to take responsibility for learning, career, and life. The third aim is to become an actual entrepreneur: how to start and manage a business. Entrepreneurship education as an exercise in the strengthening of autonomy refers first and foremost to the second aim, learning to become entrepreneurial. However, the other two aims are obviously important if enterprising initiatives are to succeed. Having the central focus on the capacity for autonomous action will mean that the personal relevance of course activities serving the first and the third aim are enhanced, which furthers integrated and identified regulation.

Another issue is whether autonomy-guided entrepreneurship education may be especially suitable for students at university. Compared with students in vocational education, university students are trained to develop independent and critical thinking skills and to rely more on self-management to conduct their studies. In these respects, university students may have a head start. On the other hand, it should be noted that students in vocational education live the same enterprising way of life (Gibb, 2002a, 2002b) as university students do. They are equally in need of a developed capacity for autonomous action.

## CONCLUSION

What does it actually mean if an entrepreneurship student graduates with straight As? Obviously, this student is expected to have gained knowledge about various aspects of entrepreneurship in general and of setting up a new venture in particular. But unlike a medical doctor, an engineer, or an accountant, the fulfillment of graduation criteria does not result in a qualification for the profession. Perhaps above all, the top student in entrepreneurship can be expected to have a developed capacity for autonomous action. This chapter has presented several arguments for putting autonomy center stage; it has offered theories and practices that aim at autonomy support and has discussed various implementation issues.

Key to students experiencing and exercising their sense of autonomy are educational processes that individualize and empower. Autonomy may serve as a generic focus for entrepreneurship education, yet it can only be practiced and developed in circumstances and conditions that are unique to each individual. Rather than decontextualizing education in the belief that learning in abstract form will promote generalization, autonomy-supportive teachers will attempt to present learning activities in individualized contexts (Cordova & Lepper, 1996).

Unfortunately, today's pressures on the educational system put severe strains on the individualization of education. Budget cuts typically result in standardization and less attention for individual student circumstances, needs and preferences. It is observed that the increased use of high-stakes testing results in teachers and schools feeling pushed into implementing controlling strategies, rather than being concerned with individual students' self-determination (Ryan & Brown, 2005). Entrepreneurship education without a strong focus on autonomy is doing individual students and society at large a disservice. The entrepreneurs of tomorrow face elevated levels of uncertainty and risk. They need a fully developed capacity for autonomous action in order to have a fighting chance.

## ACKNOWLEDGMENT

Ralph Bathurst and Karen Verduyn provided valuable comments. This chapter was a paper presented at the *IntEnt Conference* 2010 in Arnhem, the Netherlands. This chapter builds on an article presenting similar arguments that has been published in *Education + Training, 52*, (8/9).

## NOTES

1. In this chapter, the term 'entrepreneurship' refers to both types.

## REFERENCES

Ames, C. (1992). Classrooms: Goals, structures, and student motivation. *Journal of Educational Psychology, 84*(3), 261–271.

Anderson, C. (2006). *The long tail: Why the future of business is selling less of more*. New York: Hyperion.

Assor, A., & Kaplan, H. (2001). Mapping the domain of autonomy support. In A. Eflikes et al. (Eds.), *Trends and prospects in motivation research* (pp. 101–120). Amsterdam: Kluwer.

Assor, A., Kaplan, H., & Roth, G. (2002). Choice is good, but relevance is excellent: Autonomy-enhancing and suppressing teacher behaviours predicting students' engagement in schoolwork. *British Journal of Educational Psychology, 72*, 261–278.

Baumann, N., & Kuhl, J. (2005). How to resist temptation: The effects of external control versus autonomy support on self-regulatory dynamics. *Journal of Personality, 73*(2), 443–470.

Benz, M., & Frey, B. S. (2008a). Being independent is a great thing: Subjective evaluations of self-employment and hierarchy. *Economica, 75*, 362–383.

Benz, M., & Frey, B. S. (2008b). The value of doing what you like: Evidence from the self-employed in 23 countries. *Journal of Economic Behavior & Organization, 68*, 445–455.

Bird, B. (2002). Learning entrepreneurship competencies: The self-directed learning approach. *International Journal of Entrepreneurship Education, 1*, 203–227.

Brookfield, S. (1985). *Self-directed learning: From theory to practice*. San Francisco: Jossey Bass.

Cordova, D. I., & Lepper, M. R. (1996). Intrinsic motivation and the process of learning: Beneficial effects of contextualization, personalization, and choice. *Journal of Educational Psychology, 88*(4), 715–730.

Deci, E. L., & Ryan, R. M. (2000). The "what" and "why" of goal pursuits: Human needs and the self-determination of behaviour. *Psychological Inquiry, 11*(4), 227–268.

Gibb, A. A. (1993). The enterprise culture and education. *International Small Business Journal, 11*(3), 11–34.

Gibb, A. A. (1999). Can we build effective entrepreneurship through management development? *Journal of General Management, 24*(4), 1–21.

Gibb, A. A. (2002a). In pursuit of a new 'enterprise' and 'entrepreneurship' paradigm for learning: Creative destruction, new values, new ways of doing things and new combinations of knowledge. *International Journal of Management Reviews, 4*(3), 233–269.

Gibb, A. A. (2002b). Creating conducive environments for learning and entrepreneurship. *Industry and Higher Education, 16*(3), 135–147.

Gimeno, J., Folta, T. B., Cooper, A. C., & Woo, C. Y. (1997). Survival of the fittest? Entrepreneurial human capital and the persistence of underperforming firms. *Administrative Science Quarterly, 42,* 750–783.

Hundley, G. (2001). Why and when are the self-employed more satisfied with their work? *Industrial Relations, 40*(2), 293–316.

Katz, I., & Assor, A. (2007). When choice motivates and when it does not. *Educational Psychology Review, 19,* 429–442.

Knowles, M. S. (1975). *Self-directed learning: A guide for teachers and students.* Englewood Cliffs, NJ: Prentice-Hall.

Lange, T. (in press). Job satisfaction and self-employment: Autonomy or personality? *Small Business Economics.*

Loyens, S. M. M., Magda, J., & Rikers, R. M. J. P. (2008). Self-directed learning in problem-based learning and its relationships with self-regulated learning. *Educational Psychology Review, 20,* 411–427.

Markus, H., & Nurius, P. (1986). Possible selves. *American Psychologist, 41*(9), 954–969.

Mezirow, J. (1985). *A critical theory of self-directed learning.* In S. Brookfield (Ed.), *Self-directed learning: From theory to practice* (pp. 17–30). San Francisco: Jossey Bass.

Niemiec, C. P., & Ryan, R. M. (2009). Autonomy, competence, and relatedness in the classroom: Applying self-determination theory to educational practice. *Theory and Research in Education, 7,* 133–144.

Prottas, D. (2008). Do the self-employed value autonomy more than employees? *Career Development International, 13*(1), 33–45.

Reeve, J., & Jang, H. (2006). What teachers say and do to support students' autonomy during a learning activity. *Journal of Educational Psychology, 98*(1), 209–218.

Reeve, J., Jang, H., Carrell, D., Jeon, S., & Barch, J. (2004). Enhancing students' engagement by increasing teachers' autonomy support. *Motivation and Emotion, 28*(2), 147–169.

Ryan, R. M., & Brown, K. W. (2005). Legislating competence. In A. J. Elliott & C. S Dweck (Eds.), *Handbook of competence and motivation* (pp. 354–374). New York: Guilford.

Ryan, R. M., & Deci, E. L. (2000). Self-determination theory and the facilitation of intrinsic motivation, social development, and well-being. *American Psychologist, 55*(1), 68–78.

Sarasvathy, S. D. (2004). Making it happen: Beyond theories of the firm to theories of firm design. *Entrepreneurship Theory and Practice, 28*(6), 519–531.

Schjoedt, L. (2009). Entrepreneurial job characteristics: An examination of their effect on entrepreneurial satisfaction. *Entrepreneurship Theory and Practice, 33*(3), 619–644.

Shane, S., Locke, E., & Collins, C.J. (2003). Entrepreneurial motivation. *Human Resource Management Review, 13*(2), 257–280.

Sheldon, K. M., & Elliot, A. J. (1998). Not all personal goals are personal: Comparing autonomous and controlled reasons for goals as predictors of effort and attainment. *Personality and Social Psychology Bulletin, 24*(5), 546–557.

Skinner, E. A., & Belmont, M. J. (1993). Motivation in the classroom: Reciprocal effects of teacher behaviour and student engagement across the school year. *Journal of Educational Psychology, 85*(4), 571–581.

Stefanou, C. R., Perencevich, K. C., DiCintio, M., & Turner, J. C. (2004). Supporting autonomy in the classroom: Ways teachers encourage student decision making and ownership. *Educational Psychologist, 39*(2), 97–110.

van Gelderen, M. W., & Jansen, P. G. W. (2006). Autonomy as a startup motive. *Journal of Small Business and Enterprise Development, 13*(1), 23–32.

5 Contextualizing Entrepreneurship
in Administered Markets
## New Entrants' Stakeholder
## Mobilization and Legitimacy
## Generation in Dutch Health Care

*Eveline Stam-Hulsink and Willem Hulsink*

## INTRODUCTION

Over the last decades, the field of entrepreneurship has been dominated by actor-centered perspectives and the related pictures of the great man (or woman) equipped with extraordinary qualities. Occasionally, this is referred to as the 'myth of the lonely only entrepreneur' (Schoonhoven & Romanelli, 2009). Psychologists and economists have infused the body of entrepreneurship knowledge with key concepts such as specific entrepreneurial traits, unique motivations, and distinctive entrepreneur behaviors. In addition, theoretical research relating to the entrepreneurs' alertness to opportunities, innovativeness of their strategies and business models, and the macroeconomic effects of their firm-founding activities are being called upon to explain entrepreneurial activity. Overall, the heart of entrepreneurship theory is said to consist of the study of opportunity-based behavior by creative individuals with special attention to the relationship between the opportunity and the individual differences in explaining the origins of entrepreneurial activity (Stevenson & Gumpert, 1985; Shane & Venkataraman, 2000).

This dominant psychological-economic approach does not fully take into account how history and context shape the new ventures and market-creating activities of entrepreneurs. It neglects to show how business partners of entrepreneurs take part in the founding process and fails to take into account the overall entrepreneurial dynamics within a sector, field, or population. The fact that contextual, historical, and social factors also play a part in the emergence of new industries has been overlooked and their importance undervalued. The discipline that studies these related phenomena, sociology, and in particular its subdiscipline, organization theory, has largely ignored the creation of new organizations and the transformative behavior of entrepreneurs (Aldrich, 1999). The new sociological contribution defines entrepreneurship as a collective phenomenon that recognizes the actions and contributions of dynamic actors but simultaneously acknowledges the substantive impact of the larger social network and institutional community in which these actors are embedded, constraining or facilitating their behavior. Besides the actions and strategies of individuals, entrepreneurship also depends on collective action whereby entrepreneurs draw upon local, regional, sectoral, and/or professional communities (Schoonhoven & Romanelli, 2009).

In order to successfully introduce new products or services into the market to make their ventures succeed, entrepreneurs not only require good ideas, resources, and contacts but also social acceptance from their community of stakeholders. Founders of innovative ventures face a greater risk of failure than established organizations because they are operating in situations with few, if any, precedents in the population. This notion of 'liability of newness' refers to the higher risk of failure faced by young organizations (Stinchcombe, 1965). For that reason, young ventures need to develop acceptance and legitimacy. The sources and origins of organizational legitimacy, especially of new entrants with entrepreneurial firms, are an emerging field of research (Deephouse & Suchman, 2008).

As are many Western countries, the Netherlands is confronted with a growing and aging population while affordable, high-quality, and accessible health-care services and products are not keeping pace. Restructuring the Dutch health-care sector is the topic of heated political debate. Embarking on the generation of social acceptance, new ventures and the innovations they bring to market can actually induce change in the standards of efficiency and quality of Dutch health care. Some claim that health care should not be reformed and condemn moves toward liberalization, privatization, and regulatory reform because it conflicts with the Dutch welfare-state tradition. In order to improve the quality, affordability, and accessibility of merit goods such as health care and education, these highly institutionalized markets are increasingly opening up to new, innovative organizations. Thus, in these administered contexts, the competition between ambitious entrepreneurs and established market players is slowly being shaped. New entrants to these markets not only have to seize and capture the opportunity, mobilize substantial resources, build up strategic partnerships, and attract the larger public like any other entrepreneur, but they also have to overcome strong competition from powerful players and skepticism among regulators and policy makers. A growing number of entrepreneurs continue to introduce new ways of organizing and offering health-care innovations, whether successful or not. Their motivations, however, are openly questioned, indicating the lack of legitimacy or social acceptance these entrepreneurs and their activities endure. As such, private Dutch health-care entrepreneurs receive considerable press attention in the Netherlands and have been referred to as the 'Cowboys of Dutch healthcare' (e.g., NRC, 2009).

To sum up, in this chapter we examine strategies and processes in legitimacy generation by new ventures, with special relevance to the study of the social networking behavior of entrepreneurs in the Dutch health-care community. Our research question is this: How do health-care entrepreneurs strategically engage with institutional and organizational stakeholders to generate organizational legitimacy for innovative (private) health-care ventures? We adopt a behavioral theory on entrepreneurial networking and relate the question of how entrepreneurs in highly institutionalized and regulated markets, such as health care, generate social acceptance through active stakeholder mobilization. For this, we analyze and compare three qualitative case studies of distinctive health-care ventures and their founders. We investigate differences in the engagement of stakeholders and the networking styles of these health-care entrepreneurs, and we analyze subsequent differences in the venture's development and path toward success.

## LITERATURE REVIEW

Within the entrepreneurial process, three subprocesses can be identified: opportunity recognition, preparation, and exploitation (Van der Veen & Wakkee, 2004). The recognition of opportunities involves the development of initial ideas into more refined conceptualizations of new combinations to be offered to the market. Opportunity preparation involves the building of a resource base and the creation of an organization through which the opportunity is exploited. During the exploitation process, actual products and services are produced and sold in the marketplace, and social and economic value is created. Whereas alert entrepreneurs usually copy and adjust existing business models, innovative entrepreneurs pursue more radical innovations in highly institutionalized markets. Both types of entrepreneur must learn about new markets and develop knowledge and capabilities to exploit them in order to survive and grow. However, entrepreneurs of radical innovations have to overcome substantive levels of liabilities of newness. These innovative entrepreneurs need to obtain cooperation from strangers, recruit and train employees, raise capital from skeptical investors, and compete effectively against established rivals (Stinchcombe, 1965).

These new entrants first need a place in the institutional framework defining a particular sector in order to successfully bring novel products and services to the market. Institutions refer to the rules of the game in a society that, when stable, can reduce uncertainty and risk for individual behavior as well as transaction costs (North, 1990). Institutions include both formal rules, such as constitutional, legal, and organizational frameworks for individual actions directly under the influence of the state, and informal rules referring to cultural codes of conducted values and norms that the state can indirectly influence (North, 1990; Scott, 2001). Institutions hold distinctive logics that indicate the concealed agreement on conventional ways of social action or 'the accepted ways of how things get done'(Thornthon & Ocasio, 2008).

De Clercq and Voronov (2009) conceive of legitimacy attributed to entrepreneurs as consisting of elements that capture both stability and change, that is, an expectation to 'fit in' (institutional legitimacy) as well as to 'stand out' (innovative legitimacy). Overall, organizational legitimacy indicates the social acceptance resulting from the organization's stakeholders' evaluation of the comprehensibility, desirability, and appropriateness of its practices. The concept has been categorized by identifying three primary dimensions: pragmatic legitimacy, based on audience self-interest; cognitive legitimacy, based on comprehensibility and taken-for-grantedness; and moral legitimacy based on normative approval of an organization's practices (Suchman, 1995). It is likely that obtaining legitimacy depends on how the entrepreneur demonstrates the innovation's potential for creating economic and social value—the innovation's value propositions—to different stakeholders groups. The innovation's value proposition can be structured along the same dimensions of legitimacy discussed previously. Pragmatic legitimacy—its basic prerogative and social acceptance—can be derived from stakeholders when the innovation contains obvious potential for social and economic profit for stakeholders. If the innovation is difficult to comprehend by stakeholders (e.g., due to its technical complexity or increased levels of tacit knowledge necessary to operate and understand it), the innovation's cognitive legitimacy and interpretability may be lacking. An innovation can have difficulties in obtaining moral legitimacy if the innovation simply does not abide by laws and regulations and goes against accepted norms.

Cheney and Christensen (2001) call attention to the interdependence of organizations and stakeholders and demonstrate the necessity of engaging stakeholders in the organization's decision-making process. A legitimate organization is one that is perceived to be pursuing socially acceptable goals in a socially acceptable manner in addition to their basic quality, efficiency, and performance requirements. One will expect that health-care entrepreneurs, deliberately acting upon this necessity and engaging stakeholders during the start-up and early growth phases, are more successful in generating legitimacy from their institutionalized health-care system than those new entrants who act on their own.

Entrepreneurial decisions are not exclusively made through economic contracting relations, but rather evolve in sociocultural contexts of stakeholder mobilization and active networking (Starr & MacMillan, 1990). In new small ventures, interactions between entrepreneurs and their venture's stakeholders often take place on a personal level, which indicates that resource exchanges of new ventures occur in one-on-one social network relationships (Elfring & Hulsink, 2003). The network dimension of tie-strength categorizes social relations on levels of interaction frequency, emotional intimacy, and cognitive understanding (Granovetter, 1983). Weak ties are theoretically those relations in which an actor, and in our case, the entrepreneur, do not often meet and are characterized by low levels of the aforementioned characteristics. Yet weak ties can be vital sources of information and can function as bridges between groups of strong relations. Strong ties are characterized by frequent interactions and higher levels of emotional intimacy and/or cognitive understanding of the actors that allow for fine-grained information transfer, joint problem-solving, and trustworthiness.

Facing the demographic challenges of ageing populations, European health-care policies work toward the realization of key issues of availability, affordability, and quality of health-care systems (e.g., De Gooijer, 2007). Health-care sectors contain multifaceted sets of relations between the national policy and individual health-care demands. Currently, demographic changes, new efficiency demands, and increased availability of new medical technologies put pressure on health-care systems and force realignment of organizational processes (Camps & Kenis, 2010). Within this complex setting of dependencies, rules, and regulations, health-care entrepreneurs run into high regulatory institutional entry barriers when looking for market openings for their alternative and innovative services and products. New ventures in Dutch health care deliver health-care services and products for profit reasons; they have private management structures and use innovative techniques and practices while consistently serving patients as care customers.

Successful health-care innovations rock the status quo in norms and routines in Dutch health-care delivery by questioning and challenging current interaction patterns of health-care delivery within the current institutional framework. In regulated market environments like health care, entrepreneurs repeatedly encounter the scrutiny of regulators, policy makers, and other stakeholders, such as patient communities and specialized and general care-practitioners. These stakeholders have different expectations regarding the practices and output of an entrepreneurial health-care venture and the innovation it is putting forward. Yet legitimacy granted by these stakeholder groups is vital for a venture's growth. How well an entrepreneur handles the venture's early growth phases, characterized by these vulnerabilities, and successfully generates social acceptance in the form of familiarity, credibility, and commitment from heterogeneous stakeholder groups in the market may well influence the venture's chances of survival. Thus, Dutch health-care initiatives are undertaken by entrepreneurs within interorganizational chains and overlapping networks while being governed by strict regulations and institutional arrangements.

To illustrate the restrictions health-care entrepreneurs face, Putters (2009) portrays innovative entrepreneurs in Dutch health care as being entrepreneurial yet bounded by regulations. We can deduce that the generation of organizational legitimacy by private ventures is at the heart of these complex arrangements. As stated by Christensen, Bohmer, and Kenagy, health-care industries are considered to be among the most entrenched, change-averse industries: "The innovations that will eventually turn around health-care service delivery processes are ready in a lot of cases; but they can't find the backers" (2000, p. 105). For this reason, in this chapter, we study networking strategies of health-care entrepreneurs in the creation of alignment between their venture and stakeholder groups. We analyze how their efforts in mobilizing support for their venture's present and future business activities bring us closer to establishing sources and origins of organizational legitimacy.

## CASES AND DATA COLLECTION

The data from our three cases is part of a greater qualitative research sample on the process of the legitimation of new Dutch health-care ventures.[1] In the selection of these cases, we applied theoretical sampling logic (Eisenhardt, 1989). Our three cases differ between product and process innovations and/or a combination of the two. Product innovations are new or better goods, as well as new intangible services. Process innovations are new ways of providing health-care services. These may be technological or organizational. In this chapter, we compare three cases of innovative health-care ventures. The entrepreneur of venture Alpha introduces a product innovation in the form of medical technological innovation for use in large medical facilities. Venture Beta belongs to an entrepreneur introducing an innovative health-care process within the traditional system through which patients choose their health-care provider. Our third case, venture Gamma, is run by an entrepreneur introducing a combined product and process innovation around a track-and-trace system for surgical instruments. Table 5.1 displays the characteristics of the entrepreneurs and their innovations.

Our data and results are based on the collection of primary data in the form of interviews with health-care entrepreneurs and experts in Dutch health care as well as on secondary data derived from online studies of websites, discussion forums, newspaper content, and expert magazines. The interview sessions contained three separated yet integrated parts: an ego-network analysis, a stakeholder analysis, and a semistructured interview section focusing on the entrepreneur's networking behavior. First, a personal network analysis (ego-network analysis) of the health-care entrepreneurs was performed. For this, a name generator (Burt, 2000) to elicit the characteristics of the age and the content of the entrepreneur's network ties with important network members (alters) of the entrepreneur was used. With the name generator, we brought about the entrepreneur's key network members in the venture's areas of strategic advice, operational support, knowledge, and miscellaneous issues. Second, a data-collection method that permits the inventory of the entrepreneur's cognitive map of the venture's stakeholders from the entrepreneur's point of view was implemented. We also asked how the entrepreneur maintained these relationships and how

*Table 5.1* Case Characteristics

| Case | Innovation | Entrepreneur | Year of launch | Phase in entrepreneurial process | Prior experience |
|---|---|---|---|---|---|
| Venture Alpha Product innovation | Mobile operating-room unit | Kees, male, 41 years of age | 2005 | Exploitation | Optometrist, no prior entrepreneurial experience. |
| Venture Beta Process innovation | Online health-care auction | Paul, male, 50 years of age | 2005 | Abandoned original idea | HR manager and health-care consultant with prior entrepreneurial experience. Started and managed his own unsuccessful business in health-care venture consultancy. |
| Venture Gamma Product and product/process innovation | Track-and-trace system for surgical instruments | Bonny, female, 36 years of age | 2008 | Exploration/preparation | Dietician, prior entrepreneurial experience launching a successful technical service company for the maintenance of endoscopic instruments. |

advantages or disadvantages were created from the development or maintenance of these relationships. Third, semistructured interview questions were asked about the entrepreneur, the venture's general characteristics, and the entrepreneur's networking behavior. The full sets of data permitted us to construct significant pictures of the social networking behavior and stakeholder engagement in the innovative ventures. In the following section, we describe the innovation and the business model of the venture and present our findings.

## CASE DESCRIPTIONS

### Case Venture Alpha: The Mobile Operating-Room Unit

Kees, a 41-year-old former optometrist, is the driving force behind the exploitation of the technological innovation of the mobile operating-room unit (MOU) for small surgeries. In 2003, he met the inventor of the MOU, an ophthalmologist who had designed a prototype and wanted to sell the MOU to other ophthalmologists starting home-based practices. The MOU offers an innovative way of performing microsurgery outside the conventional operating room and can be implemented independent of location. Small-surface surgeries and microsurgeries can be performed in any part of a hospital, outpatient center, or private clinic, or even at a medical office or residence without being dependent on a complex operating room organization, logistics, and other structural challenges. The innovation is that the airflow in the MOU is cleaner than in conventional operating rooms. For hospitals or clinics, the MOU offers the option to move the bulk of the high-volume microsurgical interventions to alternative treatment environments, which results in considerable relief for the operating-room complex and an increase in surgery capacity and turnover. For operating surgeons, the accessibility of the MOU is similar to that of a dentistry unit, a treatment area in which routine interventions can be performed without complex operating-room logistics. Although the initial purchase of the unit is more than €100,000, it is only a fraction of the cost of adding a conventional operating room to a large hospital. The MOU simplifies the infrastructure around the treatment space, and medical staff can be used more effectively. The MOU is a radical innovation; it opens up the possibility of small-surface surgery anywhere, and the quality of the air is even better then in regular operating rooms.

### Case Venture Beta: The Online Auctioning System of Maternity Care

Paul, age 50, is the owner of Beta, an Internet-based maternity-care auctioning venture. Paul is the driving force behind an attempt to introduce the radical innovation of online auctioning in the process of delivering maternity services in Dutch health care. Traditionally, Dutch women have had to arrange maternity services with their health-care insurance companies, which have fixed contracts with several maternity companies to provide maternity care in a given geographical location. This has resulted in restrictive price arrangements and long waiting lists. Women who have just given birth sometimes have to wait several days before receiving the necessary maternity care. Between 1992 and 1996, maternity services were among the first Dutch health-care services where competitive forces and entrepreneurial opportunities were permitted. Since then, maternity nurses have been able to join private maternity service companies, but their services are still covered by Dutch health-care insurances.

Because babies do not arrive at set times, it is difficult to plan maternity care. Paul's original concept of online maternity-service matching was supposed to work in the following way: An online maternity care management application would permit maternity-care providers to offer their services directly to pregnant women, who could call for services online, at the price that had been set, when the baby was born. Available maternity-care providers could offer their services at a price they themselves had established. The price level would depend on several issues: how much the maternity nurses wanted or needed to work at that time, how much available time they had, how competitive they wanted to be, online quality descriptions of their delivered care, and registered evaluations of the quality of their work. The online matching or auctioning program had a full quality-control application containing the registration of the maternity nurses' regulatory qualifications as well as quality record statistics obtained through continuous follow-ups with their clients. Quality reports were displayed in the online maternity-care site. New mothers or their partners would be able to apply electronically for maternity services when they needed them and choose from the maternity-care providers who responded to the call. Every maternity-care provider qualified and registered with the Internet auctioning site could react because the call for care was public. The idea of the maternity-care auctioning service is radical: Instead of giving the power to health-care insurers to decide who will work for them, the power went to the women and also set prices for health-care services. The venture's goal would be to offer high-quality maternity care established through market principles. Due to automating the process of matching supply and demand, administrative costs of care supply would be a fraction of the old arrangement.

## CASE VENTURE GAMMA: A TRACK-AND-TRACE SYSTEM FOR SURGICAL INSTRUMENTS

Bonny, a 34-year-old former dietitian, started a venture with her husband, a surgical instrument technician. She and her husband had already run a successful specialized and innovative company in the endoscopic surgery instrument-servicing field. They seized an opportunity in the servicing process of endoscopic surgical instruments by increasing the speed and service level at a reasonable price. Bonny was looking for a sales manager for this company when Janna applied for the job. Janna is also an entrepreneur but, at the time, was bound up in a legal fight over a previous venture that had introduced a track-and-trace system in life-science laboratories with 2-D matrix inscription. She needed a break from her entrepreneurial endeavors. The two women began discussions, and Bonny convinced Janna to investigate if Janna's innovative idea could be applied to sets of surgical instruments in operating rooms. Bonny knew from her own experience servicing medical devices that current track-and-tracing routines either consisted of the operating-room staff weighing full sets of instruments before and after surgery or just recounting full sets. Both methods have proved to be subject to human error, and operating room instruments tend to disappear. These routines do not sufficiently guard the patient's safety and lead to an increase in medical claims due to instruments being left behind in patients. Currently, no law or protocol on this issue exists in the Netherlands.

## ANALYSIS

We will describe our results using the three dimensions of the interviews. First, we discuss the ego-network inventory of the entrepreneurs. Second, we describe the inventory of the entrepreneur's cognitive map of the venture's stakeholders. Third, we discuss the entrepreneur's general characteristics as well as the entrepreneur's intentional social-networking behavior. Table 5.2 contains an overview of our findings.

### Venture Alpha: Actively Engaging with Stakeholders

Health-care venture Alpha is in the exploitation phase of the entrepreneurial process. Kees's ego network shows how he actively upholds social relationships with four different social networks for strategic advice and knowledge. He has no business exchange relations with his advice partners, to whom he is strongly related; he has developed solid relations with three of them, whom he has known for several decades; and he quickly developed solid relations with a fourth, whom he met six months ago. Kees's advice and knowledge contacts are from different backgrounds and different countries. By engaging staff from hospitals that were already familiar with working with an MOU, the entrepreneur was able to generate normative legitimacy for the MOU. As the entrepreneur mentioned, "these people in the field become sort of 'my people.'" Overall, we describe the activity of actively restructuring social-network contacts as a stakeholder

*Table 5.2*  Ego Network, Stakeholder Engagement Strategy, and Generated Legitimacy

| Venture | Entrepreneur | Ego network | Stakeholder engagement strategy | Generated Legitimacy |
|---|---|---|---|---|
| Alpha Mobile operating room unit | Kees, male, 41 years of age | Strong ties to multiple alters for strategic advice and knowledge provision. Uses and finds weak ties for resources on a need base. | Activating stakeholder engagement | Pragmatic, subsequently cognitive, which is followed by moral legitimacy. |
| Beta Online health-care auction | Paul, male, 50 years of age | Little or no strong ties, uses weak ties and supportive networks for day-to-day business. | Reticent stakeholder engagement | None. |
| Gamma Track-and-trace system for surgical instruments | Bonny, female, 36 years of age | Variety of strong network ties to strategic advisors and former financiers. Calculative in network development. | Early aligning stakeholder engagement | Pragmatic legitimacy originally, subsequently some problems with generation of cognitive legitimacy. Moral needs to follow further in entrepreneurial process. |

engagement strategy and social-network development for organizational legitimacy generation as the activating stakeholder strategy in generating organizational legitimacy.

## Venture Beta: Reticent Strategy Toward Stakeholders

The innovation of the online health-care service auction went as far as the introduction of the exploitation phase in the entrepreneurial process. Paul's story about introducing the idea is very different to the other two cases. The entrepreneur of venture Beta, Paul, chose to 'fly under the radar' until his innovation was ready to start. Unfortunately, the product launch was unsuccessful. The ideas of the health-care auction and ready-to-go ICT programming were not positively received. The innovation prompted many political actors to comment on the innovative idea. On this, Paul commented: "A few months after the kick-off, I asked for my first advice; I knew then that I had a problem. . . . And now I realize I have a communication problem." The antagonistic attitude of the entrepreneur toward informing the venture stakeholders for the sake of protecting the idea was a deliberate strategy that did not turn to the venture's advantage. We call this a 'reticent strategy' of the venture demonstrating a nonalignment between the innovation's value propositions and the context. In this case, the entrepreneur's engagement strategy toward the stakeholder groups had an impeding effect. It can be noticed that the entrepreneur missed out on the opportunity to benefit from the collective action of its stakeholder group by failing to engage them in the value propositions of the innovation. The unsuccessful reticent stakeholder engagement strategy of venture Beta's entrepreneur illustrates the need for an active and strategic development of social acceptance to overcome the venture's liabilities of newness.

## Venture Gamma: Aligning Stakeholders Early

Venture Gamma is working toward the introduction of the innovative track-and-trace system for surgical instruments and can be designated to handle issues in both the exploration phase and preparation phase of the entrepreneurial process. Bonny was in the phase of visiting potential clients—hospitals with the need to improve their track-and-trace systems in operating rooms. She was also in the active process of designing the full ICT system of the product and was actively getting in contact with stakeholder groups in order to discuss the potential of the innovation and to receive feedback. Bonny's ego network turned out to be a social network with active relationships with strategic advisors, and she was still in contact with others who had helped her financially with her previous venture. In the case of venture Gamma, moral legitimacy has not yet been generated because the venture is still in its exploration and preparation phase. However, in Bonny's case, we witnessed the use of stakeholder involvement and collaboration in order to influence the existing norm on how surgical instruments should be tracked and traced. Bonny was thus able to identify the names and faces of her active network ties to significant stakeholders. She had intentionally sought out social-network contacts with multiple institutional players to inform them of the product and sponsor events for them. We call this process of early engagement with stakeholders through concrete social-network development the 'aligning strategy.' In this, value propositions of the innovation are being made explicit by the entrepreneur to diverse groups of stakeholders through processes of actively giving information and gathering advice. With this approach, the generation of legitimacy forms a strategic goal of the entrepreneur early on in the entrepreneurial process. The chances are greater that pragmatic legitimacy can be generated from stakeholder groups for the obvious value added by the innovation. Consequently, demonstrating and communicating improved working routines as a result of incorporating the innovation into current work practices facilitates the subsequent generation of cognitive and normative legitimacy.

## Cross-Case Analysis

The case descriptions demonstrate how successful generation of organizational legitimacy is generated; the social acceptance by stakeholders of the organization's practices and norm starts in the exploitation and preparation phases of the entrepreneurial process with an aligning strategy of stakeholders and develops into an active stakeholder engagement strategy in the exploitation phase of the innovation. We also demonstrated that a reticent and unforthcoming attitude in stakeholder engagement can be detrimental to the introduction of an innovation with objectively considered high levels of pragmatic legitimacy but low levels of moral (normative) and cognitive legitimacy. Those entrepreneurs that aligned their innovation's value propositions, enclosing the foundations for their innovation's legitimacy generation and subsequently actively engaging their stakeholders, seemed more successful in recognizing their innovation's dependence on trust and the commitment of community and institutional stakeholders.

The new entrants' conscious social-network contact selection and the subsequent influence of community and institutional stakeholders seemed to work in their favor in the generation of social acceptance for their innovation. These entrepreneurs recognized the importance of these contacts as much as the importance of organizational stakeholders for capital or other organizational resources. These new entrants closely and consciously monitored their social relations to key stakeholder groups. Consequently, these social contacts naturally assumed ambassador roles for the value propositions of the health-care innovation. In this way, these key stakeholders helped new entrants translate their innovation's assets to the greater community and institutional public. The value propositions of the innovation, considering it pragmatic value, are being transmitted through this strategic social network interaction and subsequent changes in work practices and routines are thus more easily accepted by stakeholders. Working with and acceptance of the innovation's practical value leads to the natural acceptance of the innovation and the new social structures around the innovation lead to the generation of normative approval of the new routine. Entrepreneurs engage deliberately in personal network relations with key stakeholders from the community that endorse and consequently support the entrepreneur with the design and execution of proliferating strategies. In the exploitation phase, successful health-care entrepreneurs both maintained the links represented by personal network ties to the organization set as well as indirect and direct contact with the stakeholders in the greater context. Such a process of new venture legitimation results from well-thought-out communication and social-network strategies for their venture's survival.

## CONCLUSION

According to their collective view of entrepreneurship, Schoonhoven and Romanelli (2009) argue that it takes a community of people and organizations to mount the successful launch of a new firm. Our three cases demonstrate that rather than being individual actions, successful entrepreneurship and innovation realizations are extraindividual phenomena including collaborative activities from active stakeholders. Acquiring organizational legitimacy is the first result of collaborative activities between an entrepreneur and stakeholder groups. The social acceptance generated through this collective process is essential for innovative ventures as it grants the venture access to necessary resources such as funding, know-how, and government support. From our cases, we see how the necessity of generating social acceptance and organizational legitimacy is easily underestimated by entrepreneurs. We sought to answer the question of how health-care entrepreneurs strategically engage with institutional and organizational stakeholders to generate organizational legitimacy for innovative health-care ventures. We recognized the different strategies of active, reticent, and early-aligning stakeholder engagement through social-networking behavior in the early phases of new health-care ventures.

Overall, we conclude that the process of embedding an innovative venture into existing social structures and practices is strategically executed by entrepreneurs who consciously incorporate the innovation into the institutionalized context through active social networking. A successful introduction of the innovation takes more than merely presenting the idea to the environment. It requires individual entrepreneurs to employ and engage into collective action. Through this, entrepreneurs draw upon the local, regional, sectoral, and/or professional communities and their dynamics as early as the exploration and preparation phase of the innovation. Comprehension, commitment, and trust are generated by means of the development of direct social relationships with stakeholders. The engagement of and communication with stakeholders through these direct network ties provide the basis for positive evaluation of the venture's potential and practices and generates necessary organizational legitimacy.

## ACKNOWLEDGMENTS

We thank Peter Groenewegen, Ingrid Wakkee, and the editors of this volume for their comments on earlier versions of this chapter. We also thank Syntens (Human Health Group) and the participating entrepreneurs for supporting access to the research field.

## NOTES

1. The data from this research is part of the qualitative phase of a multimethod PhD research of one of the authors, Eveline Stam, Department of Organization Science, Vrije Universiteit, Amsterdam, into entrepreneurial social networking and the process of new venture legitimation in administered market environments.

## REFERENCES

Burt, R. (2000). The network structure of social capital. In R. I. Sutton & B. M. Staw (Eds.), *Networks and organizations* (pp. 125–161). Greenwich, CT: JAI.
Aldrich, H. (1999). *Organizations evolving.* London: Sage.
Camps, T., & Kenis, P. (2010). Healthcare, chains and networks. *Journal on Chain and Network Science, 10*(2), 87–88.
Cheney, G., & Christensen, L. (2001). Organizational identity at issue: Linkages between 'internal' and 'external' organizational communication. In F. Jablin & L. Putnam (Eds.), *New handbook of organizational communication* (pp. 231–270). Newbury Park, CA: Sage.
Christensen, C., Bohmer, R., & Kenagy, J. (2000). Will disruptive innovations cure healthcare? *Harvard Business Review, 78*(5), 102–112.
De Clercq, D., & Voronov, M. (2009). Toward a practice perspective of entrepreneurial legitimacy as habitus. *International Small Business Journal, 27*(4), 395–419.
De Gooijer, W. (2007). *Trends in EU healthcare systems.* New York: Springer.
Deephouse, D., & Suchman, M. (2008). Legitimacy in organizational institutionalism. In C. O. R. Greenwood, K. Sahlin & R. Suddabay (Eds.), *The Sage handbook of organizational institutionalism* (pp. 49–78). London: Sage.
Eisenhardt, K. (1989). Building theories from case study research. *Academy of Management Review, 14*(4), 532–550.
Elfring, T., & Hulsink, W. (2003). Networks in entrepreneurship: The case of high technology firms. *Small Business Economics, 21*(4), 409–422.
Granovetter, M. (1983). The strength of weak ties: A network theory revisited. *Sociological Theory, 1*, 201–233.

North, D. (1990). *Institutions, institutional change and economic performance.* Cambridge: Cambridge University Press.

NRC (2009) 'Kabinet maakt Eind aan 'Cowboys in Zorg'. http://www.nrc.nl/binnenland/article2295722.ece/Kabinet_draait_liberalisering_zorg_deels (Retrieved August 2011).

Putters, K. (2009). *Besturen met duivelselastiek.* Rotterdam: Inaugural Lecture Erasmus University.

Schoonhoven, C. B., & Romanelli, E. (2009). Advances in entrepreneurship, firme-mergence and growth. In G. T. Lumpkin & J. A. Katz (Eds.), *Entrepreneurialstrategic content.* Vol. 11 (pp. 225–259). Stanford CA: Stanford University Press.

Scott, W. (2001). Institutions and organizations (2nd ed.). Thousand Oaks, CA: Sage.

Shane, S., & Venkataraman, S. (2000). The promise of entrepreneurship as a field of research. *Academy of Management Review, 25*(1), 217–226.

Starr, J.A., & MacMillan, I. (1990). Resource cooptation via social contracting: Resource acquisition strategies for new ventures. *Strategic Management Journal* 11, 79-92.

Stevenson, H., & Gumpert, D. (1985). The heart of entrepreneurship. *Harvard Business Review, 2,* 85–94.

Stinchcombe, A. (1965). Organizations and social structure. In J. March (Ed.), *Handbook of organizations* (pp. 153–193). Chicago: Rand-McNally.

Suchman, M. (1995). Managing legitimacy: Strategic and institutional approaches. *Academy of Management Review, 20*(3), 517–610.

Thornton, P.H., & Ocasio, W. (2008). Institutional Logics. In R. Greenwood, C. Oliver, K. Sahlin & R. Suddaby (Eds.), *Handbook of Organizational Institutionalism* (pp. 99-129). London: Sage.

Van der Veen, M. & Wakkee, I. (2004). Understanding the entrepreneurial process. In D. S. Watkins (Ed.), *Annual Review of Progress in Entrepreneurship Research* (pp. 114–152). Brussels: European Foundation of Management Development.

# 6 Entrepreneurship for Environmentally Sustainable Design

*Bart Bossink*

## INTRODUCTION

This chapter proposes that the environmental design process needs both entrepreneurial designers as well as a context of entrepreneurial stakeholders who finance, support, produce, and sell the designs. The designer's capability to develop environmentally sustainable designs are vital, along with his/her capacity to gain access to, become a member of, and cooperate with members of entrepreneurial networks within environmentally aware governmental, institutional, and commercial organizations.

The chapter is presented in six sections. This section introduces the central theme. The second section presents the methodology and research methods with which the entrepreneurial process of environmentally sustainable design is studied. The third section builds the analytical framework with which entrepreneurial environmental design can be described. The next section applies this framework to setting out the entrepreneurial environmental design process in the Dutch house-building industry. Then, the case study findings are discussed and analyzed, and the final section summarizes the main conclusions.

## RESEARCH DESIGN

The case study in this chapter analyzes cooperation in entrepreneurial networks that develop environmentally sustainable designs. The study's basic research question is this: Which factors stimulate the entrepreneurial activities of the stakeholders in the environmentally sustainable design process? To search for answers to this question, a framework has been derived from the literature to serve as the analytical framework for the study.

The Dutch house-building industry was selected to serve as the setting for the case study. It was selected because it has a long history of entrepreneurial activity by SMEs, gives a high priority to environmental sustainability, and has by nature an orientation toward design.

The analysis of entrepreneurial firms' cooperative environmental design activities was based on document studies and observations of one of the nation's 33 demonstration projects for buildings that are environmentally sustainable or 'green,' that is, energy-efficient and material-saving. The common denominator of all 33 demonstration projects was the fact that members of a small entrepreneurial network of firms had cooperatively developed the green designs. The project that was studied encompassed the design process for more than 350 dwellings, which were designed by combinations of architects, real estate agents, contractors, and consultants. This was studied by the following means:

- Seventy hours of observation in 13 design/build meetings. In several meetings, the architects presented and discussed their design output with the municipal manager, other architects, real estate agents, contractors, and consultants. The observer only observed and had no obligation to offer advice or intervene.
- Thirty-one design documents were collected and analyzed. The projects included eight different building types. For every type, at least three design versions, that is, rough draft, preliminary design, and final design, were studied. The study examined the aesthetics, materialization, and environmental orientation of the designs.

The case study research project specified the interaction and cooperation processes between the entrepreneurial architects and stakeholders in the environmentally sustainable building design process. A within-case analysis, in which the analytical framework structured the case study findings and resulted in a description of entrepreneurial, environmentally sustainable housing design processes (Yin, 2004), is presented in the case study section.

## ANALYTICAL FRAMEWORK: ENTREPRENEURSHIP FOR ENVIRONMENTALLY SUSTAINABLE DESIGN

The analytical framework with which the case study is structured and analyzed is based on a review of the literature on entrepreneurial networks for green innovation (e.g., Moensted, 2006; George & Farris, 1999; Håkanson, 1993). Four factors that can stimulate entrepreneurship for environmentally sustainable design were distinguished:

1. Environmental cooperation routines
2. Environmental technology policies
3. Environmental regulations
4. Environmental incentives

## Environmental Cooperation Routines

Cooperation between entrepreneurial governmental, institutional, scientific, and commercial organizations often facilitates the development of environmentally sustainable design in both emerging clusters of new organizations as well as in existing networks of established organizations. According to Smith, Stirling, and Berkhout (2005), the transition of industries toward environmental sustainability is dependent upon these networks of cooperating firms and institutions and the coordination of their assets to transform traditional processes into ecologically friendly ones. In addition to this, Chiffoleau (2005) showed that these firms rely upon daily dialogue and the frequent exchange of environmental services and knowledge. Tsoutsos and Stamboulis (2005) suggested that intensive environmental communication, environmental service provision, and environmental knowledge exchange typically take place in specialized niches, separated from the settings that are dominated by mainstream and the more traditional organizations. Lambert and Boons (2002) also stressed the importance of clusters of firms in self-sufficient, industrial areas. They argued that there is a symbiotic relationship between environmentally entrepreneurial firms and demonstrated this using a case in which residual products from one firm are used as raw materials in another. Besides this, the literature also reports that some mainstream organizations are becoming increasingly entrepreneurial in the field of environmental sustainability. Knot, Van den Ende, and Vergragt (2001), for example, argued that although traditional industries were often resistant to 'greening' initiatives, they were willing to change when their counterparts offered robust technologies that were capable of performing in accordance with new environmental standards.

## Environmental Technology Policies

Environmentally sustainable innovative design can also be stimulated by a nationwide environmental technology policy in which both public entrepreneurial and private entrepreneurial organizations cooperatively develop and execute environmental action plans. Sigurdson and Cheng (2001) and Watanabe (1999), for example, describe how governments and institutions develop a national innovation policy. Such a policy induces research, invention, development, and the adoption of new environmentally friendly technologies by entrepreneurial governmental, institutional, scientific, and commercial parties. Furthermore, an analysis of Finnish national technology policies by Kivimaa and Mickwitz (2006) illustrates how environmental issues become part of a national technology policy. They showed that the integration of environmental goals in a national policy, in combination with an action-and-assessment program in which institutional and commercial entrepreneurs cooperated, produced considerable environmental results. Although it is difficult to neutralize the friction between sustainability as a public interest and profitability as an individual interest of the entrepreneurial commercial firms, to a certain degree a national technology policy is capable of doing so (Dewick & Miozzo, 2004).

## Environmental Regulations

Environmental regulation forces, guides, and stimulates entrepreneurs' environmentally sustainable design activities. Environmental regulation is often used to both force and invite entrepreneurs to increase the environmental sustainability of their operations (Biondi, Iraldo, & Meredith, 2002; Brío & Junquera, 2003; Cetindamar, 2003; Clark & Paolucci, 2001; King & Lenox, 2000; Nameroff, Garant & Albert, 2004; Newton & Harte, 1997; Noci & Verganti, 1999). Although it is a common premise that regulation in terms of norms, procedures, laws, and control is useful and appropriate, there is also evidence for the opposite argument that suggests it hinders environmental innovation. McKay (2001), for example, argued that most firms react strategically to environmental regulation. Firms scan which competitors and counterparts in their environment respond to regulatory pressure and then decide to proceed in the same way or differently, based on their competitive strategy. In addition, Cetindamar (2003); Cordano and Frieze (2000); Rothwell (1992); and Tenbrunsel, Wade-Benzoni, Messick, and Bazerman (2000) substantiated the premise that firms that are confronted with environmental regulation just comply with the rules—nothing less, nothing more. To neutralize this effect, Rothwell (1992) argued that governments should adopt environmental performance standards instead of environmental standardization guidelines. Performance standards benefit from the fact that they simply define the measures of the company's expected environmental performance. Firms decide for themselves 'how' to comply. Sharma (2000) went a step further and discussed the option of using regulation that encourages entrepreneurial firms to embrace environmental issues as new competitive opportunities. Regulation could facilitate the development of objective data on the comparative environmental performance of entrepreneurial activity in the industry and stimulate and reward the most innovative organizations in industry.

## Environmental Incentives

Financial incentives also support cooperative entrepreneurship for environmentally sustainable design. According to Bansal and Roth (2000) and Kassinis and Vafeas (2006), organizations primarily act on the social and economic pressure that is exerted by governments, institutions, and communities. A stream in the literature emphasizes the stimulating effects of economic incentives on the environmental innovativeness of scientific and commercial organizations. Clark and Paolucci (2001), for example, stressed the importance of funding commercial R&D activities for new environmentally aware technology. The financial incentives provided by the government and institutions enable entrepreneurial research institutes and companies to direct some of their R&D efforts toward 'greening' their strategies, processes, products, and services. Although the literature stresses that funding and subsidies are a means to stimulate environmentally sustainable development, it also argues that environmental innovation can be profitable by itself. Judge and Douglas (1998), for example, studied the effects of the integration of environmental issues into a company's strategic management processes. They argued that investments in environmental sustainability, particularly in waste-prevention practices, could result in a reduction of the costs associated with waste processing and emissions. However, not every entrepreneurial organization is able to profit from environmentally sustainable innovation. According to Christmann (2000), organizations need a strong foundation of entrepreneurial and innovative capabilities to create the financial advantages of environmental management.

## CASE STUDY: ENTREPRENEURSHIP FOR ENVIRONMENTALLY SUSTAINABLE HOUSING DESIGN

In this section, the above analytical framework is used to structure the outcomes of the empirical research project. The description, which is the result of this methodology of case description and within-case analysis, is summarized in table 6.1.

*Table 6.1*   Factors That Stimulate Cooperative Entrepreneurship for Environmentally Sustainable Housing Design

---

*Environmental cooperation routines:*

Public-private partnerships realize environmentally sustainable design practices.

*Environmental technology policies:*

National environmental policy plans stimulate the creation of designs with green building materials.

*Environmental regulation:*

Environmental performance standards stimulate the development of designs with high energy-efficiency scores.

*Environmental incentives:*

Financial subsidies stimulate the development of cost-neutral green designs.

---

## Environmental Cooperation Routines

Public-private partnerships were used to stimulate entrepreneurship for green design. Thirty-three distinctive, multistakeholder, public-private partnerships were formed and these realized 33 environmentally sustainable housing estates. In these demonstration projects, the Dutch Ministry of Housing, Spatial Planning, and Environment and the Dutch Ministry of Economic Affairs cooperated with the National Steering Group for Experiments in Housing and the Dutch Organization for Energy and Environment. Together they initiated, funded, and coordinated all thirty-three of the ecological building projects in the country. All projects were developed, designed, and built by commercial consortia, in which an entrepreneurial municipality and various entrepreneurial firms cooperated. Most of these firms had strong cooperative ties before 'going green.' They had coinnovated before and were used to the routines and habits of their traditional counterparts. The demonstration projects aimed to demonstrate the possibilities of green design, and on the whole, this national stimulation plan for cooperative green design was very successful. Overall, 30 municipalities, 37 real estate agents, 45 architects, 23 consultants, and 28 contractors participated in the 33 demonstration projects. This is a rather small network, however, for a national industry that consists of approximately 86,000 firms. The participants invested heavily in networking activities to create contacts and become members of this small network of green entrepreneurial organizations. Each public-private partnership incorporated a municipality and one or more real estate agents, architects, and construction firms. Additionally, in 29 of the 33 projects, one or more green consultants also joined the partnership. The municipalities and firms shared the desire and the need to cooperatively experiment with green design, and they all developed a collaborative, green design practice.

## Environmental Technology Policies

National environmental policy plans, issued by the Dutch government, were used to initiate and stimulate environmentally sustainable design. The plans directed the green materialization of the designs in the demonstration projects. This created a substantial reservoir of innovations. The demonstration projects encompassed entrepreneurial municipalities, architects, real estate agents, and builders who cooperated on the basis of mutual trust and shared responsibility. During the eighties, nineties, and 'noughties,' the Dutch Ministry of Housing, Spatial Planning, and Environment; the Dutch Ministry of Economical Affairs, Traffic, Water and Agriculture; and the Dutch Ministry of Natural Preservation and Fishery published five National Environmental Policy Plans. The Dutch Ministry of Housing, Spatial Planning, and Environment also issued a sustainable building report and two action schemes for sustainable building. The ministries considered the building industry one of the major industries that had to improve in terms of environmental performance. The ministries used the 33 demonstration projects to experiment with ecological building materials in building designs. Materials were classified as 'environmentally sustainable' if they met several environmental criteria. These included, for example relatively low embodied energy or high material renewability. The green materialization scores of 24 projects were measured and calculated by a nationally recognized public institution using a nationally acknowledged method. The designs developed by the cooperating entrepreneurs scored a weighted average of 93.2 on a sustainability scale of 0 to 100 (with 0 being least sustainable and 100 being most sustainable). The dwelling design with the lowest score achieved 76.5 and the design with the highest score, 98.5.

## Environmental Regulations

Environmental performance standards were used to stimulate cooperative entrepreneurship for environmentally sustainable design. Environmental regulations were put in place to increase the energy efficiency of the building designs and provided remarkable results in terms of innovation diffusion. The best energy-efficiency practices developed within the national demonstration projects were made part of new national environmental legislation. Most commercial firms—that is, the majority, of the 86,000 firms—obeyed these new rules. Most of the late adopters did not participate in the demonstration projects. To benefit from the knowledge that was developed herein, they hired one or more members from the small network of entrepreneurial architects and consultants in order to commercialize the green design capabilities that had been obtained from the demonstration projects. By means of direct or indirect consultation with these experts, the less entrepreneurial organizations also became capable of designing energy-efficient dwellings. Since 1996, Dutch housing design has had to comply with a strict energy efficiency standard that was prescribed by the so-called Building Decree that became law. The energy efficiency standard defined a measure for the minimum energy-efficiency of housing designs. Since 1996, housing designs have had to score less than or equal to 1.4, which is equal to a maximum annual use of 850 cubic meters of natural gas to heat an average house. In 1998, the energy-efficiency standard was lowered to 1.2, in 2000 to 1.0, and in 2006 to 0.8. The energy-efficiency standard was a performance measure that forced traditional architects to meet the requested energy-efficiency level, but it also enabled them to choose the energy-saving technologies themselves. In 1997, the energy-efficiency scores of the 3,886 building designs in the 33 demonstration projects were measured and calculated by a nationally recognized public institution using a nationally acknowledged method. The dwellings had to score equal to or less than 1.4. On the whole, the building designs scored a weighted average of 1.11 per dwelling. The dwelling with the best score achieved 0.93. The dwelling with the worst score still achieved 1.23.

## Environmental Incentives

Financial subsidies were used to neutralize the extra costs of the environmentally sustainable options used in the design process. The financial subsidies had a stimulating effect on the innovativeness of the demonstration projects. The Dutch Ministry of Housing, Spatial Planning, and Environment and the Dutch Ministry of Economical Affairs introduced a subsidy program for the 33 demonstration projects (and 17 nonresidential demonstration projects) totaling €8,500,000 to cover a substantial percentage of the extra costs. The program was coordinated and the subsidies assigned by the National Steering Group for Experiments in Housing and the Dutch Energy and Environment Organization. Most of the subsidies neutralized the extra costs of the green designs incurred by the entrepreneurial firms cooperating in the 33 national demonstration projects. Based on the experiments in the demonstration projects, the ministries introduced a national package of sustainable options for housing design. Although the government and most of the pressure groups in the industry encouraged the implementation of the package by the whole industry, the majority of firms did not adopt the innovations developed by the small network of entrepreneurial organizations. They continued working in a traditional way and, as a result, illustrated the fact that all four factors primarily stimulate 'green' entrepreneurial firms but have a weak impact on companies that are less open to entrepreneurialism.

## DISCUSSION

The empirical research showed that although entrepreneurial architects had a central position in the environmental design process, cooperation, or the absence thereof, with other stakeholders can be either a success factor or a source of failure. Environmental design is created at different contextual levels by several entrepreneurial stakeholders and can be stimulated with various methods. This process is highly dependent upon cooperation between the entrepreneurial government bodies, institutions, and commercial firms. The demonstration projects, the context in which the entrepreneurial stakeholders cooperated, realized substantial results.

One of the propositions that can be derived from the literature review is that green design is dependent upon a context of entrepreneurial networks involving cooperating governments, institutions, and firms; the frequent exchange of knowledge between these parties, and sufficient innovative options to serve emerging markets. The empirical research, indeed, found that governmental ministries played an entrepreneurial role in the transformation of the interests of the organizations in the industry. These ministries initiated a dialogue with the institutions and firms in the building industry. This dialogue was situated within the context of a small set of highly innovative demonstration projects. Although the demonstration projects' results were substantial, this niche was relatively small compared to the size of the industry as a whole.

A second proposition that can be based on the literature review is that environmentally sustainable entrepreneurship is dependent upon a context encompassing national environmental technology policies, action plans, and assessment programs. The empirical research traced just such an environmental technology policy that provided new technological directions. It stimulated the development of new green technology, developed demonstration projects, and consequently created a small market with commercial possibilities for environmentally sustainable design. The national assessment of the demonstration project showed the innovative performance of the entrepreneurial firms in these projects.

A third proposition resulting from the literature review is that environmentally sustainable innovation is affected by a context that comprises environmental regulations and performance standards. The empirical research certainly found new environmental legislation for energy efficiency and discovered that it was very effective. It also found evidence that supported the importance of performance standards. The entrepreneurial firms in the demonstration projects all worked with performance standards and even achieved results that exceeded the estimated targets.

The fourth and final proposition that can be derived from the literature review is that environmental innovation is stimulated by a context of social and economic pressures and incentives. In reality, most of the environmentally conscious technology that was used in the designs for the demonstration projects was more expensive than less environmentally aware alternatives. In most cases, these extra costs were covered by governmental subsidies.

## CONCLUSION

Cooperation routines between entrepreneurial governmental, institutional, and commercial firms are needed in order to create a context of organizational networks that collectively develop environmentally sustainable designs. Research also shows that a context consisting of environmental technology policies guides the cooperative design practices of entrepreneurial firms toward an estimated set of environmentally sustainable goals. In addition to this, research confirms that a context that incorporates environmental regulation and incentives has a stimulating effect on the collaboration of participants in small entrepreneurial green design networks.

Although the designer traditionally has a central position in the contextualized design process, the government, institutions, and firms have substantial control over the environmental innovativeness of the design process. It is not just the designer's capability to develop environmentally sustainable designs but also his or her capacity to gain access to, become a member of, and cooperate with other members of networks of environmentally aware governmental, institutional, and commercial organizations that is important for successful innovative environmentally design.

## REFERENCES

Bansal, P., & Roth, K. (2000). Why companies go green: A model of ecological responsiveness. *Academy of Management Journal, 43*(4), 717–736.

Bernasconi, M., Harris, S., Moensted, M. (2006) *High-tech Entrepreneurship: Managing Innovation, Variety and Uncertainty.* New York: Routledge.

Biondi, V., Iraldo, F., & Meredith, S. (2002). Achieving sustainability through environmental innovation: The role of SMEs. *International Journal of Technology Management, 24* (5/6), 612–626.

Brío, J. A., & Junquera, B. (2003). A review of the literature on environmental innovation management in SMEs: Implications for public policies. *Technovation, 23*(12), 939–948.

Cetindamar, D. (2003). The diffusion of environmental technologies: The case of the Turkish fertilizer industry. *International Journal of Technology Management, 26*(1), 68–87.

Chiffoleau, Y. (2005). Learning about innovation through networks: The development of environment-friendly viticulture. *Technovation, 25*(10), 1193–1204.

Christmann, P. (2000). Effects of "best practices" of environmental management on cost advantage: The role of complementary assets. *Academy of Management Journal, 43*(4), 663–680.

Clark, W. W., & Paolucci, E. (2001). Commercial development of environmental technologies for the automotive industry: Towards a new model of technological innovation. *International Journal of Technology Management, 21*(5/6), 565–585.

Cordano, M., & Frieze, I. H. (2000). Pollution reduction preferences of U.S. environmental managers: Applying Ajzen's theory of planned behavior. *Academy of Management Journal, 43*(4), 627–641.

Dewick, P., & Miozzo, M. (2004). Networks and innovation: Sustainable technologies in Scottish social housing. *R&D Management, 34*(3), 323–333.

George, V. P., & Farris, G. (1999). Performance of alliances: Formative stages and changing organizational and environmental influences. *R&D Management, 29*(4), 379–390.

Håkanson, L. (1993). Managing cooperative research and development: Partner selection and contract design. *R&D Management, 23*(4), 273–286.

Judge, W. Q., & Douglas, T. J. (1998). Performance implications of incorporating natural environmental issues into the strategic planning process: An empirical assessment. *Journal of Management Studies, 35*(2), 241–262.

Kassinis, G., & Vafeas, N. (2006). Stakeholder pressures and environmental performance. *Academy of Management Journal, 49*(1), 145–159.

King, A. A., & Lenox, M. J. (2000). Industry self-regulation without sanctions: The chemical industry's responsible care program. *Academy of Management Journal, 43*(4), 698–716.

Kivimaa, P., & Mickwitz, P. (2006). The challenge of greening technologies: Environmental policy integration in Finnish technology policies. *Research Policy, 35*(5), 729–744.

Knot, J. M. C., Van den Ende, J. C. M., & Vergragt, P. J. (2001). Flexibility strategies for sustainable technology development. *Technovation, 21*(6), 335–343.

Lambert, A. J. D., & Boons, F. A. (2002). Eco-industrial parks: Stimulating sustainable development in mixed industrial parks. *Technovation, 22*(8), 471–484.

McKay, R. B. (2001) Organizational responses to an environmental Bill of Rights. *Organization Studies, 22*(4), 625–658.

Nameroff, T. J., Garant, R. J., & Albert, M. B. (2004). Adoption of green chemistry: An analysis based on US patents. *Research Policy, 33*(6–7), 959–974.

Newton, T., & Harte, G. (1997). Green business: Technicist kitsch? *Journal of Management Studies, 34*(1), 75–98.

Noci, G., & Verganti, R. (1999) Managing 'green' product innovation in small firms. *R&D Management, 29*(1), 3–15.

Rothwell, R. (1992). Industrial innovation and government environmental regulation: Some lessons from the past. *Technovation, 12*(7), 447–458.

Sharma, S. (2000). Managerial interpretations and organizational context as predictors of corporate choice of environmental strategy. *Academy of Management Journal, 43*(4), 681–697.

Sigurdson, J., & Cheng, A. L. P. (2001). New technological links between national innovation systems and corporations. *International Journal of Technology Management, 22*(5–6), 417–434.

Smith, A., Stirling, A., & Berkhout, F. (2005). The governance of sustainable sociotechnical transitions. *Research Policy, 34*(10), 1491–1510.

Tenbrunsel, A. E., Wade-Benzoni, K. A., Messick, D. M., & Bazerman, M. H. (2000). Understanding the influence of environmental standards on judgments and choices. *Academy of Management Journal, 43*(5), 854–866.

Tsoutsos, T. D., & Stamboulis, Y. A. (2005). The sustainable diffusion of renewable energy technologies as an example of an innovation-focused policy. *Technovation, 25*(7), 753–762.

Watanabe, C. (1999). Systems option for sustainable development-effect and limit of the Ministry of International Trade and Industry's efforts to substitute technology for energy. *Research Policy, 28*(7), 719–749.

Yin, R. K. (2004). *Case study research: Design and methods* (3rd ed.). Thousand Oaks, CA: Sage.

# 7 Reducing Food Waste
## An Opportunity for the Innovative Catering Entrepreneur

*Gerry Kouwenhoven, Sergej Bulterman, and Vijayender Reddy*

## FRAMEWORK: ENTREPRENEURSHIP, FOOD WASTE, AND THE CATERING SECTOR

Sustainable development is the development that meets the needs of the present without compromising the ability of future generations to meet their own needs (WCED, 1987). Corporate Social Responsibility (CSR) or sustainable entrepreneurship means that entrepreneurs act in accordance with this principle. One of the most striking issues within the scope of CSR is (future) global food production. Challenges to be met in terms of future food production are continuous population growth, the scarcity of land, desertification and deforestation, and growing carbon dioxide production as a result of food production. Because it is the food industry that will have to cope with these problems, sustainable entrepreneurship in this sector is of vital importance. The two crucial entrepreneurial challenges are finding ways to (a) increase food production with minimal environmental load and (b) reduce food waste.

In highly developed countries in Europe and the United States approximately 30% to 40% of all produced food is wasted every year; this refers to both economical and environmental waste. Consumers and governments expect the entrepreneurs who run the food businesses to behave and act in an environmentally friendly and sustainable manner. The aforementioned reasons indicate that the entrepreneur of the future will not be able to avoid sustainable entrepreneurship and cooperation with the other partners in the value chain. On the contrary, in fact, the food industry entrepreneur of the 21st century has to be a sustainable entrepreneur.

This study clearly demonstrates opportunities for existing entrepreneurs in the food service business to increase profitability by reducing food waste. We regard this as direct encouragement for the entrepreneur to sustain his business by realizing higher economic returns. Moreover, the framework and cases discussed within this paper present opportunities for aspiring entrepreneurs to build new business by adding value to the created food waste and coming up with new and innovative products and services. In this way, we would like to position this article as a real contribution to entrepreneurship insofar as it helps existing entrepreneurs to sustain their businesses and provides scope for new entrepreneurial possibilities.

Food-waste management is one of the most critical sustainable-entrepreneurship topics in the catering industry. Drivers and forces from within a caterer's company and from outside (the environment in which an entrepreneur operates) stimulate and restrict the implementation of food-waste reduction measures in the business. External pressure regarding the reduction of food waste, of course, mandates the entrepreneurs to take action. From an opportunity-based perspective, food-waste reduction can also be seen as a chance for a strategic action. External forces are also important in enlarging the entrepreneur's consciousness of and knowledge about food waste. At the same time, uncertainty over the outcomes or surplus value of possible measures, particularly if they involve substantial investments, often prevent entrepreneurs from taking concrete action. Furthermore, the current character of a catering business and its organization has a greater influence on the need and possibilities for food-waste reducing measures (see figure 7.1). This is the

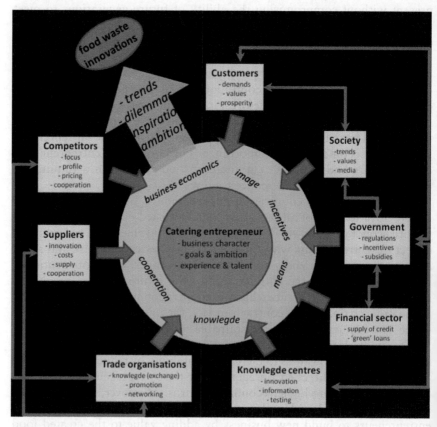

*Figure 7.1*   Food-waste innovation from the entrepreneur's contextual viewpoint.

context in which an entrepreneur needs to decide whether dealing with food waste is a priority for his company.

## Dutch Catering Industry Overview

In this chapter we focus on sustainable entrepreneurship within the Dutch food-service industry (hotel, catering, and restaurants). The Dutch food-service industry is fragmented and consists of about 36,000 active catering companies (hotels, restaurants, cafés, lunchrooms, cafeteria, catering companies, and recreation residences) of which 99% are an SME (Pleijster, Mooibroek, De Kok, & Wennekers, 2009). The catering group consists of the bistro, the restaurant, café, and transport café. In total there are roughly about 15,500 restaurants. In 2009, total catering turnover declined by 4.75% to €13.6 billion. The categories most significantly affected were the liquor business (7.5%), the hotel sector (7.75%), and the restaurant sector (4.25%). Only the fast-food sector demonstrated a slight positive growth of about 1.25%. At the same time, this sector is producing masses of food waste. In the Dutch case, companies are responsible for a waste value of over €235 million (Luitjes, 2007).

The combination of fierce competition within an SME market and food-waste problems gives rise to the need for innovation in terms of organizing and positioning a caterer's business. Entrepreneurship as a behavior means openness to change and a willingness to take risks within the objectives/goals of the business. A new dimension of innovative and renewable entrepreneurship is a change in the attitude/behavior of the entrepreneur toward carrying out his/her business activities in a sustainable and environmentally friendly manner.

## Innovation Profile of Dutch Catering Entrepreneurs

Dutch catering company owners are unambiguous in that all of them consider high-quality service a key element of their business and about 45% consider innovation a business-critical element. The innovative entrepreneur within the catering industry has a clear understanding of his/her own market and the challenges facing his/her business. The innovative entrepreneur pays good attention to evolving market trends, has a clear understanding of the challenges facing his/her business, and demonstrates a willingness to change (Pleijster et al., 2009). The prime sources of information for innovative entrepreneurs are consumers, the Internet, employees, and suppliers. The innovative entrepreneur works toward improving business results through increasing efficiency and improving service and image. The innovative entrepreneur believes that continuous improvement is the key to growth and profits. Research suggests that investment in continuous change/improvement is certainly effective; almost 74% of innovative catering entrepreneurs report that change/improvement initiatives have contributed positively to their bottom line, namely, profits.

## Entrepreneurship, Strategy, and Focus

Entrepreneurs can innovate on two levels. The first is the more practical one, which focuses on minor process improvements/adjustments and smaller investments. To stimulate this kind of innovation, only the entrepreneurs' awareness of such simple innovation possibilities is needed. Practical innovation will be relatively popular within the SME-dominated Dutch catering industry, where the focus is on local competition, most caterers possess a low to medium level of education, it is relatively easy to start up a catering business, and catering itself requires a hands-on approach.

The second level can be described as strategic innovation in which the entrepreneur needs to reconsider positioning, customer focus, market approach, and CSR. In this case, innovation can lead to food-waste reduction measures in two ways. The first involves repositioning or changing the concept of the business. This will then have the knock-on effect of reducing food waste. The reconstruction of the businesses profile and organization will, in fact, lead to 'accidental' opportunities for reducing food waste. The second is making CSR an important or even the main driver in the business strategy and allowing it to determine the identity of the catering company itself. In this case, food-waste reduction is an important topic and is regarded as one of the main business objectives.

## The Relationship Between Corporate
## Sustainability and Loss Reduction

Food-waste reduction is positively related to all three dimensions of sustainable entrepreneurship: people, planet, and profit:

1. People: Social responsibility also refers to conscious usage of scarce natural resources; poverty is a widespread problem, and it is very uncertain whether expansion of the world's food production can keep up with the world's population growth. Within a catering business, this means informing and training one's personnel about food treatment and valuing food as an important asset.
2. Planet: With less waste, more products can be delivered by consuming the same amount of raw materials. This also impacts upon logistics, which in turn has a positive influence on the environment.
3. Profit: Wasting food is equivalent to wasting money, particularly if this occurs before the food has been ordered by and actually sold to a client. Even waste disposal of unconsumed food is costly, however, due to the time and attention required. Hence, food waste has a direct influence on the financial performance of a company. A positive impact on financial performance as a result of less food waste can have an indirect positive effect on employment.

## FRAMEWORK TO GUIDE ENTREPRENEURS IN FOOD-WASTE REDUCTION

The main objective of this chapter is to suggest innovative approaches and tools for food service entrepreneurs to reduce food waste within their businesses. Another of our objectives is to facilitate and motivate the entrepreneurs to incorporate food waste into their business strategies. To achieve this goal we will use the framework below.

In this four-step framework, the first step is to define the food waste from the food service business perspective. This will help the entrepreneurs create awareness of and understanding about food waste. The second step is to quantify the cost implications of the food waste by calculating the economic implications of food waste that have been defined in the first step. The third step is to analyze the causes for such waste, and finally, in the fourth step, we suggest different improvement possibilities. In our view, this framework represents a very simple way for food service entrepreneurs to understand food waste, identify the benefits of reducing food waste, and implement strategies that can help them achieve food-waste reductions.

### Step 1: Define/Understand

This first phase concerns the entrepreneurs' awareness and knowledge of food waste as a relevant topic, both in terms of society and their own businesses. At present, most entrepreneurs are unaware of the true cost of waste and its effect on competitiveness and profitability (Envirowise, 2009). It must be made clear that sustainable entrepreneurship is as much about making profit as 'traditional' entrepreneurship. Sustainable entrepreneurs have to think in terms of financial profit without forgetting both the input of and the effects on the planet, people, and pleasure. An all-encompassing view of food waste as a cost factor within a catering company covers discarded materials, raw materials, energy and water, products, wasted labor, wasted processes, and waste disposal.

The Dutch Ministry of Agriculture, Nature, and Food Quality defines waste as all food that is produced and destined for people but ultimately not consumed by people (including a lower value; Ministry of Agriculture,

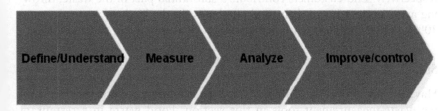

*Figure 7.2* Four steps to accomplish food-waste reduction.

Nature and Food Quality). Food becomes waste when (a) the supply chain players including end consumers throw it away and inefficiently use leftover food, or (b) there is a demand-supply mismatch (chain inefficiency).

Waste production still takes place in different links of the supply chain. The majority of waste is produced at the consumer level. Some studies have estimated waste percentages to be around 40% in the agrifood sector (meat, fish, dairy, vegetables, fruit, bread, pastry). The vast majority of the aforementioned waste is not consumed at all, and the rest is not consumed by the consumers for whom it was intended. In the Netherlands, the value of total food wastage is estimated to be around €4.4 billion a year, of which €2.4 billion worth of food (10% of all purchased food) is thrown away by the end-consumers, and €2 billion worth of food is wasted in different links of the food chain (excluding the end-consumers).

These waste figures are quite alarming and have unintended repercussions on costs, the environment, the carbon footprint, energy, water, and other ethical aspects such as animal well-being and food security. Prevention and minimization of food waste would definitely have positive economic implications for all of the players in the supply chain. In addition to economic implications, it can also make a business sustainable and socially responsible, that is, it can address all three critical societal dimensions: people, planet, and profit.

Research has identified three prime reasons for such high waste figures (Waarts, Onwezen, Wiersinga, & Hiller, 2009):

1. Businesses in different links of the chain are not aware of the food waste they create.
2. They do not know how they can prevent and/or reduce waste.
3. They are not aware of the environmental impact caused by the food waste they produce.

A study conducted by a research center at Wageningen University showed that restaurants in the Netherlands are wasting around 51,000 tons of food annually with a value of €235 million (Luitjes, 2007). In the same study it was estimated that vegetables contribute between 25% and 35% of total food waste, whereas fruit makes up about 32%. Starch products such as potatoes, rice, and pasta account for about 15% of waste, and meat and fish 7% and 8%, respectively. End-customers contribute a substantial part of the waste, throwing away up to 15% of their total purchases. In the kitchen, we waste up to 10% of our purchases of perishable items such as fish, meat, and vegetables.

## Step 2: Measure

Having understood the different waste possibilities, we now provide simple waste-measurement tools in this section. Food waste in a restaurant occurs at three separate moments during the process (figure 7.3). The first

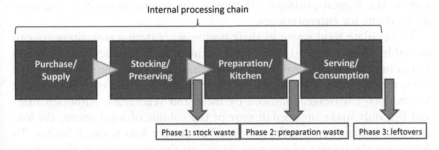

*Figure 7.3* Moments of food waste during the business process.

moment is during the stocking period, that is, before the food or ingredients are actually used in the kitchen. This waste does not reach the preparation stage. The second moment is during the food preparation stage in the kitchen. In this instance, food waste does not find its way to the restaurant table and the customer. The third moment refers to leftovers after dinner has been served to the customer. These three moments are the focus points for entrepreneurs who want to accurately measure food waste.

In general, of the 25% to 35% of the food that is wasted in restaurants, a rough estimate shows that this is split over the three wastage moments as follows:

1. 5% to 10%      food waste in phase 1
2. 10%            food waste in phase 2
3. 10% to 15%     food waste in phase 3

Table 7.1 provides a more elaborate analysis of food waste for different food products. The table suggests a dilemma: the first (visual) impression is that bread and vegetables make up most of the food waste. Commercially, however, meat and fish are focus products. But environmentally,

*Table 7.1* Food Waste of Different Food Products

|  | Volume (%) | Euros (%) | Carbon dioxide equivalents (%) |
|---|---|---|---|
| Meat | 8 | 20 | 60 |
| Fish | 7 | 23 | 5 |
| Starch | 15 | 6 | 16 |
| Bread | 25 | 11 | 11 |
| Vegetables and fruits | 32 | 29 | 2 |
| Sundries | 13 | 11 | 6 |

meat is the biggest problem. Of course, the second measure is the most relevant one for entrepreneurs.

To calculate food waste in their businesses, catering entrepreneurs can use table 7.1 as a tool to derive and estimate their product-specific losses by multiplying their actual wastage (purchase and stock) numbers with the given ratios. Table 7.1 also makes clear that fish is the most susceptible for shrinkage/wastage, followed by meat and vegetables. Although meat and fish only make up a small part of the volume of food waste, the loss in Euros is high because the products' prices per kilo is much higher. To determine the impact of catering 'litter' on the environment, the volume is changed into equivalent carbon dioxide. Food waste amounts to about 0.1 billion tons a year in terms of carbon dioxide equivalent, and meat is responsible for about 60% of this (Westhoek, Van Oostenbrugge, Faber, Prins, & Van Vuuren, 2008).

An entrepreneur can value or score each type of ingredient, stock item, and dish by classifying it according to the waste-management strategy currently in place. To do so, he/she can make use of the three *R*s, that is, reduce, reuse, and recycle, which are listed in order of importance. The complete hierarchy is as follows:

1. Eliminate: Avoid producing waste in the first place.
2. Reduce: Minimize the amount of waste produced.
3. Reuse: Use items as many times as possible.
4. Recycle: Recycle everything possible, only after it has been reused.
5. Dispose: Dispose of what is left in a responsible way.

The first step toward better waste management is to identify the waste currently being generated as part of a business activity, and the best way to do this is to carry out a waste 'walk-around.'[1] The formula below can be used to obtain the most objective estimate of the cost of food waste:

True cost of waste = cost of wasted raw materials + lost time + cost of utilities used + waste treatment costs + disposal costs

In the next section, we discuss how an entrepreneur can analyze the waste within a business.

## Step 3: Analysis

It is important that the entrepreneur makes a thorough analysis of causes as well as sources of food waste in order to take effective measures. The following are various causes for unnecessary waste:

- More processed and sliced (composite) products to increase convenience.
- Purchasing products that are not required or that will not be used.
- Purchasing more than the required quantities.

- Not transporting and storing the product at optimal and favorable conditions.
- Incorrect estimates of the product (failed recipe).
- Faulty or improper packaging.
- Wrong product quality.
- Errors during the processing stage (failed batches).
- Serving large quantities of food to the customers.

In addition to the above general guidelines, an entrepreneur's self-assessment is also critical. Entrepreneurs should generally be in a position to assess the strengths and weaknesses of the business. The following are a few critical internal success factors:

- Experience.
- Ambitious and friendly attitude of the staff/employees.
- The client orientation of the company.
- Good cooking, good food, presentation of the dishes.
- Ambience and interior of the restaurant.
- Price versus product and service, and the customer's value perception.
- Storage tips, storage procedures, product space, kitchen and storage facilities.
- Procurement times, delivery times, suppliers, order frequency.
- Number and variety of menus, different ingredients, garnish, products (local or season), portion size, capabilities adapted to customer wishes.

An *external* analysis provides clarity on the opportunities and threats and below we summarize a number of factors which are relevant for the food service business. These factors correlate with the information given in figure 7.1.

With this information it is possible (although not easy!) to draw up a SWOT analysis and a 'confrontation matrix.' This is a way for the entrepreneur to become more aware of the determining drivers in the current businesses policy and the current size of food waste as an outcome of that policy. By doing so, the entrepreneur discovers where food-waste reduction and other interests come into conflict as well as which drivers and motivators may support new reduction measurements. At the very least, it is a way for the entrepreneur to become familiar with the determining drivers in the current businesses policy and food-waste situation in the company.

## Step 4: Improve

In this chapter we propose that there are opportunities for reducing food waste in every phase of the internal production cycle (figure 7.4). Here, we will focus on the second and fourth phases, namely, stocking management and consumption.

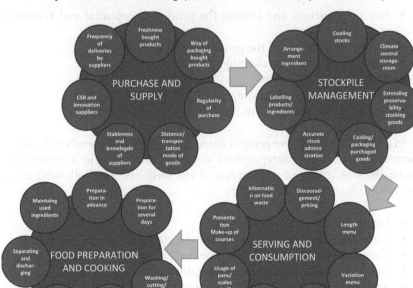

*Figure 7.4*  Points of interest for food-waste reduction measures in the production cycle.

In every phase of the internal production cycle, an entrepreneur has opportunities to reduce food waste. On average, however, the largest amount of food waste occurs during the serving and consumption phase. This is because commercial motives focus on efficiency gains during the process up to the point where the food is actually selected by (sold to) the customer. Furthermore, caterers feel cautious and reserved about confronting their customers with the food-waste phenomenon. They do not want to trouble them with the issue. However, even for entrepreneurs who do not explicitly want to profile themselves as socially responsible, there are numerous ways to reduce food waste in the consumer phase without annoying guests and risking standards of hospitality.

The basic principle for waste reduction in this phase is to ensure that the right product is served to the right taste and at the right moment:

- Prepare tailor-made amounts of food per guest; labels indicate the quantity per person.
- Serve seasonal products and limit the size of the menu.
- Display half-portion options on the menu and provide the option to reorder.
- Allow starters to be ordered as main courses.

- Minimize buffet arrangements and 'unrestricted' eating, if necessary, by demanding a penalty for not eating the plate clean.
- Minimize serving starch-based side dishes that are meant to prevent guests complaining about small courses.
- Do not automatically serve (free) side dishes such as fries or salads, but mention on the menu that side dishes are available for free if the guest is interested.
- Limit the amount of garnish used on dishes, and focus on clearly fresh and edible products.

To elaborate further on the relevance of above approach in practice, we have provided several waste-management case studies in the appendix. In the next section, we conclude the study.

## CONCLUSION

In this chapter, we have addressed the importance of sustainable entrepreneurship in the Dutch food-service industry in order to reduce food waste. To achieve this, the provision of food must be regarded as one of the main topics affecting the world's sustainable future. The case of the catering sector shows that food-waste management is a relevant and interesting approach to enhancing innovation based on sustainable entrepreneurship.

We have provided a detailed framework and the necessary tools for entrepreneurs to effectively manage food waste and position their business as environmentally responsible by addressing the elements of planet, people, profit, and pleasure. Although the study presents cases and statistics from the Dutch food-service industry, the insights and the frameworks from this study are relevant for the hospitality industry in general. A series of interviews held with Dutch catering entrepreneurs have suggested numerous practical and innovative waste-improvement tools.

Food-waste management can help catering entrepreneurs learn to think and act more sustainably and in a more socially responsible manner. By doing so, entrepreneurs will hopefully embrace sustainable entrepreneurship because sustainable development is the best way forward.

This study clearly demonstrates opportunities for existing entrepreneurs in the food service business to increase profitability by reducing food waste. In our opinion, this is direct encouragement for entrepreneurs to sustain their businesses by realizing higher economic returns. Moreover, the framework and cases discussed within this chapter present possibilities for aspiring entrepreneurs to build new business by adding value to the food waste created and coming up with new and innovative products and services.

An easy way for catering entrepreneurs to demonstrate that they are taking their responsibilities seriously is to reduce food wastage. The result manifests itself as improvements to planet, people, pleasure, and profit.

## APPENDIX: SOME EXAMPLES OF BEST PRACTICES

### Free Meals Against Overproduction

The action group Food Not Bombs collects food just past the sell-by date from supermarkets, wholesalers, and restaurants. Volunteers make vegetarian and vegan meals and distribute them for free. Food Not Bombs is an international organization operating out of the Netherlands, with eight active groups spread over the entire country. This organization's objective is to protest against the ease with which people throw away good food, says Christaan Verweij of the Amersfoort section. Furthermore, retailers are very happy with this initiative. Unfortunately, some supermarkets lock the containers of food because they do not want anyone rummaging around inside. The only reservation is from the consumers because they do not trust something that is being given away for free. Ask a euro and they think it is inexpensive. If it is free, they often think, there is something wrong with it.

### McDonald's

McDonald's is a well-known fast-food chain with franchise ventures all over the world. The venture at Delft Noord is very aware of the food they waste. They have a very tight system in the kitchen, which is necessary because of the large number of employees working there. They work very accurately with production systems that are optimally adjusted to expected customer demand. The kitchen employees prepare burgers in advance, based on the expected demand. Burgers are allowed to stay in the 'bin' for approximately 10 minutes; after that they are no longer allowed to be served and must be thrown away. The kitchen employees are required to keep a record of all the ingredients and burgers they throw away. This record is then entered into the production system so that it can continuously readjust expected demand. McDonald's Delft Noord is also planning to review its stock system for fresh ingredients in order to reduce waste in this area.

### Spirit

Spirit (Rotterdam) is a vegetarian and organic restaurant in a small, so-called 'green passage' in Rotterdam. They serve food buffet style, and customers can fill their plates with whatever they wish. The plates are weighed by the cashier, and the customers pay for the weight of their food. Because of this innovative billing mechanism, the customers do not overfill their plates and thereby do not waste a great deal of food.

The chef of the restaurant estimates that approximately 5% of the buffet food is thrown away. This amount could be reduced if the range were reduced, but this would also mean a reduction in profit. The only other option for cutting back waste could involve the kitchen employees taking greater care when cleaning, cutting, and preparing the food.

## Café du Midi

At Cafe du Midi (Delfgauw), the lifestyle of the owners is clearly evident throughout the entire business, even without conscious efforts being made toward corporate social responsibility. The owners prioritize taste and quality and have a strong preference for local and sustainable products. Discarding products without using them is expensive and does not feel good. Various measures to reduce food wastage have been introduced in the first year of their entrepreneurial endeavor. Side dishes are served in small portions, and the customer can reorder. The lunch menu is tailored to the dinner menu so that materials can be used on both occasions. The owners have consciously chosen a small pantry for better visibility and lower stock levels and have also trained the staff to manage the refrigerator effectively and reduce the wastage of milk, yogurt, and buttermilk. For them, CSR is not a strategy, but a way of life.

## Het Friethoes

In Haarlem, in the second half of 2009, caterer Joost Hoes opened his first corner 'chip stand' in the Netherlands, making and selling organic chips. He uses organically produced potatoes, most of the ingredients for his mayonnaise are organic, and he also sells organically produced croquettes. This focus on organic products suggests that Het Friethoes pays attention to sustainable entrepreneurship in general, including minimizing food waste. Indeed, this is an important topic for Joost Hoes. First, he had to become more acquainted with the use of organically produced potatoes, which have a lower supply reliability compared to conventional ones. He rapidly managed to reduce the quantity of unused potatoes by making continuous improvements in his supply chain. He makes his mayonnaise on a daily basis to prevent leftovers. Furthermore, he uses average-sized chip bags to make sure that people do not get too large a portion, as starchy flour/fecula based products are quite filling. He also uses little bags for children and for patrons who just want to have a 'taste' of his quality product. His high-quality standards partially conflict with his waste-management goals, however. He does not use cooking oil for long periods because it has an impact on the taste quality of the chips. So in the end, quality prevails over optimal waste prevention. Nevertheless, he estimates his food waste to be only about 5% of total production.

## De Bokkedoorns

Having been active in the catering sector for more than 20 years, John Beeren, owner of two Michelin-starred restaurants De Bokkedoorns in Overveen, is a very experienced and well-known entrepreneur in the catering sector. Having a high-class restaurant implies that De Bokkedoorns is maintaining the highest professional standards in the Dutch catering sector.

This should also apply to the topic of food-waste management. The most logical drive for food-waste minimization is a commercial one, namely, optimization of the gross profit of the business. In his experience, concrete waste-management improvements are usually an 'accidental' outcome of learning by doing and of practical developments, instead of being a result of deliberate innovations on this topic. For instance, he discovered that meat has a longer shelf life if it is seasoned and vacuum packed after delivery. Unexpectedly, he also found out that eliminating the immediate filleting of fish after delivery had a positive effect on its shelf life. Because of the high quality standards and relatively high salary costs at his restaurant, a waste-reduction concept does not always compare favorably against the costs involved. For instance, the use of remaining/leftover products from prepared meat and fish in soup dishes or sauces is too labor intensive and risky in terms of the quality standards adhered to in the restaurant. De Bokkedoorns does not actually measure its food-waste production, but John Beeren estimates it at 3% to 4%.

## NOTES

1. An unstructured approach also known as 'management by wandering around,' wherein the managers directly participate in the work-related affairs of their subordinates with a purpose to collect qualitative information.

## REFERENCES

Envirowise. (2009). *Self-assessment review for food and drink manufacturers.* Envirowise report EN284. Retrieved March 17 2011 from http://envirowise. wrap.org.uk

Ministry of Agriculture, Nature, and Food Quality. (2010). Fact sheet about food waste in the Netherlands. Retrieved March 17 2011 from http://english.minlnv. nl

Luitjes, H. (2007). *Voedselverspilling in de horeca.* AFSG Research Group report. Wageningen: Wageningen University.

Pleijster, F., Mooibroek, M., De Kok, J. M. P., & Wennekers, A. R. M. (2009). *Innovatief ondernemerschap binnen de horeca.* Zoetermeer: EIM.

Rudzki, R. E. J. (2008). Beyond the Brundtland Report: Founding principles for international business and global economics in the 21st century and beyond. Paper presented at Oxford Business and Economics Conference, St. Hugh's College, Oxford University, England, June 22–24, 2008.

Waarts, Y., Onwezen, M., Wiersinga, R., & Hiller, S. (2009). *Voedselverspilling, waarden van voedsel in de keten.* Delft: Hogeschool INHolland.

WCED (World Commission on Environment and Development) (1987). *Our common future.* Oxford: Oxford University Press.

Westhoek, H. J., Van Oostenbrugge, R., Faber, A., Prins, A. G., & Van Vuuren, D. P. (2010). *Voedsel, biodiversiteit en klimaatverandering: Mondiale opgave en nationaal beleid.* PBL No. 500414004. The Hague: PBL.

## Part IV

# Entrepreneurship as Context

## 8 Muslim Businesswomen Doing Boundary Work
### The Negotiation of Islam, Gender, and Ethnicity Within Entrepreneurial Contexts

*Caroline Essers and Yvonne Benschop*

## INTRODUCTION

Religion is a largely underresearched theme in entrepreneurship, yet religion is not simply 'left at home' but infuses working life too. As a result of both globalization and migration, Islam features prominently in Western European organizations. In the Netherlands, where this study is situated, the largest group of Muslims is of Moroccan and Turkish origin. Participation of the women in this group in the labor market is strongly increasing; labor participation of Moroccan women doubled to 36%, and labor participation of Turkish women increased from 17% to 41% in the Netherlands between 1995 and 2009 (CBS, 2011).[1] Some of these migrant women also started their own businesses.[2]

As argued elsewhere (Essers & Benschop, 2007), it is important to study the intersectionality of social categories of exclusion such as gender and ethnicity within entrepreneurial contexts. Intersectionality is a useful notion for understanding how these axes of difference are simultaneously implicated in the construction of entrepreneurial identities (Crenshaw, 1997). This chapter contributes toward contemporary debates about entrepreneurship by exploring the role of Islam as an axis of difference in relation to gender and ethnicity within entrepreneurial identity construction. It studies how Islamic identification intermeshes with gender-based and ethnic practices and experiences of inclusion and exclusion in entrepreneurial activities. Because people of Turkish and Moroccan origin are often studied as one group in the Netherlands due to their Islamic background, similar migration history and comparable Mediterranean culture (see also Essers & Benschop, 2007), the focus of this chapter is on the 'variance' within this group of Muslim businesswomen.

This chapter is situated in a context in which immigration and integration are contested topics. Gender, specifically femininity, often serves as a symbolic marker to illustrate the tensions between Western and Islamic norms and values. In the public debate, Islamic women are often depicted as either the admirable counterparts of their derailed criminal brothers, as hard-working students, or as the victimized and oppressed second sex (Van der Spek, 2004). It is in this atmosphere that migrant[3] women contemplate the role of Islam at work. The concurrent existence of gender, ethnicity, and Islam within these women's entrepreneurial contexts may bring about oppositional demands and role expectations (Sveningsson & Alvesson, 2003). Therefore, this chapter seeks to understand how the intersectionality of these identity categories requires businesswomen of Moroccan and Turkish origin to carry out identity work to sustain their entrepreneurial identities. Identity work "refers to people being engaged in forming, repairing, maintaining, strengthening or revising the constructions that are productive of a sense of coherence and distinctiveness" (Sveningsson & Alvesson, 2003, p. 1165). We contend that the identity work of these businesswomen is mostly boundary work, which refers to strategies for cultivating differences between groups (Lamont & Fournier, 1992). This boundary work consists of creating boundaries between Islam, gender, and ethnicity, as well as generating margins within Islam. This kind of identity work shows that entrepreneurial identity construction is complicated when multiple social categories are involved and that their simultaneity results in both restrictions and possibilities.

## INTERSECTIONALITY WITHIN THE CONTEXT OF ENTREPRENEURSHIP

Generally, gender and ethnicity seem to be regarded as important identity categories for understanding the identities of female migrants (Buitelaar, 1998). Entrepreneurship and Islam are other salient categories when studying the multiple identities of migrant Muslim businesswomen.

We view identity construction as a socially accomplished process dependent upon place, time, and context. Identities are fluid, multiple (Haraway, 1991), and discursively constructed. Although people have agency in their identity construction, they are also constrained by societal structures and discourses.

Furthermore, identities are intersectionally constructed. The concept of intersectionality stresses the importance of simultaneous categories of oppression that constitute differences in power for groups at neglected points of intersection such as black, migrant women (Crenshaw, 1997). "Women (or men) are never just women, but always also located within a particular class and of a particular ethnicity and sexuality" (Mirchandani, 1999, p. 229).

Accordingly, intersectionality adds to the traditional entrepreneurship debate, in which both gender and ethnicity have been underresearched. Popular and scientific discourses on entrepreneurship have contributed to the creation of an archetypical white male entrepreneur (Ogbor, 2000).

Yet when people are involved in entrepreneurship they are also involved in identity construction related to gender and ethnicity as well as religion (Essers, Benschop, & Doorewaard, 2010). Studies concerning gender, ethnicity, and entrepreneurship have addressed either gender or ethnicity in relation to entrepreneurship but have not addressed both simultaneously. Neither female entrepreneurship nor migrant entrepreneurship studies (which both often construct an essentialist category of the 'other' entrepreneur) have focused on the interrelationship between gender and ethnicity, let alone Islam, in the experience of entrepreneurship. By applying intersectionality, we provide a greater insight into the complexity of lived multiple identities and the identity work necessitated by the simultaneity of socially orchestrated identity regulations. This identity work can be regarded as boundary work that people do in order to respond to processes of inclusion and exclusion tied to various identity categories (Lamont & Fournier, 1992).

The intersection of ethnicity and Islam is important in this study. Various authors have examined the identity constructions of ethnic minorities in organizations that face discrimination and disqualification (Bell & Nkomo, 2001; S. Friday, E. Friday, & Moss, 2004). Friday et al. (2004) point to the psychological self-categorization that ethnicity entails: People construct their ethnic identities by incorporating specific 'symbolic elements' such as cultural practices and values, nationality, language, and religion into their sense of self. Some authors specifically distinguish ethnic identity from religious identity (Jacobson, 1997), separating culture from a universal understanding of religion. Eickelman (1998), however, argues that religion and ethnicity can either be invoked as different sources of distinctiveness or that Islamic identification can be part of ethnicity. The construction of ethnicity in relation to Islam is highly variable as ethnic identities are also subject to social identifications by others. Anthias contends that "the term 'ethnic' group is always constructed relationally as it only makes sense in the context of the ethnicization of another population" (2001, p. 629). Ethnicization thus refers to the formation of social boundaries aiming to differentiate between (presumed) ethnic-cultural or religious heritages. Although Islam is not confined to one society/cultural tradition, today Muslims have become ethnicized as a homogeneous group in many European societies, often for political reasons.

Islam also connects with gender, which is "about how women and men make their femininities and masculinities known to themselves and to each other, through saying and doing things in specific instances" (Torab, 1996, p. 238). Businesswomen of Moroccan and Turkish descent have agency in the construction of their gender identities, but they are also affected by structural constraints provided by gender socialization and patriarchal processes. How does Islam relate to gender identities? The Qur'an provides various guidelines for gender relations that have been interpreted both dogmatically and progressively. In reaction to detrimental representations of

Muslims, women have increasingly started to wear head scarves to ideo-
logically mark the boundaries between Muslims and non-Muslims (Brown
& Humphreys, 2002). Often as the result of social marginalization (Lutz,
1991), references to 'honor and shame' are frequently made in relation to
Islam. Honor is associated with masculinity, *religion*, and public life; and
shame with femininity, sexuality, and privacy (Bourdieu, 1966). Hence, the
honor-and-shame discourse excludes women from honor (Gilmore, 1987),
and women can only diminish shame through the preservation of chas-
tity and modesty. This explains the desire to separate women and men in
different spheres and why feminine identities are most contested in public
settings that traditionally have masculine connotations, such as entrepreneurship. Yet there are alternative interpretations that note how 'honor and
shame' should not be regarded as a dichotomy and that women can also
claim honor (Abu-Lughod, 1986).

In the dominant academic entrepreneurship discourse, Islam has been
negatively related to successful entrepreneurship. Thomas and Mueller
(2000) note that a culture of individualism and achievement has dominated the entrepreneurial worldview as this relates back to Weber's Protestant work ethic. Calvinists were perceived as potentially successful
entrepreneurs (Weber & Kalberg, 2002) because of skills congruent with
the virtues and practices of Calvinism: using time carefully, innovating,
having an internal locus of control, and reinvesting earnings (Arslan,
2001). According to Weber, Islamic societies could not produce the 'spirit
of capitalism' because of the warrior ethic, otherworldly Sufism, Oriental
despotism, and a lack of individualism (Arslan, 2001, p. 321). Yet authors
such as Shane and Venkataraman (2000, p. 220) stress that entrepreneurial opportunities come in a variety of forms and do not necessarily equate
with capitalism. And for immigrant business people that focus on ethnic
market niches, entrepreneurship can be a way to retain one's self-esteem
as this economic mobility does not entail cultural assimilation (Porter &
Washington, 1993).

Additionally, postcolonial theorists, such as Said (1978) and Prasad
(2003), take note of a typical Orientalist discourse in organization studies
that perceive certain non-Western business practices as residues of 'traditional' and backward cultural practices that are an obstacle to organizational efficiency/effectiveness. In many Orientalist discourses, Islam does
not go together with honest, ethical, and straightforward ways of doing
business (Said, 1978). In contrast to the alleged entrepreneurial asset of
individualism, the literature on ethnic minority entrepreneurship stresses
the advantages of sociability (Portes, 1995). Yet although a few authors
(for example, Sloane, 1999) discuss the realities and opportunities of
Islam-entrepreneurship, the existing entrepreneurship literature constructs
a hegemonic discourse suggesting the incompatibility of Islamic and entrepreneurial identities. What this means for the identities of 'our' businesswomen will be discussed in the empirical section.

METHODOLOGY

Studies on Muslim female entrepreneurs or on the interrelationship between gender, ethnicity, entrepreneurship, and religion are very few and far between. Therefore, an explorative approach is applied in which these women's life stories are the point of departure. This chapter focuses not only on the similarities but also on the multiplicity, situational contingency, and inconsistencies in these women's voices that produce 'situated knowledge' in close interaction with the researcher (Haraway, 1991). Inspired by poststructuralist feminism, we therefore paid attention to the discursive constructions of identities. We also looked into the construction of their multiple identifications by reading and rereading the biographical narratives concerning the behaviors and episodes in their lives that related to the question 'who am I?' (Buitelaar, 1998).

Using specific networks for migrant women, migrant entrepreneurs, and the 'snowballing' method, 20 life stories were gathered. Following MacAdams's approach (1993), the migrant businesswomen were asked to organize their life stories into life chapters, just like a book, and focus where possible on the messages they received from their family and peers regarding gender and ethnicity. Through a qualitative content analysis (Lieblich, Tuval-Mashiach, & Zilber, 1998), all 20 stories were first analyzed to uncover common patterns and themes, one of which was Muslim identity. After distinguishing the subthemes of Muslim identity, we moved to a more holistic content analysis to interpret these subthemes in light of the complete life story of the individual (Lieblich et al., 1998). The parts of the stories that referred to various subthemes of Muslim identity were discursively analyzed to interpret why and how things were said in a particular context. Ambiguities within and among the narratives were sought using this method. For this chapter, we have selected four illustrative life stories with regard to Muslim identity.

ISLAM IN PRACTICE

Four women are cited below, all of whom identify themselves as Muslims. The first is Mouria, age 47, who was 17 when she married her Moroccan husband and came to the Netherlands. Together they have two sons and one daughter. Mouria owns a beauty shop and has one employee. Aylin, age 33, is originally Turkish and owns a driving school. She was 3 when she came to the Netherlands. She and her Turkish husband are expecting their second child. Fatna, age 25, is of Turkish descent and came to Holland when she was age 11. Together with her two sisters. she has a wholesale company in vegetables and a greengrocery employing two relatives. Farah, age 26, was born in the Netherlands, is single, of Moroccan descent, and together with a Dutch woman, set up an environmental issues consultancy.

In this section we analyze how the intersections of Islam, gender, and ethnicity are experienced as a site of limitations, opportunities, and legitimizations and how these may enable as well as constrain entrepreneurial activities. We also demonstrate the types of boundary work these businesswomen apply in their identity work.

## Between Opportunity and Restriction

In contrast to the hegemonic discourse on entrepreneurship, being a Muslim and an entrepreneur is quite feasible for the interviewees; they can say their prayers and close their business during Ramadan whenever they want. However, simultaneously being a Muslim, an entrepreneur, *and* a woman seems to bring a dilemma to some migrant businesswomen, as Mouria sometimes experiences:

> Well, I do not know, but in the Qur'an it is indeed stated that you cannot touch men, and of course I do just that; I massage men, etc. Hence, I sometimes think, 'Oh yes, that is actually not allowed.' But hey, that's my job, and nurses do this too. And yes, he [the male client] has made an appointment for it. But I stick to my limits, and just tell men I'm fully booked when I don't trust them. I want to defend my business against gossip; I do not want people to talk 'dirty' about me. . . . Some were against me becoming a businesswoman since they feared I would 'play the boss' and leave my husband. People from the circles of Islam, you know. But I don't care. . . . I was rebellious when talking about the rights of women, or the Islam. . . . I sometimes also fight about that with my husband. Because when you read the Qur'an, it says something completely different. But the man never loses, and they see it differently then.

This statement shows how Mouria, who started her company because she always wanted to work with her hands, is sometimes confused when in contact with male clients. She realizes that somewhere in the Qur'an, it is stated that women cannot touch men. By massaging men, therefore, she might be acting contrary to her religion. She only contemplates this occasionally, however, and her attitude ("But hey, that's my job") illustrates that Mouria generally deals pragmatically with these Islamic behavioral codes. Furthermore, her comparison to nursing helps her present her business as respectable in response to people who may gossip (talk "dirty") about her. Sticking to her limits implies that she tries to keep a certain distance from her male clients. Besides, *he* (the male client) is the one who approached *her*, so she is not to be blamed for getting in touch with strange men. Moreover, she is in control because she decides *whom* she massages, that is, not disrespectful men. At the same time, she rejects this idea of improper behavior and adds that the Qur'an "says something completely different" than men and "people from the circles of Islam" make of it. She defends herself against such gendered dogmas by pragmatically and symbolically creating a boundary between her and men.

Mouria's ambiguity about being a Muslima and a hairdresser/beautician leads her to defend herself in dialogue with her Muslim 'audience' that might discard her as a 'bad Muslima.' Telling the Dutch female researcher that men never lose implies that Mouria sees how men use the Qur'an to exert power over women. Yet her references to her rebellion and fights with her husband in particular help her vindicate her female entrepreneurship.

Aylin, who owns a driving school, also sometimes feels friction between her religion and profession, though in a different way:

> The purpose was that, hey, there are so many Turkish women here, or Moroccan women, that do not dare to take lessons from a man. . . . And perhaps this is a bit easier for them. . . . Well, now with the Ramadan it is an advantage that I'm pregnant because pregnant women do not have to fast. If I weren't pregnant, I would perhaps be tempted to discuss the fact that I don't fast. That is the last thing that I want, going into debate about that. For I do what I want to. . . . Furthermore, I do pray before I step into my car, that everything will go fine, in that sense I am religious. . . . But Alevi are less extreme regarding religion. If I would marry a Sunni, then one way or another you would be disadvantaged because you're an Alevi. . . . Coincidentally, my uncle has married a Sunni wife. That is possible. However, not the other way around; as a woman you have far less freedom.

Aylin's story illustrates how Islamic identification may enable Muslims to discover new entrepreneurial opportunities (see also Shane & Venkataraman, 2000). Before she started her company, she taught Turkish and Dutch as a volunteer at a social center. She then started a driving school because she really liked teaching and setting her own hours. Noticing that many Muslimas hesitate to take driving lessons from a male instructor provided her, as a Muslim businesswoman, with a new market niche.

However, it also illustrates that her Alevi religion could put her in difficult situations; if she were not pregnant, she would have to defend her behavior to Sunni clients, possibly complicating her business. Therefore, it is convenient for her as an entrepreneur not to have to discuss whether she is a 'real' Muslima or not. For her, religion is an individual matter, and she uses it mostly instrumentally: She prays when she needs it. In her opinion, marrying a Sunni would unacceptably restrict her female autonomy.

This quote illustrates the diversity in Islam. Alevi constitute a minority (around 25%) in Turkey and in the Turkish community in the Netherlands (Sunier, 1998). Many Sunni consider Alevi outsiders, non-Muslims even, for their beliefs and practices center on the role of Ali, the prophet's son-in-law (Eickelman, 1998). Alevi are not required to pray five times a day, and they consider the Ramadan an 'overdone' ritual and fast twelve days in the month of Muharram instead. Furthermore, they criticize "the pilgrimage to Mecca as 'external pretense,' as the real pilgrimage takes place in one's heart" (Eickelman, 1998, p. 272). Moreover, during festivities men and women dance together and drink alcohol, which is regarded with suspicion by many Sunni (Eickelman, 1998).

The fact that certain Islamic guidelines are generally more predominant in the daily lives of Sunni is illustrated by Fatna, who always dresses herself inconspicuously and frequently contemplates wearing a head scarf:

> It is important for us what other people say because we have to remain businesslike; they look at our lives. So you have to be careful because everyone knows you. . . . I don't want that yet [wearing a head scarf]. Yes maybe, don't know, not yet.

In a second private conversation, Fatna expresses her qualms about the head scarf:

> People will think of you differently, and I do not want to deviate even more from the rest, I do that too much already! . . . Moreover, the Qur'an only prescribes that you have to dress decently. Women are often not suppressed by the Qur'an, but in the name of the Qur'an. Women are being oppressed by the culture, by men!

Fatna, who started a company with her sisters because her father did not want them to work for a male boss, is clearly highly affected by the Turkish community. It became clear in her life story that her employees, clients, and suppliers are predominantly of Turkish descent. They all expect her to behave in an 'appropriately' feminine, modest way. Paradoxically, she gains some freedom through her business, although she simultaneously loses some as well because a businesswoman who moves in public places might be considered shameful. As both her entrepreneurial and Muslim identity are predominant in her narrative, she is ambivalent about wearing the head scarf: On the one hand she postpones it, but on the other hand she denies its necessity. The fact that her sisters do wear head scarves is confrontational. Reflecting on the interview situation, Fatna may diplomatically state she does not want to wear a head scarf *yet*, as she does not want to oppose her sisters' convictions as they walk in and out during the first interview. However, when interviewed alone, Fatna refers to the head scarf as a bothersome symbol of contrast ("deviation from the rest"). Apparently, Fatna feels more comfortable expressing her criticism about what is expected from Muslimas when she is alone with the non-Muslim female interviewer.

Fatna's deliberation fits into a context where postponing the head scarf is a generally accepted practice. In a way, just like Aylin in response to

Sunni Muslims, Fatna creates boundaries within Islam by individualizing the relationship between Allah and herself in order to acquire more female autonomy. In Islamic orthodoxy, the head scarf symbolizes devoutness to Allah and other typically Islamic feminine virtues, such as modesty and shyness.[4] Three Qur'anic verses are often quoted (Sura 24:24, 33:53, and 33:59) to demonstrate that women should wear a head scarf (Bartkowski & Read, 2003). However, more liberal, feminist interpretations of Islam contextualize the prescription of the head scarf in pre-Islamic periods, stating that the word 'head scarf' is not found anywhere in the Qur'an. These arguments help Fatna justify her reservations as she emphasizes that it is not necessary to wear a head scarf in Islam and that it is not Islam who restrict women, but culture and men.

## LEGITIMIZING FEMALE ENTREPRENEURSHIP THROUGH ISLAM

Farah is perfectly able to combine her Muslim identity with her gender and entrepreneurial identities, as the following quote illustrates:

> I am a woman, but that does not limit me in what I would like to do. . . . It [the Qur'an] is a guideline; people want power, and then you have people that abuse the Qur'an and this is how, for instance, women are oppressed. . . . For me, they [women and men] are equal; in the Qur'an they are seen as equal, providing that the Qur'an states that women should remain indoors, but that pertains to that period, and the wife of the Prophet was even an entrepreneur . . . so who can tell me that I cannot work outside the home?

Farah emphasizes that the Qur'an is interpreted with different consequences. She critiques the interpretations that lead to oppression and proposes an alternative reading that historicizes the Qur'an ("that pertains to that period"), stressing gender equality. She can be a woman, a Muslim, and an entrepreneur at the same time ("being a woman does not limit me"). Reacting to an imaginary Muslim audience that might think otherwise, she uses her knowledge of the Qur'an and invokes the female role model of Khadisha to legitimize her entrepreneurship.

Farah's reading of the Qur'an relates to feminist interpretations of Islam. Muslim feminists try to revise Islam, arguing that the Hadith (the passed-down and therefore debatable traditions concerning the Prophet) are the source of most misogynous Islamic rulings and not the Qur'an, which was allegedly transmitted to the Prophet by Allah. By "reading the Qur'an and the Hadith as a woman," or *Ijtihad* (Najmabadi, 1998), diverse linguistic explanations of verses are provided, patriarchal interpretations are exposed, and gender equality is proven. By historicizing religious texts,

Muslim feminists state that the head scarf predates Islam (Bartkowski & Read, 2003). For instance, famous Muslim feminist Fatima Mernissi criticizes the male mentality that considers it 'dishonorable' if a female family member works outside the home (Mernissi, 1996). Farah both stretches the boundaries of what is acceptable work within gendered and religious regulations through feminist Islamic interpretations and demarcates earlier societies from contemporary societies by historicizing the Qur'an. Unlike Fatna, Farah does not feel that her head scarf restricts her entrepreneurship; in fact it accommodates her:

> This is part of my identity; I have chosen it because it gives me a feeling of being a Muslim. . . . Later, I went to live on my own, and I was completely gone from the Moroccan circuit, did not know at all what was going on there. It was on purpose that I distanced myself. . . . Ah, culture, yes, I am someone who does not care too much about what others think, and my mother doesn't either. . . . She is also more a Muslim than a Moroccan who lives according to culture. . . . I had just done an internship at a consultancy and been in touch with new soiling policies, so it seemed nice to do something with it, as it was new. . . . Yes, often when I call, they [potential clients] don't know that [about her head-scarf], and when I enter, you get all those looks! Really, people who stare! And that is what you use to do your story because they are totally out of balance.

These quotes demonstrate that Farah distinguishes between Islam and Moroccan culture and identifies herself much more with Islam. She expresses her Muslim identity with her head scarf. Living outside a socially controlling community and adhering to Islam enables Farah to discard the rules and expectations for Moroccan women. Her mother is her role model in this. Her entrepreneurial and Muslim identities seem to enforce each other. She captures an entrepreneurial opportunity by entering a new environmental business, and she uses her head scarf as an entrepreneurial trademark to distinguish herself.

Van Nieuwkerk (2006) argues that Islam offers distance from an ethnic background through a discourse on the universality of Islam and the irrelevance of the ethnic, cultural dimension. Many young women seem to feel more attracted to a Muslim identity than to a Moroccan or Turkish identity because the "Islamic community is open to anyone" (Buitelaar, 1998, p. 44), and they want to resist parental and communal restrictions on behavior.

Fatna refers to different parts of Islam in another way to legitimize her concurrently being an entrepreneur, a woman, and Turkish:

> Allah knows everything and respects you as long as you don't harm anyone. . . . That is also one of the five pillars of Islam: You have to be

a Muslim; you have to pray; you have fast 30 days a year; you have to give alms to the poor; and if you can, you should do the hadj once in your lifetime. . . . We do not think so materialistically. But just standing on your own feet and helping poor people, that is what I want. It will be enough for me to have a house. The rest to the poor. . . . Entrepreneurship in the Turkish community provides women with legitimization to develop themselves and gives them the opportunity to socialize with men, even if it is only in a pure business context.

Earlier we saw Fatna's doubts in relation to wearing a head scarf, as more orthodox people of the Turkish community could perceive her not wearing a head scarf as not being a devout Muslima. She deals with the expectations of her community regarding the head scarf by claiming she is still considering it. Moreover, her 'otherness' may not be advantageous for her business. Thus, Fatna seems to prioritize her entrepreneurial identity; yet she presents this in line with her Muslim identity and legitimizes her wish to 'stand on her own feet' by claiming that helping others is in line with Islam. Helping others through her business and stressing she does not think so materialistically gives an honorable and moral sound to her entrepreneurship and might also compensate for her not remaining in the private sphere. Therefore, Fatna uses her religious identification and separates this from her ethnic identity to legitimize her being a female entrepreneur.

In many Arab countries, women legitimize their public behavior in the labor market by describing their work as 'helping.' In Algeria, for instance, *Ajr* ('a heavenly reward from Allah,' or gifts instead of wages) is provided to women for "doing good deeds and providing services to others" (Jansen, 2004). By referring to *Ajr*, women can compensate for their public manifestation. *Ajr* relates to what Fatna seems to be doing; as a woman in a masculine/public profession, she compensates for her entrepreneurship by helping others. She uses her religion to give her job a moral sound by claiming she does not work for materialistic ends, but for others. Apparently, Fatna's boundary work involves separating her religion from her ethnicity and tying her entrepreneurial identity to her religion.

## CONCLUSION

This chapter has explored how Islamic identification relates to the multiple identity constructions of female entrepreneurs of Moroccan and Turkish origin. The contribution of this chapter to theory development within entrepreneurship is threefold.

First, the concept of intersectionality helps to clarify how entrepreneurial identities are situationally and dialogically constructed at different axes of difference such as gender and ethnicity. This chapter advances entrepreneurship studies by including and combining the hitherto largely neglected identity categories of religion and entrepreneurship and interlocking them with gender and ethnicity. It has demonstrated how these businesswomens' gender, ethnic, entrepreneurial, and/or religious identities are dynamic coconstructions, not merely accumulations of womanhood, entrepreneurship, ethnicity, and religion. We have seen that this intersectionality within entrepreneurship requires extensive identity work to cope with structural inequalities and create room for agency and opportunities as diverse constituencies steer in opposite directions. For instance, Mouria combines her entrepreneurial and gender identities in her beauty salon but refrains from dogmatic behavioral codes for Muslim women because this disturbs her entrepreneurship. Aylin connects her Muslim, ethnic, and gender identities to target a new market niche for her driving school: Muslim women. Farah uses her head scarf as a trademark to emphasize that her gender and religious identities go well together with her entrepreneurial identity. She discards her ethnic Moroccan identity because this hinders her ability to develop an entrepreneurial identity. Fatna seems to deploy her Muslim identity to underline the ethics of her business and to distance herself from ethnically gendered norms on entrepreneurship. Our analysis of the lived practices of intersectionality has demonstrated the importance of including particular social contexts to come to a better understanding of entrepreneurial identities.

Second, this chapter furthers the understanding of boundary work within entrepreneurship. The expectations of various constituencies related to these diverse identity categories exhibit particular, sometimes conflicting, identity regulations that give rise to boundary work (see also Sveningsson & Alvesson, 2003). Boundary work in the context of migrant Muslim businesswomen entails strategies in which Islam is used as a basis for distinction, stratification, and demarcation to facilitate entrepreneurship. Although some expressions of Islam, such as the head scarf, may be experienced as a bothersome symbol of 'otherness' within entrepreneurship, all interviewees resist dogmatic approaches of Islam and negotiate their Muslim identity in relation to entrepreneurship. We distinguish four kinds of boundary work. One strategy is to resist the strict sex segregation as advocated by certain sections in Islam. Mouria pragmatically relates her job to respectful professions and defines her 'limits' by keeping appropriate distance from male clients. She symbolically creates a boundary between herself and male clients to conform to gendered norms without jeopardizing her business. Another strategy to deal with gender regulations ascribed to Islam is to emphasize the individuality of faith. The women in this study do this by claiming the right to decide for themselves which religious rules apply to their entrepreneurship and which rules can be disregarded. Thus, they craft an individual Muslim identity and build boundaries within Islam; different Islams are distinguished to stretch the boundaries for religious individualism and, accordingly, their female entrepreneurship. The third form of boundary work involves embracing feminist progressive interpretations of the Qur'an, such as referring to Qur'anic female role models and stressing the morality of work. This provides women with the opportunity to stretch the boundaries of what is acceptable within gendered and religious regulations. The latter not only pertains to the businesswomen; for instance, Marshall (2005, p. 114) notes that reformist Muslim women in Turkey also claim the ability to work outside the home as long as they serve their families and society. The final form of boundary work involves historicizing and contextualizing the Qur'an by stating, for example, that the strict gender relations as described in several Qur'anic verses pertain to ancient periods. Demarcating earlier societies from contemporary societies helps these women shield themselves from dogmatic interpretations of the Qur'an. Accordingly, they are able to counter more universal interpretations within Islam regarding appropriate gender behavior.

Finally, exploring the lived practices of a hitherto marginalized and understudied group of entrepreneurs demonstrates what kind of power processes emerge in entrepreneurship at the crossroads of gender, ethnicity, and religion. Yet the context of entrepreneurship shows that there is more than inequality and exclusion when the social categories of gender, ethnicity, and Islam intersect. We have seen our businesswomen create and use ample opportunities and possibilities to craft their 'selves.' Analogous to Bartkowski and Read (2003) who observe that Muslim women often negotiate the cultural prescriptions that produce their social marginality as women, these businesswomen gain agency from the intersectionality of their gender and ethnic identities while identifying with Islam. Moreover, in contrast to the Orientalist discourse that suggests the incompatibility of Islam and entrepreneurial identities, this chapter has shown that Islamic identification can go well with gender, entrepreneurial, and ethnic identities, although this sometimes requires creative identity work. As Shane and Venkataraman (2000) note, entrepreneurial identities can even be strengthened by using religion to identify new innovative market niches. Our study of these Muslim women's completion of entrepreneurship makes for a situated contribution to the revision of the archetype of the white, male, individualistic, Calvinist entrepreneur.

# NOTES

1. The degree of participation of Turkish and Moroccan women, however, remains low compared to that of women of native Dutch origin, which was 62% in 2009.
2. Of all entrepreneurs of Moroccan and Turkish origin (5,500 and 13,700, respectively), 14.5% and 17.5% are women, whereas 31% of all 899,000 entrepreneurs of native Dutch origin are female (statline.cbs.nl).
3. In this study, migrant women (or ethnic minority women, or in Dutch *allochtone vrouwen*) are women for whom at least one parent was born abroad and who belong to either the first or second generation of migrants.

4. In the Netherlands, almost 50% of all Turkish and Moroccan women between the ages of 15 and 64 wear a head scarf (Merens, 2006).

# REFERENCES

Abu-Lughod, L. (1986). *Veiled sentiments: Honor and poetry in a Bedouin society.* Berkeley and Los Angeles: University of California Press.
Anthias, F. (2001). New hybridities, old concepts: The limits of 'culture.' *Ethnic and Racial Studies, 24*(4), 619–641.
Arslan, M. (2001). The work ethic values of Protestant British, Catholic Irish and Muslim Turkish managers. *Journal of Business Ethics, 31*(4), 321–339.
Bartkowski, J., & Read, J. (2003). Veiled submission: Gender, power, and identity among evangelical and Muslim women in the United States. *Qualitative Sociology, 26*(1), 71–92.
Bell, E., & Nkomo, S. (2001). *Our separate ways: Black and white women and the struggle for professional identity.* Boston: Harvard Business School.
Bourdieu, P. (1966). The sentiment of honour in Kabyle society. In J. G. Peristiany (Ed.), *Honor and shame: The values of Mediterranean society* (pp. 211–240). Chicago: University of Chicago Press.
Brown, A., & Humphreys, M. (2002). Nostalgia and the narrativization of identity: A Turkish case. *British Journal of Management, 13*, 141–159.
Buitelaar, M. (1998). Between ascription and assertion: The representation of social identity by women of Moroccan descent in the Netherlands. *Focaal, 32*, 29–50.
CBS (2011). *Archief Beroepsbevolking.* Retrieved July 8, 2011, from http://statline.cbs.nl.
Crenshaw, K. (1997). Intersectionality and identity politics: Learning from violence against women of color. In M. Lyndon Shanley & U. Narayan (Eds.), *Reconstructing Political Theory* (pp. 178–193). University Park: Pennsylvania State University Press.
Eickelman, D. (1998). *The Middle East and Central Asia: An anthropological approach.* Upper Saddle River, NJ: Prentice Hall.
Essers, C., & Benschop, Y. (2007). Enterprising identities: Female entrepreneurs of Moroccan and Turkish origin in the Netherlands. *Organization Studies, 28*(1), 49–69.
Essers, C., Benschop, Y., & Doorewaard, H. (2010). Female ethnicity: Understanding Muslim migrant businesswomen in the Netherlands. *Gender, Work and Organization.*
Friday, S., Friday, E., & Moss, S. (2004). Multiple dimensions of racioethnicity. *Journal of Management Development, 3*(6), 500–517.
Gilmore, D. (1987). *Honor and shame and the unity of the Mediterranean.* Arlington, VA: American Anthropological Association.
Haraway, D. (1991). Situated knowledges: The science question in feminism and the privilege of the partial perspective. In D. Haraway (Ed.), *Simians, cyborgs and women: The reinvention of nature* (pp. 183–201). London: Free Association.
Jacobson, J. (1997). Religion and ethnicity: Dual and alternative sources of identity among young British Pakistanis. *Ethnic and Racial Studies, 20*(2), 238–256.
Jansen, W. (2004). The economy of religious merit: Women and Ajr in Algeria. *Journal of North African Studies, 9*(4), 1–17.
Lamont, M., & Fournier, M. (Eds.). (1992). *Cultivating differences: Symbolic boundaries and the making of inequality.* Chicago: University of Chicago Press.

Lieblich, A., Tuval-Mashiach, R., & Zilber, T. (1998). *Narrative research: Reading, analysis and interpretation.* London: Sage.

Lutz, H. (1991). *Migrant women of «Islamic background»: Images and self-images.* Amsterdam: Stichting MERA—Middle East Research Associates.

MacAdams, D. (1993). *The Stories we live by: Personal myths and the making of the self.* New York: William Morrow.

Marshall, G. (2005). Ideology, progress, and dialogue: A comparison of feminist and Islamist women's approaches to the issues of head covering and work in Turkey. *Gender & Society, 10*(1), 104–120.

Merens, A. (2006). Betaalde arbeid. In S. Geuzenkamp & A. Merens (Eds.), *De sociale atlas van vrouwen van etnische minderheden.* The Hague: CBS

Mernissi, F. (1996). *Islam en democratie: De angst voor het moderne.* Breda: De Geus.

Mirchandani, K. (1999). Feminist insights on gendered work: New directions in research on women and entrepreneurship. *Gender, Work and Organization, 6*(4), 224–235.

Najmabadi, A. (1998). Feminism in an Islamic republic: Years of hardship, years of growth. In Y. Haddad & J. Esposito (Eds.), *Islam, Gender and Social Change* (pp. 59–84). New York: Oxford University Press.

Ogbor, J. (2000). Mythicizing and reification in entrepreneurial discourse: Ideology-critique of entrepreneurial studies. *Journal of Management Studies, 37*(5), 605–635.

Porter, J., & Washington, R. (1993). Minority identity and self-esteem. *Annual Review of Sociology, 19*, 139–161.

Portes, A. (1995). *The economic sociology of immigration: Essays on networks, ethnicity, and entrepreneurship.* New York: Russell Sage Foundation.

Prasad, A. (Ed.). (2003). *Postcolonial theory and organizational analysis: A critical engagement.* London: Palgrave Macmillan.

Said, E. (1978). *Orientalism.* London: Routledge and Kegan Paul.

Shane, S., & Venkataraman, S. (2000). The promise of entrepreneurship as a field of research. *Academy of Management Review, 25*, 217–226.

Sloane, P. (1999). *Islam, modernity and entrepreneurship among the Malays.* New York: St. Martin's.

Sunier, T. (1998). *Turkije: Mensen, politiek, economie, cultuur.* Amsterdam: Koninklijk Instituut voor de Tropen.

Sveningsson, S., & Alvesson, M. (2003). Managing managerial identities: Organizational fragmentation, discourse, and identity struggle. *Human Relations, 56*(10), 1163–1193.

Thomas, A., & Mueller, S. (2000). A case for comparative entrepreneurship: Assessing the relevance of culture. *Journal of International Business Studies, 31*(2), 287–301.

Torab, A. (1996). Piety as gendered agency: A study of Jalaseh Ritual discourse in an urban neighbourhood in Iran. *Journal of the Royal Anthropological Institute, 2*(2), 235–252.

Van der Spek, I. (2004). Als religie niet alleen maar sexy en smaakvol is . . . : Een drieluik over vrouwen en religie in Nederland. *Tijdschrift voor Genderstudies, 7*(1), 8–17.

Van Nieuwkerk, K. (2006). *Gender and conversion to Islam in the West.* Austin: University of Texas Press.

Weber, M., & Kalberg, S. (2002). *The Protestant ethic and the spirit of capitalism.* Los Angeles: Roxbury.

# 9 Social Capital as Networks of Networks
## The Case of a Chinese Entrepreneur

*Peter Peverelli and Lynda Jiwen Song*

## INTRODUCTION

The social embeddedness of entrepreneurs has been a theme in contemporary debates on entrepreneurship for some time (Granovetter, 1995; Kloosterman & Rath, 2001; Lin, 2001; Portes & Sensenbrenner, 1993; Rath & Kloosterman, 2000; Waldinger et al., 1990). Due to the rapidly increasing influence of China on the global economy, understanding the embeddedness of the emerging class of Chinese entrepreneurs has become more than a merely academic endeavor (Batjargal & Liu, 2004; Xiao & Tsui, 2007; Yang, 2007).

In most of these debates, the notion of embeddedness is linked to social networks. Entrepreneurs are seen as people who combine various resources (capital, knowledge, people, etc.) to create surplus value. These resources can be accessed through the different social networks of which the entrepreneur is a member (Kloosterman & Rath, 2001, p. 192).

The sum of the potential access to resources an entrepreneur accumulates in social networks is often referred to as social capital. Bourdieu distinguishes between economic capital, cultural capital, and social capital. The capital of each individual is a specific mix of these three (Bourdieu, 1986, p. 114). Lin (2001, p. 119) uses a definition that is more focused on the financial meaning of the word 'capital' when he states that the premise behind the notion of social capital is rather simple and straightforward: investment in social relations with expected returns to the market place. Lin follows Burt (1992) here in linking social capital to social networks. Network locations are seen to "represent and create competitive advantages" (Lin, 2001, p. 22; see also Batjargal & Liu, 2004).

However, the majority of the discussions use the term 'social network' but do not engage in social-network analysis. The minority that do (e.g., Granovetter, 1995; Lin, 2001) use mainstream social-network analysis that describes social relationships in terms of nodes and ties, wherein the nodes are the individual actors and ties are the relationships that exist between the actors (Brass & Burkhard, 1992; Kilduff & Tsai, 2003, pp. 13–16; Scott, 2000, p. 89).

Social-network analysis is a useful tool to study how individuals form alliances on the micro level. However, when trying to apply it to higher-level problems, this method of analysis seems to deviate from the way people form relationships in social practice. People tend to form relationships on the basis of inclusion in social groups. For example, an interior decorator who has worked as an employee of a firm specializing in decorating private homes for a number of years may decide to start his own consulting company in the same business. Another option would be to start a similar company in another market segment, such as corporate offices. In both cases, this person would be using the same skills, typically acquired through education, but in the first case he would also use the experience accumulated during his employment, whereas in the second option he would have to make an additional effort to get into the world of corporate interior decoration. Our entrepreneur could also leave the decorating business and decide to venture into a completely different field, which would require an even heavier investment in accessing and combining resources. This explains why people who exchange a salaried job for a private business would be more likely to take the first option: doing what one is used to do, but as one's own boss.

Burt (1992, 2005) has attempted to address the problem of links between groups of people by introducing the concept of structural hole, a gap between tighter networks. In this view, society is imagined as consisting of networks of tightly related individuals that can be linked by brokers, people who have ties within different networks. Although we believe this is a major step forward, this model is problematic because it still takes individuals as nodes; it puts the broker in the relatively isolated position of linking groups while apparently not belonging to any of them. Xiao and Tsui also highlight this problem (2007, p. 20). A more natural solution would be to conceive the role of brokers as people who are members of multiple networks. This chapter attempts to use concepts from social integration theory (Peverelli, 2000; Peverelli & Verduyn, 2010) to add such a model to existing social-network analysis.

Combining Kloosterman and Rath's (2001) view of the entrepreneur as someone who combines resources with Lin's (2001) model of social capital, we would like to redefine entrepreneurs as people with a strong capability to create value from their social capital by linking their social networks in various ways. To support this definition, our problem is to find a way to enrich existing social-network models with a module that takes into account the multiple social inclusions of the same person. In this chapter, we will turn to social integration theory to find such a module and test the enriched model on the building of social capital by a Chinese entrepreneur.

## SOCIAL INTEGRATION THEORY

This study uses social integration (SI) theory to bridge that gap and enrich social-network theory with a module that links networks on the basis of multiple inclusions of actors in several social-cognitive groups (networks).

SI theory has been developed on the basis of Weick's organization theory (1979, 1995), enriched with concepts from postmodern philosophy and psycholinguistics (Peverelli, 2000; Peverelli & Verduyn, 2010). In this theory, organizing is defined as "the reduction of equivocality in ongoing social interaction between actors to couple their behavior to perform a certain task more efficiently" (Peverelli & Verduyn, 2010, p. 5). One consequence of this process is the emergence of groups of actors who frequently interact around a specific theme and therefore make sense of that topic in a more or less similar way. Those actors are said to be 'included' in such groups. Each actor is involved in a large number of such groups, which is referred to as 'multiple inclusion.' Two or more groups are connected by actors with inclusions in each of the groups.

SI theory includes a graphic convention. As soon as two or more actors start interacting about a certain theme, they will create a configuration consisting of the actors and the cognitive matter they share (typical language, symbols, ways to do things, etc.). Figure 9.1 represents a situation in which two configurations are linked by the fact that actor A is included in both.

Mainstream social-network analysis would not be able to handle this situation because at least two actors are required to draw a basic network. In SI research, one observes who interacts with whom and the nature of that interaction. While observing, the researcher gradually becomes aware of the social-cognitive groups, the key actors, and each actor's multiple inclusions. SI researchers build up their insight in the social construction of the object of their research by laying down the observed data into graphs such as figure 9.1, which can be regarded as a representation of the social embeddedness of actors.

As such, the SI model is a tool to map and link the social capital of each key actor involved in the case under investigation and simultaneously see how the social capital of all these actors is organically integrated.

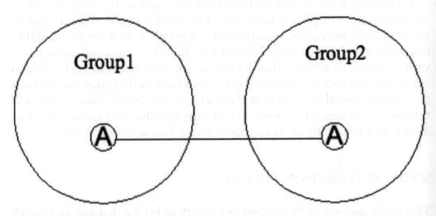

*Figure 9.1*   A simple SI network indicating that actor A is included in two groups.

## RESEARCH METHOD

The research method used in this study is naturalistic inquiry (Lincoln & Guba, 1985). To maximize our exposure to actors involved in the case, extensive use has been made of unstructured observations and in-depth conversations documented by detailed field notes. These stories are the containers for the shared perception of reality, the symbols, and so on of each group. They define the role of each actor and describe the relationships between the actors (Bojé, 2001; Czarniawska, 1998; Van Eeten, Twist, & Kalders, 1996). In the SI framework, each social-cognitive group is regarded as having its own story of the case. Such stories only pertain to one particular group and are linked to one particular moment in time (Gergen, 1992, p. 220). The groups are then integrated by the multiple inclusions of the actors involved.

As the study of social-capital building by Chinese private entrepreneurs is still in its initial stage, we are coping with a relatively high number of variables of potential interest and a large number of sources of data. In such a context, the case study is the most appropriate approach (Yin, 2004). The combination of a case study and naturalistic inquiry will generate a framework that can be applied to a larger number of cases in the future, and this will gradually lead to the construction of a model of social capital in relation to Chinese private entrepreneurs.

The company used in this case, Yihai Garden, is a privately managed condominium in Beijing that has established a series of schools on its premises to create additional value for its clients. The condominium is located in the Fengtai District of Beijing, and according to current Chinese regulations, the schools should be supervised by the education bureau of that district. However, in practice the Fengtai Education Bureau has a very low profile in the operation of the schools, whereas another district's education bureau takes a much more active role in Yihai's schools. We will use our model to show that this situation is a consequence of the way the entrepreneur, in this case, has gradually built up social capital by enabling key people to link their various networks.

## YIHAI GARDEN

Fengtai District had been looking for a party interested in investing in the development a piece of wasteland for some time without success before it finally attracted Wang's attention. One impediment that prevented people from buying apartments in Yihai was the lack of proper education in the vicinity. Wang decided to develop a complete set of schools within Yihai as a way to relieve the Yihai residents of this mental and physical burden, so they could focus on their jobs to earn a living for their families.

Establishing and operating schools involves a lengthy bureaucratic procedure. Government approval is required, and one must comply with the relevant rules. In line with Chinese practice, Wang proposed her idea to the appropriate administrative level, Fengtai District. She was mainly met with opposition, with the exception of one official, Li Yingwei. The authorities claimed they did not have the funds to build new schools. Wang, in her own words, then decided to "help the government" and finance the schools herself, as long as she was granted permission to do so.

To access educational knowledge, Wang sought relationships for her primary and secondary schools with existing schools. As a result of Li Yingwei's connections, Beijing Number 2 Experimental Primary School (Beijing 2) and Beijing Number 8 Middle School (Beijing 8) were thus contracted. The Yihai schools were established as subsidiaries of these schools. In the remainder of this chapter, Yihai 2 will refer to Yihai's primary school and Beijing 2 to its parent organization.

During the initial stage, in particular, a significant number of teachers, including current principals, were assigned to Yihai from the partner schools. This created a peculiar situation with regard to the administrative affiliation of the Yihai schools. According to administrative practice, the Fengtai Education Bureau would be the expected supervising agency of the Yihai schools. Our research revealed this was not the case, however. The West City District Education Bureau, on the other hand, had visited Yihai once with an official delegation of school principals to learn from Yihai's experience. During that visit, a representative of the West City Education Bureau mentioned the links with the West District as the motivation for the visit.

The following section will describe the process of ongoing social interaction that constructed the West City identity of the Yihai education system.

## THE SOCIAL CONSTRUCTION OF YIHAI EDUCATION

In terms of SI theory, the educational activities of Yihai constitute a separate cognitive space, which will be referred to here as Yihai Education. This space started as an idea by Wang and was gradually expanded through her interaction with various people. All these people added to the cognitive matter of that space through their multiple inclusions.

People do not develop ideas from scratch. They emerge on the basis of existing inclusions. As the CEO of Yihai, Wang needed to attract buyers for her apartments and realized that political practice required her to contact the Fengtai government. She talked to a number of Fengtai officials, but only one supported her, Li Yingwei. Li Yingwei has been the governor of Fengtai District and has always been a supporter of developing education, which made him more open than his colleagues to Wang's initiative. Together, they conceived Yihai Education. Wang is included in Yihai and the newly created Yihai Education space, Li in the Fengtai Government space and Yihai Education. The resulting situation is graphically represented in figure 9.2.

Of core importance to the realization of her educational ambition was the establishment of a primary and a secondary school. Wang wanted to establish

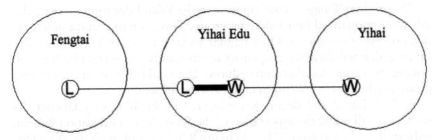

*Figure 9.2*  Basic situation during the initiation of Yihai Education.

cooperation with existing schools to utilize their experience. Because Wang had already established a strong bond with Li, she once more turned to him for advice. Li had inclusions in Beijing 2 and Beijing 8. He is an alumnus of Beijing 8, and his son had been educated at Beijing 2. It was then natural for Li to introduce these schools to Yihai as potential partners.

As part of the cooperation, Beijing 2 and Beijing 8 sent a number of teachers to Yihai, including the current principals, Shi and Yin, respectively. Overall, Shi is included in Yihai 2 and Beijing 2. The same holds for Yin in Yihai 8 and Beijing 8, resulting in figure 9.3. We have added a traditional social-network analysis of the same for comparison.

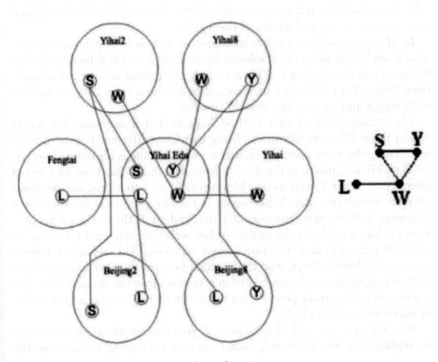

*Figure 9.3*  All actors involved in Yihai Education.

The original Wang–Li configuration in the Yihai Education space gradually institutionalized into a steering group. This is an important milestone in a process of emergence. Once regular social interaction has been institutionalized, it will have the propensity to constantly reconstruct itself by following the institutionalized procedures. The establishment of the steering group marks the consolidation of Yihai Education.

Both Beijing 2 and Beijing 8 are located in the West City District. As such, they fall under the supervision of the West District Education Bureau, indicated by the interrupted line in figure 9.3. This link with the West District was not intended, but it is a consequence of the gradual social construction of Yihai Education.

## SI VERSUS SOCIAL NETWORKS

When we look at the two graphs in figure 9.3, both say something about the relationships between the five actors. However, the strength of the left-hand graph is that it demonstrates that all of these actors are linked to all others and also indicates the nature of the linkages. An SI graph is a not a network of individuals but of social groups. Although the SI graph only includes 5 actors, the graph actually represents a much larger group of people. For example, Fengtai represents a large number of people, although in this case only Li is relevant. The linkages between the groups are people who are included in at least two of the groups. We can determine what each pair of actors share and what sets them apart.

In SI theory, inclusion refers to cognitive inclusion. A person like Yin, who is no longer officially employed by Beijing 8, can still be regarded as being included in Beijing 8. This is exactly the reason why Li could introduce Beijing 2 and Beijing 8 to Wang, although he was no longer a student of Beijing 8 and his son was already an adult.

The strong point of this methodology is that it accounts for actors acting from different identities. Wang can have different points of view concerning the same issue depending on whether she is regarding it as the CEO of Yihai Garden, as the driving force of Yihai Education, as a board member of Yihai 8, and so on. Moreover, in all situations, she occupies all roles simultaneously. What varies is that in any given situation, one inclusion will be more prominently invoked than the other inclusions. Wang is like a spider in the middle of her web with the most relations (in terms of quantity) and the most intense relations. This reflects her position as the driving force, and it also corroborates that her interpersonal skill of forging strong bonds has been a key factor in her success. This has a stronger explanatory power than the mathematical notion of centrality in social-network analysis.

We are not arguing that standard social-network analysis should be replaced by the SI model, rather we are attempting to increase the explanatory power of both by combining them. The social groups indicated in SI graphs by circles usually represent networks. The social-cognitive group Yihai Education consists of Wang and Li, and actors such as the principals of Yihai 2 and Yihai 8. The members of Yihai Education form a social network that can be described as using standard social-network analysis, as we have in the graph of figure 9.3. In fact, the graph of figure 9.3 can be regarded as a description of the situation inside the Yihai Education space in the graph on the left.

## RESULTS AND DISCUSSION

We recognize the use of social-network analysis to determine the social capital of entrepreneurs. However, we noted that the current social-network models that take individuals as nodes do not properly reflect the way people form networks in social practice. We sought a solution by applying the concept of multiple inclusion from SI theory, which regards actors included in two or more networks as the links between those networks.

We tested the new model on a peculiar aspect of the educational activities at Yihai Garden. The core problem in the Yihai Education case is that the government organization that would be expected to control the schools was in fact hardly involved in their operation, whereas another one, although not officially empowered with such jurisdiction, showed certain aspects of the behavior of a supervising organization.

We understand this situation as a consequence of the concatenation of interactions related to the establishment of Yihai Garden in a particular institutional environment. Wang's decision to help Fengtai District develop a piece of wasteland without using any government funding formed the basis on which Yihai Garden could emerge as an enterprise operating with only marginal interference from the local government.

Through her configuration with Li in Yihai Education, Wang could access Li's other inclusions, in particular the ones in Beijing 2 and Beijing 8 as partners for Yihai 2 and Yihai 8, respectively. As both schools were located in the West District, the inclusions of the staff that were assigned from Beijing 2 and Beijing 8 to Yihai, in particular the two principals, formed many channels to access the cognitive matter of the West District.

As a result, the West District Education Bureau gradually perceived the Yihai schools as 'like' their own and felt a natural urge to exercise some form of control. However, they could not do so directly because Yihai was under Fengtai jurisdiction. Instead, the West District Education Bureau organized the study visit of West District school principals to Yihai.

It seems that the entrepreneurship of Wang lies in her ability to sense the commercial possibilities created by linking her multiple inclusions (sources of resources) in various ways and picking the set of inclusions that can produce the desired results in the quickest way.

Our findings seem to support those by Xiao and Tsui (2007), who found that the notion of broker as proposed by Burt (2005) did not fit with social practice in China. In Western individualist societies, brokers typically try to retain that position, which they regard as a vital asset. In more collectivist societies like China, such people would be better regarded as *integrators* who work in their own interest as well as the interests of the groups they link (Xiao & Tsui, 2007, p. 20). However, Xiao and Tsui still fail to escape the bonds of the notion that social networks are based on individuals. Their 'integrators,' regardless of their altruistic intentions, are still perceived as lingering between networks. Social integration theory regards all people as integrators, links between their various social inclusions.

## SHORTCOMINGS, FUTURE RESEARCH, AND RELEVANCE

This is only a preliminary study. The new methodology has only been applied to a single case. However, the results of the analysis of the Yihai Education case can serve as a model to analyze a much larger number of different cases of the social capital of Chinese private entrepreneurs. Variety must be sought in the type of business, size of company, geographic location, and so on.

Another aspect we have not yet taken up is that our analysis of social capital may also reveal opportunities missed by the entrepreneur. In Wang's case, her low-profile relationship with the Fengtai government may have caused her to miss interesting opportunities. This has to be addressed in future research.

The results of this study are highly relevant for the advancement of social-network analysis and academic realms that use social-network analysis, in particular the study of social capital. Instead of studying the various social identities of actors and the way they are involved in networks separately, the model developed in this study combines these two into an organic whole. This method seems to fit more 'naturally' to the way in which human actors behave. This has to be corroborated by future research. A large-scale follow-up project has already started.

The results also contribute to the growing body of literature on Chinese entrepreneurship.

## ACKNOWLEDGMENTS

We are highly indebted to the large number of people who gave us so much of their valuable time. This includes employees of Yihai Garden and various officials of Fengtai District. We would also like to thank Chen Aini, Sunny Wen, Zhiqiang Sun, and Jianfeng Yu of Renmin University for their valuable assistance and input. The project is supported by a grant from

China National Natural Science Foundation (project no. 70702024) and the China National Education Bureau's Humanities and Social Science Youth grant (project no. 07JC630063).

## REFERENCES

Batjargal, B., & Liu, M. (2004). 'Entrepreneurs' access to private equity in China: The role of social capital. *Organization Science, 15*(2), 159–172.
Bojé, D. (2001). *Narrative methods for organizational and communication research.* London: Sage.
Bourdieu, P. (1986). *Distinction: A social critique of the judgement of taste.* London: Routledge.
Brass, D. J., & Burkhard, M. E. (1992). Centrality and power in organizations. In N. Nohria & R. G. Eccles (Eds.), *Networks and Organizations* (pp. 191–215). Cambridge, MA: Harvard Business School Press.
Burt, R. S. (1992). *Structural holes: The social structure of competition.* Cambridge, MA: Harvard University Press.
Burt, R. S. (2005). *Brokerage and closure: An introduction to social capital.* Oxford: Oxford University Press.
Czarniawska, B. (1998). *A narrative approach to organization studies.* Thousand Oaks, CA: Sage.
Daft, R. L. (2007). *Understanding the theory and design of organizations.* Mason: Thomson.
Gergen, K. J. (1992). Organization theory in the postmodern era. In M. Reed & M. Hughes (Eds.), *Rethinking organization: New directions in organization theory and analysis* (pp. 207–226). London: Sage.
Granovetter, M. (1995) The economic sociology of firms and entrepreneurs. In A. Portes (Ed.), *The economic sociology of immigration: Essays on networks, ethnicity and entrepreneurship* (pp. 128–165). New York: Russell Sage Foundation.
Kilduff, M., & Tsai, W. (2003). *Social networks and organizations.* London: Sage.
Kloosterman, R., & Rath, J. (2001). Immigrant entrepreneurs in advanced economies: Mixed embeddedness further explored. *Journal of Ethnic and Migration Studies, 27*(2), 189–201.
Lin, N. (2001). *Social capital: A theory of social structure and action.* New York: Cambridge University Press.
Lincoln Y., & Guba, E. G. (1985). *Naturalistic inquiry.* Beverly Hills, CA: Sage.
Peverelli, P. J. (2000). *Cognitive Space: A social cognitive approach to Sino-Western cooperation.* Delft: Eburon.
Peverelli, P. J., & Verduyn, K. (2010). *Understanding the basic dynamics of organizing.* Delft: Eburon.
Portes, A., & Sensenbrenner, J. (1993). Embeddedness and immigration: Notes on the social determinants of economic action. *American Journal of Sociology, 98*(6), 1320–1350.
Rath, J., & Kloosterman, R. (2000). 'Outsiders' business: A critical review of research on immigrant entrepreneurship. *International Migration Review, 34*(3), 657–681.
Scott, J. (2000). *Social network analysis.* London: Sage.
Scott, W. R. (2001). *Institutions and organisations* (2nd ed.). London: Sage.
Van Dongen, H. J., De Laat, W. A. M., & Maas, A. J. J. A. (1996). *Een kwestie van verschil* [A matter of difference]. Delft: Eburon.

Van Eeten, M. J. G., Twist, M. J. W., & Kalders, P. R. (1996). Van een narratieve bestuurskundenaar een postmoderne beweerkunde? *Bestuurskunde, 5*(4), 168–188.
Waldinger, R., Aldrich, R., Ward, R., & Associates. (1990). *Ethnic Entrepreneurs: Immigrant Business in Industrial Societies*. Newbury Park, CA: Sage.
Weick, K. E. (1979). *The social psychology of organizing*. New York: McGraw Hill.
Weick, K. E. (1995). *Sensemaking in organizations*. London: Sage.
Xiao, Z., & Tsui, A. S. (2007). When brokers may not work: The cultural contingency of social capital in Chinese high-tech firms. *Administrative Science Quarterly, 52*, 1–31.
Yang, K. (2007). *Entrepreneurship in China*. Aldershot: Ashgate.
Yin, R. K. (2004). *The case study anthology*. Thousand Oaks, CA: Sage.

## Part V
# Wider Contextual Influences

## 10 Regions, Families, Religion
### Continuity and Change in Social Contexts of Entrepreneurship Between 1800 and 2000

*Karel Davids*

### INTRODUCTION

Over the past 200 years, Western countries have been through a series of radical economic and social transformations. They have undergone a structural transformation from a preindustrial to an industrial (and partly, postindustrial) economy; they have experienced several 'ups and downs' in terms of globalization; and they have suffered a number of violent fluctuations in business cycles, the latest of which was more vehement than anything witnessed in the last 80 years. Meanwhile, they have also seen various upturns and downturns in inequality, a drastic decline in birth and mortality rates, a significant rise in life expectancy, an unprecedented increase in living standards, the growth of individualism, and in Europe at least, a steady advance of secularization. Western societies have certainly changed more significantly since 1800 than previously.

This contribution discusses continuity and change in social contexts of entrepreneurship against the backdrop of these transformations. It examines, more specifically, how and to what extent entrepreneurship has been persistently influenced by traditional forces such as regional identities, family values, and religion. The key question addressed in this article is this: Given the radical economic and social changes between 1800 and 2000, in what ways and to what degree has entrepreneurship continued to be shaped by regional, familial, and religious networks and cultures? The approach taken in this chapter will be as follows: For each of these contextual factors, first the most relevant economic and sociohistorical research will be briefly discussed. Next, concepts, insights, and questions based on this body of research will be brought to bear on a particular Western society, the Netherlands. The extent to which these general notions can help us understand the effects of regions, families, and religion on entrepreneurship in the Netherlands in the 19th and 20th centuries will also be discussed. We will also investigate what the Dutch case can contribute to the general debate on social contexts of entrepreneurship after 1800. The conclusion summarizes the findings on the various contexts of entrepreneurship and discusses a few implications.

## REGIONAL CONTEXTS OF ENTREPRENEURSHIP

The key concept in the historical analysis of regional effects on entrepreneurship is the notion of 'industrial districts.' Since its reintroduction by Giacomo Becattini some 30 years ago, the concept of 'industrial districts' has become firmly established in scholarly debates on industrial development and regional economic disparities. Although the revival of this concept, originally coined by Alfred Marshall, first appeared among economists, sociologists, and political scientists, it has increasingly found acceptance among economic historians as well.

The immediate cause of its resurrection was the need for a convenient tool to analyze regional economic developments in Italy. It is not surprising that Italy still is the country where the phenomenon is most intensely studied and where many of the new ideas in methods and theory with regard to industrial districts first emerge and find application in empirical research. Yet Italy, or more precisely, the regions in north-central and northeastern Italy dubbed 'la Terza Italia,' certainly does not present the only example of industrial districts. Industrial districts have also been identified and analyzed in various other countries in Europe and across the Atlantic (Pyke, Becattini, & Sengenberger, 1990; Pyke & Sengenberger, 1992). As the notion of industrial districts gained wider currency, the tendency to refashion what Jonathan Zeitlin called "the canonical model of the Marshallian district" grew stronger too (Zeitlin, 1992, p. 281). Although the essence of the phenomenon is generally still taken to be the long-term combination of competition and cooperation between industrial producers in a specific regional setting, the contents of the concept have been elaborated, adapted, and refined. As more and more cases of industrial districts have been made the subject of inquiry, the greater the diversity of organizational models and trajectories of development there turned out to be. Some scholars now conceive of industrial districts simply as a special case of a larger set of 'territorial production complexes' or prefer to use terms such as 'regional network-based industrial systems' or 'urban industrial subsystems' to describe districtlike industrial localities that have not shown a specialization in a single sector (Capecchi, 1997; Saxenian, 1994; Storper & Walker, 1989).

Whereas the definition of 'industrial districts' has thus become more flexible than previously, serious efforts have also been underway to obtain a sharper picture of an aspect of these regions that was usually deemed to be of central importance but hitherto has always remained somewhat elusive, namely, the aspect of 'industrial atmosphere.' In Italy, recent research on the 'atmosphere' of industrial districts, such as the textile district of Prato or the footwear district in Vigevano, has particularly focused on the role of 'intermediate institutions' between central governments and individual firms, such as credit banks, employers' associations, and local governments, that could provide local networks of firms with some measure of coordination. Alberto Guenzi, Carlo Marco Belfanti,

Sergio Onger, and other economic historians have shown that the roots of the present-day districts can often be traced back to the 19th century (and sometimes even before) and that the forms and functions of the intermediate institutions in these districts can vary widely over time (Belfanti & Onger, 2002; Guenzi, 1997, 1999).

The Netherlands has also known industrial districts in the sense used in international literature. The most important one was a region northwest of Amsterdam called the Zaanstreek. In the 17th century, the Zaanstreek became one of the leading industrial centers in Europe. Within the space of a few decades, this cluster of villages in a wet, flat, treeless landscape along the River Zaan developed into a busy hub of industry, including shipbuilding, timber sawing, canvas weaving, oil milling, barley hulling, paper making, and paint manufacturing. Nearly all of these industries used wind energy as their main source of power. The total population of the region increased from about 7,000 in 1550 to roughly 27,000 by the middle of the 18th century. By 1900, the Zaanstreek was home to more than 47,000 people and nearly twice that number in 1950. Unlike most industrial districts in Italy, the Zaanstreek was never specialized within a single sector. The Zaan district has always consisted of various clusters of firms that, to some extent, were linked by a relationship of vertical integration. As far as the approach to production or the format of manufacturing is concerned, the Zaanstreek during the greater part of its career as an industrial district was characterized by a focus on bulk production. The Zaan district was not specialized in making small quantities of products to discrete specifications by individual customers (as in custom work) or in producing many items of varied size on the basis of aggregated advance orders (as in batch manufacturing), but rather in turning out large amounts of standardized goods that could be delivered from stock (Davids, 2006b).

Between the middle of the 19th century and World War I, the character of the region dramatically changed. In response to the rapidly growing integration of markets in the national and international economies since the 1840s, the Zaanstreek went through a radical change in its energy base as well as a fundamental shift in industrial structure. Steam replaced wind power as the principal source of energy. The Zaan industries no longer concentrated only on the production of semimanufactured goods and producer nondurables. In addition to old, established branches of industry such as oil milling, hulling, timber sawing, and starch making, there emerged a wide range of new industries that specialized in the production of durable and nondurable consumer goods such as furniture, linoleum, cacao, chocolate, soup, pastas, and biscuits. The format of manufacturing could now more aptly be described as 'mass and flow production' instead of bulk manufacturing, as the volume of output and the complexity of the production process—which notably involved increasing application of knowledge and skills in chemical and mechanical engineering—grew considerably. The raw material base of the Zaanstreek industries also underwent a remarkable change. A growing percentage of the materials used in the production process (such as rice, cocoa, timber, or oil seeds) originated from tropical or subtropical regions, instead of being imported from Europe or supplied by domestic producers. In this respect, the Zaan industry became more dependent on the services of the overseas shipping and trading network centered on Amsterdam than it had been previously (Davids, 2006b).

While the energy base and industrial structure of the Zaanstreek between approximately 1840 and 1920 were being profoundly transformed, the social networks that underpinned entrepreneurial behavior were changing too, albeit more slowly. Since the middle of the 17th century, the Zaanstreek, like industrial districts in Italy, has seen the rise of intermediate institutions that ensure a measure of cooperation between firms. The most persistent form in which this interfirm cooperation took shape was an arrangement for the mutual insurance of property. From the 1660s, an increasing number of industrial windmills in the Zaan district were included in some formal agreement concluded between owners and/or millers, by which the contracting parties committed themselves to contribute to compensation (up to a specified amount of money) to any one of the insured persons whose mill (or inventory) was wholly or partially destroyed by fire. Insurance contracts could be made between owners and/or millers either in the same branch of industry (e.g., oil milling) or in different branches of industry (e.g., sawing, hulling, and paper making; Schuddebeurs, 1948).

Insurance money could be raised in two ways. The most common method was a system of apportionment. Every time a mill covered by the contract suffered damage by fire, the costs of compensation were divided among all members of the contract, pro rata the amount for which each participant had insured his own mill. This was the system used by the oil millers. The other system incorporated the formation of a compensation fund by means of the payment of premiums, the money from which could then be invested in public bonds. The size of the fund was specified in advance; the level of the premium depended on the degree to which this target was achieved. This method was chosen by paint and snuff millers in 1739 and by paper makers, hullers, and saw millers in 1801 (Davids, 2006b). Two mutual insurance contracts, which at the time of foundation in 1733 comprised 72 and 96 mills, respectively, continued without interruption until the beginning of the 20th century. The former, which initially included mostly paper mills but later involved many hulling mills and sawing mills tool, was not disbanded until 1903. The latter, which was exclusively related to oil mills (hence nicknamed the *Olieslagerscontract*), remained in existence until 1912 (Davids, 2006b).

Mutual insurance organizations were very flexible indeed. Both the 'paper mill' contract and the *Olieslagerscontract* admitted steam-powered factories as members in the 1860s and 1870s. Both organizations adopted partial reinsurance schemes. Both organizations, over the course of time, acquired functions that went beyond their original purpose. They provided a framework for collective invention, offered a prime setting for various social activities, and from the 19th century onward, occasionally served as a springboard for collective action in defense of particular industries vis-à-vis the central authorities. The oil millers' contract eventually also became concerned with the relations between capital and labor. It was the *Olieslagerscontract* that, in 1892, founded an association for accident insurance of employees in the oil crushing industry (Davids, 2006b).

But why did mutual insurance contracts for windmills and factories nevertheless disappear from the scene before World War I? Although mutual insurance contracts until the 1890s still covered a substantial part of the hulling and sawing industries and almost the entire oil crushing trade, they were no longer dominant in the former sectors and were not represented in any of the new branches of activity that arose in the region after 1850. An ever-larger part of the Zaan industry was not involved in the network of cooperation maintained by these old, established institutions. An increasing number of industrial firms in the Zaanstreek turned to the market to satisfy their needs for insurance. They had their property insured by a commercial insurance company (or more often than not, by a group of companies) through the agency of brokers. The chief factor that induced more and more firms in the Zaanstreek to seek insurance via the market, which ultimately also became the seed of disruption within the mutual insurance institutions, was the growing capital intensity of production. The value of capital goods in Zaan firms by the end of the 19th century had increased to the extent that the capacity of the mutual insurance contracts to offer acceptable protection was ultimately deemed to be no longer sufficient. In terms of fire insurance via the market, this problem did not arise because the insured sum could be shared by a number of companies that could be extended almost at will.

New organizations for interfirm cooperation that arose in the period between 1840 and 1920, such as the Chamber of Commerce and a general employers' association (Van Dalsem, 1993; Van Waarden, 1987) never managed to replace insurance contracts as key elements in the industrial district of the Zaanstreek. They never established such strong local roots as the traditional, mutual societies. Given the scale and method of the organization of labor, by 1920 the Zaanstreek entrepreneurs considered regional associations of employers to be less effective than networks on a nationwide scale. Thus, ties between firms within the industrial district were replaced by or subordinated to ties between firms outside the industrial district in several respects.

## FAMILIAL CONTEXTS OF ENTREPRENEURSHIP

What kept interfirm cooperation in the Zaanstreek intact for several decades thereafter, however, were ties between regional family networks. By the end of World War I, it was not the ties of mutuality but the bonds of family that proved to be the bedrock of the industrial district of the Zaanstreek. Families provided the prime axis of solidarity for Zaanstreek entrepreneurs and economic life in the region was dominated by entrepreneurial dynasties like Vis, Laan, Honig, Smit, Prins, Duyvis, Dekker, Schoen, and Kaars Sijpesteijn (Arnoldus, 2002). These dynasties were interlinked by marriage connections, shared religious and political persuasions, and by a lively social intercourse focused on clubs, associations, and Masonic lodges. Such family-based networks were an essential element for the continuity of and cooperation between firms. The Zaanstreek in the 20th century depended more on family networks than it had in the preceding 300 years. Family networks proved to be adequate institutions for the provision of firms' vital needs, such as capital supply and the training and selection of leadership, in the Zaanstreek until the 1950s (Davids, 2006b).

The continued viability of family networks in the Zaanstreek seems, at first sight, to be anomalous in the light of Alfred Chandler's theory on the dynamics of business organizations. Chandler argued that the rise of modern industrial enterprises was essential in the transformation of Western economies in the late 19th and 20th centuries. Modern industrial enterprises were companies that moved quickly to build organizational capabilities to benefit fully from new possibilities for economies of scale and scope, opened up by technological advance, by investing heavily in production, distribution, and management. The crucial investment required in management, according to Chandler, was the development of a professional managerial hierarchy. In his view, family firms and personal management cultures failed to rise to the challenge posed by the changing technological environment. Economies dominated by this 'personal' type of capitalism, therefore, would be less competitive than economies characterized by 'competitive managerial capitalism' (such as the U.S.) or 'co-operative managerial capitalism' (such as Germany; Chandler, 1990).

The strength of family firms in the Zaanstreek, however, exemplified a more general pattern in Dutch business organization. Keetie Sluyterman and Len Winkelman found that industrial capitalism in the Netherlands until World War II, as in Britain, conformed more to the model of personal capitalism than to either of the other two. During this period, small-scale, family-run, networking companies were typical for Dutch industry at large. Far from being a drawback, however, personal managerial structures enabled these companies to compete successfully in foreign markets and invest in long-term growth. Families were very capable of running a business efficiently and competitively (Sluyterman & Winkelman, 1993). This remained true, to a large extent, for the second half of the 20th century as well. In the 1990s, family firms still formed some 80% to 90 % of all companies in the Netherlands. Of the 5,000 largest companies, nearly half were family firms (Sluyterman, 2005).

The resilience of family firms, however, remains puzzling in another respect, namely, its relation with the institutions of marriage and the family.

Sociologists generally agree that the ongoing process of individualization in Western societies that has been taking place since the 1960s means that these institutions, which used to lie at the very base of family firms, are no longer as strong as they used to be. If these institutions are in decline, how can family firms continue to exist? The paradox may be resolved if we take a closer look at the meaning of 'familism,' that is, the impact of family interests in the definition of business policy of family firms (Van Schelven, 1984). 'Familism' had already been losing its hold on family enterprises for a considerable period of time before the consequences of individualization began to make themselves felt in Dutch society (Davids, 1997).

Family firms were not inflexible entities. Their legal status changed over the course of time. This evolution was primarily related to the issue of succession, as the case of Zaanstreek shows. The legal structure that governed Zaanstreek firms in the middle of the 19th century had a disadvantage in the sense that the financial basis of a family enterprise at the time of generational change was intrinsically unstable. A partnership was automatically dissolved on the death of any of the partners. If the heirs of the deceased partner chose not to participate in the succeeding partnership and decided to withdraw their inheritance from the firm altogether, the total capital of the firm could be abruptly diminished. And even if these nonparticipating heirs *did* deposit their inheritance with the firm, the ratio of the firm's equity capital to debt capital could nevertheless suddenly become very unfavorable. Although the relations between heirs and the division of tasks between the succeeding managing family members within the firm could be regulated, to some extent, by drawing up elaborate contracts between family members, the risks for the continuity of the firm were thereby only partly reduced. It was precisely this wish to reduce the risks for the financial basis of the enterprise and preserve the autonomy of the firm that induced many families in the Zaanstreek, over the last decade of the 19th century, to convert partnerships into nonlisted limited companies (closed *naamloze vennootschappen*). The advantage of this new legal structure was that the financial basis of the firm was assured, whatever happened to the family (Arnoldus, 2002).

'Familism' declined further in the middle decades of the 20th century, not because of any inherent defect of this particular kind of business management, but because of specific changes in legal and fiscal systems and the opportunities and pressures of economic growth and European integration after World War II. Changes in inheritance law and death duties that have been implemented since the 1920s have strengthened the legal position of a marital partner vis-à-vis blood relatives. The introduction of corporate tax in the 1940s meant, for the family owners of a enterprise, that family property tied up in a firm would be taxed both by the established dividend tax on shareholders and by the new corporate tax. As the postwar economic boom and the emergence of new market opportunities as a result of incipient European integration in the 1950s led many firms to seek an increase in capital, family owners of firms were increasingly inclined to abandon traditional principles of 'familism.' Changes in institutional context and economic conditions thus meant that family-dominated firms were no longer regarded as the most natural way to protect family interests. Families diversified their interests outside the world of enterprise. Family firms were less family-connected than they may have seemed at first sight and thereby suffered less under the impact of individualization than might have been expected (Davids, 1997).

But the extent to which family members were involved in the ownership and management of an enterprise always remained a matter of choice. The end of a family connection with a firm was not and is not in any way predetermined. Many family firms continued to preserve a distinct familial stamp (Davids, 1997). 'Familism' can still live and thrive even in a highly industrialized and individualized society like the present-day Netherlands.

## RELIGIOUS CONTEXTS OF ENTREPRENEURSHIP

For a long time, regional ties and family bonds in the Zaanstreek were strengthened by collective religious persuasions. At the end of the 19th century, there were still relatively more Mennonites among Zaanstreek entrepreneurs than in the Dutch population at large (Arnoldus, 2002). The persistence of industrial districts or family networks, however, does not depend on a shared connection with religion, nor does a link between religion and entrepreneurship depend on the preexistence of regional or familial bonds. One of the canonical theses in the social sciences, known as 'the Weber thesis,' famously stresses the relationship between ascetic Protestantism and the growth of the spirit of capitalism, yet it does so first and foremost by looking at the motivations of individuals. Its primary angle is a psychological one (Weber, 2006). Although Max Weber's basic contention has been characterized as "arguably obtuse, practically impossible to confirm or demonstrate, and remote from twentieth-century concerns" (Barbalet, 2008), his thesis is still a frequent subject of debate among social scientists (Swatos & Kaelber, 2005). One of the reasons for its endurance is no doubt, as Jack Barbalet notes, that "every undergraduate student enrolled in a sociology course [is still] expected to know the *Protestant Ethic*" (Barbalet, 2008, p. 14).

Economists and economic sociologists have shown a lively interest in Weber's thesis in the past few years, too. Their studies usually examine empirical relations between variations in religion, on the one hand, and on the other, differences in rates of economic growth or timing of capitalist development between countries or societies in different parts of the world over a prolonged period of time, particularly in the 19th or 20th centuries. Typical examples of such studies of recent date are articles by Barro and McCleary (2003); Cavalcanti, Parente, and Zhao (2007); and Delacroix and Nielsen (2003). Robert Barro and Rachel McCleary (2003) conducted a cross-country study of the relationship between religion and economic growth, which characterized religion as church attendance and belief in heaven and hell and restricted itself by and large to the period between 1980 and 2000. Jacques Delacroix and François Nielsen (2003) tested the Weber thesis by examining the strength of the association between the religious composition of populations (defined as the percentages of Protestants and Catholics) and a wide range of dimensions of industrial capitalism in a number of European countries in the 19th century. Tiago Cavalcanti, Stephen Parenta, and Rui Zhao (2007) examined to what extent differences between Catholics and Protestants could explain delays in the beginning of industrialization by comparing the estimated performance of 'Catholic' and 'Protestant' economies (defined as a difference in the belief of whether prosperity during one's life is a barrier to reaching heaven or not), calibrated by a counterfactual study supposing that England had remained a 'Catholic' country after 1645 instead of becoming a 'Protestant' one.

All of these studies share the characteristic that they stretch the range of the Weber thesis much further than its author claimed. The thesis about the Protestant ethic was, after all, only ever intended to explain the *emergence* of a particular 'capitalist' mentality at a specific place and a specific point in time—Europe in the 16th and 17th century—and not its transference to other places or persistence through time. The relevance of such economic exercises applied to other times and places as 'tests' pro or contra Weber's thesis is therefore not entirely clear. Their value is further diminished by the design of the studies themselves. Despite their purported historical dimension, the argument of these studies is based on definitions and (often heroic) assumptions that treat religious factors merely as static, one-dimensional entities. The actual contents of religious beliefs and values are not seriously considered at all. These studies thus tell us little about continuity or change in religious contexts of entrepreneurship.

In contrast with social scientists, historians have largely withdrawn from the debate on the Weber thesis for a long time because they are only too aware of its weaknesses and inaccuracies as a credible account of historical developments. Locating a single document from an entrepreneur that really exemplifies some supposed key features of ascetic Protestantism such as "diligence in spiritual and vocational calling, making use of one's time, and material asceticism" is sometimes hailed as a veritable discovery (Benedict, 1995; Jacob & Kadane, 2003; Van Stuijvenberg, 1975).

More promising from a historian's point of view are approaches that take a more inductive, empirical perspective. In *Capitalists and Christians*, for example, David Jeremy examines the relationship between entrepreneurs and religion in early 20th-century Britain by first creating a database of chairmen and managing directors of leading companies in the country between approximately 1900 and 1960 (such as Armstrong, Vickers, Courtaulds, Dunlop, Woolworth, and Unilever) and then systematically investigating what sorts of relationships these 'captains of industry' maintained with the principal national denominations (such as the Church of England, the Methodists, or the Baptists; Jeremy, 1990). A similar approach has recently been explored on a much more modest scale with regard to a select group of Protestant entrepreneurs in the Netherlands in the 19th and 20th centuries (Van der Woude & Werkman, 2006).

Compared with their colleagues in Britain, Dutch entrepreneurs turn out to have been much less prone to openly bear witness of their faith or to use religious teachings as an inspiration or a set of guidelines for managing personnel in their own firms. Christian beliefs *did* come into play, by contrast, when Protestant entrepreneurs in the Netherlands began to build their own employers' association or when they came face to face with the growing power of organized labor. Under those circumstances, religious persuasions induced these entrepreneurs to seek consultation arrangements rather than engage in all-out confrontation (Davids, 2006a). Not all Protestant entrepreneurs chose to join an employers' association on a confessional basis, however, and not all Protestant entrepreneurs refrained from clashing with organized labor, even in the Zaanstreek in the early 20th century (Davids, 2006b; 'T Hoen, 1968). In general, however, the importance of religious ties and beliefs among entrepreneurs in the Netherlands declined as the twentieth century drew to a close.

## CONCLUSION

This essay has shown that there was more change than continuity in social contexts of entrepreneurship between approximately 1800 and 2000. The evidence discussed in this contribution leads us to conclude that regional and religious networks and cultures by the end of the 20th century influenced entrepreneurship in the Netherlands to a much lesser extent than 100 years before, whereas family bonds, insofar as these still provided a social context for entrepreneurship, have substantially changed in nature. The intermixture of regional, familial, and religious ties, as exemplified by the Zaan district in the late 19th and early 20th century, had entirely disappeared by the year 2000. Webs of 'strong ties' that once held groups of entrepreneurs tightly together have in the meantime largely been replaced by more loose networks of 'weak ties,' as Mark Granovetter famously called them (Granovetter, 1973).

The changes in social contexts of entrepreneurship described earlier have been caused by structural transformations in Dutch society at large, as summarized at the outset of this chapter; they were not an inevitable response to demands of efficiency or competitiveness. Moreover, these changes in social contexts proceeded without much visible friction. An explanation for the relative smoothness of this process may be that entrepreneurs switch rather easily from one type of tie to another as long as society at large persists in being 'a high-trust society.' This was certainly the case in the Netherlands until the dawn of the 21st century (Dekker et al., 2006; Fukuyama, 1995). It can be suggested that as long as a substratum of high trust remains in place, changes in ties at other levels can be completed without much difficulty. There is no obvious reason to assume, however, that a substratum itself can never change. Following this suggestion, it would be interesting not only to study whether changes in types of tie are harder to realize in 'low-trust' societies but also to examine whether regional, familial, or religious ties may regain importance for entrepreneurship once a high level of trust in society at large has been eroded.

## REFERENCES

Arnoldus, D. (2002). *Family, family firm, and strategy: Six Dutch family firms in the food sector, 1880–1970*. Amsterdam: Aksant.
Barbalet, J. (2008). *Weber, passion and profits: 'The Protestant Ethic and the spirit of capitalism' in context*. Cambridge: Cambridge University Press.
Barro, R. J., & McCleary, R. M. (2003). Religion and economic growth across countries. *American Sociological Review, 68*, 760–781,
Belfanti, C. M., & Onger, S. (2002). Mercato e istituzioni nella storia dei distretti industriali. In G. Provasi (Ed.), *Le istituzioni dello sviluppo: I distretti industriali tra storia, sociologia ed economia* (pp. 245–268). Rome: Donzelli.
Benedict, P. (1995). The historiography of Continental Calvinism. In H. Lehmann & G. Roth (Eds.), *Weber's Protestant Ethic: Origins, evidence, contexts* (pp. 305–325). Cambridge: Cambridge University Press.
Capecchi, V. (1997). In search of flexibility: The Bologna metalworking industry, 1900–1992. In C. F. Sabel & J. Zeitlin (Eds.), *Worlds of possibilities: Flexibility and mass production in Western industrialization* (pp. 381–418). Cambridge: Cambridge University Press.
Cavalcanti, T. V., Parenta, S. L., & Zhao, R. (2007). Religion in macroeconomics: A quantitative analysis of Weber's thesis. *Economic Theory, 32*, 105–124.
Chandler, A. (1990). *Scale and scope: The dynamics of industrial capitalism*. Cambridge, MA: Harvard University Press.
Davids, K. (1997). Familiebedrijven, familisme en individualisering in Nederland, ca. 1880–1990. *Amsterdams Sociologisch Tijdschrift, 24*, 527–554.
Davids, K. (2006a). Ondernemers en religie in Nederland: Een inleidende beschouwing. In R. E. van der Woude & P. Werkman (Eds.), *Geloof in eigen zaak. Markante protestantse werkgevers in de negentiende en twintigste eeuw* (pp. 9–21). Hilversum: Verloren.
Davids, K. (2006b). The transformation of an old industrial district: Firms, family, and mutuality in the Zaanstreek between 1840 and 1920. *Enterprise and Society, 7*, 550–580.
Dekker, P., Ederveen S., De Groot, H., Van der Horst, A., Lejour, A., Straathof, B., Vinken H., & Wennekers, C. (2006). *Divers Europa: De Europese Unie in de publieke opine & Culturele verscheidenheid, economie en beleid: Europese Verkenning 4*. The Hague: SDU.
Delacroix, J., & Nielsen, F. (2003). The beloved myth: Protestantism and the rise of industrial capitalism in nineteenth-century Europa. *Social Forces, 80*, 509–553.
Fukuyama, F. (1995). *Trust: The social virtues and the creation of prosperity*. London: Penguin.

Granovetter, M. S. (1973). The strength of weak ties. *American Journal of Sociology*, *78*, 1360–1380.

Guenzi, A. (1997). La storia economica e i distretti industriali marshalliani: Qualche considerazione su approcci e risultati. In C. M. Belfanti & T. Maccabelli (Eds.), *Un paradigma per i distretti industriali. Radici storiche attualità e sfide future* (pp. 19–29). Brescia: Grafo.

Guenzi, A. (1999). Istituzioni intermedie e sviluppo locale: Un approccio di storia economica. In A. Arrighetti & G. Servalli (Eds.), *Istituzioni intermedie e sviluppo locale* (pp. 67–92). Rome: Donzelli.

Jacob, M., & Kadane, M. (2003). Missing, now found in the eighteenth-century: Weber's Protestant capitalism. *American Historical Review, 108*, 20–49.

Jeremy, D. J. (1990). *Capitalists and Christians: Business leaders and the churches in Britain, 1900–1960*. Oxford: Clarendon.

Pyke, F., Becattini, G., & Sengenberger, W. (Eds.). (1990). *Industrial districts and interfirm cooperation in Italy*. Geneva: International Institute for Labour Studies.

Pyke, F., & Sengenberger, W. (Eds.). (1992). *Industrial districts and local economic regeneration*. Geneva: International Institute for Labour Studies.

Saxenian, A.L. (1994). *Regional advantage: Culture and competition in Silicon Valley and Route 128*. Cambridge, MA: Harvard University Press.

Schuddebeurs, H. G. (1948). *Onderlinge brandverzekeringsinstellingen in Nederland van 1663 tot 1948*. Rotterdam: 1948.

Sluyterman, K. (2005). *Dutch enterprise in the twentieth century: Business strategies in a small open economy*. London: Routledge.

Sluyterman, K., & Winkelman, L. (1993). The Dutch family firm confronted with Chandler's dynamics of industrial capitalism. *Business History, 35*, 152–183.

Storper, M., & Walker, R. (1989). *The capitalist imperative: Territory, technology, and industrial growth*. Oxford: Wiley-Blackwell.

Swatos, W. H., Jr., & Kaelber, L. (Eds.). (2005). *The Protestant Ethic turns 100: Essays on the Centenary of the Weber Thesis*. Boulder, CO: Paradigm.

'T Hoen, J.J. (1968). *Op naar het licht: De Zaanstreek in de periode van de opkomst der arbeidersbeweging, 1882–1909*. Waormerveer: Meijer Pers.

Van Dalsem, C. (1993). *"Zaansche toestanden": 150 jaar Kamer van Koophandel en Fabrieken voor de Zaanstreek*. Zaandam: Kamer van Koophandel.

Van der Woude, R. E., & Werkman, P. (Eds.). (2006). *Geloof in eigen zaak: Markante protestantse werkgevers in de negentiende en twintigste eeuw*. Hilversum: Verloren.

Van Schelven, A. L. (1984). *Onderneming en familisme: Opkomst, bloei en neergang van de textielonderneming Van Heek & Co te Enschede*. Leiden: Martinus Nijhoff.

Van Stuijvenberg, J. H. (1975). The Weber thesis: An attempt at interpretation. *Acta Historiae Neerlandicae, 8*, 50–66.

Van Waarden, F. (1987). *Problemen van machtsvorming in een heterogene belangenvereniging: De beginjaren van de Algemene Werkgeversvereniging (AWV (1919- ± 1926) als voorbeeld*. Leiden: Leiden Institute for Law and Public Policy.

Weber, M. (2006). *Religion und Gesellschaft: Gesammelte Aufsätze zur Religionssoziologie Frankfurt am Main*: Zweitausendeins.

Zeitlin, J. (1992). Industrial districts and local economic regeneration: Overview and comment. In F. Pyke & W. Sengenberger (Eds.), *Industrial districts and local economic regeneration* (pp. 279–294). Geneva: International Institute for Labour Studies.

# 11 Contextualizing Chinese Indonesian Entrepreneurship

*Juliette Koning*

## INTRODUCTION

The year 1998 was a year full of contrasts for Chinese Indonesians. It was the year that ended the authoritarian regime of President Suharto whose New Order government had installed strict policies aimed at erasing 'Chineseness.' Paradoxically, it was also the year that saw one of the more violent attacks against the ethnic Chinese minority. A lingering economic crisis of rising prices for basic foods, fuel, and energy brought people to the streets to protest; in some places these protests changed into massive attacks on people of Chinese descent. Many Chinese Indonesians were killed or raped, and houses and shops were set afire. How and why this happened is still unresolved, but it does follow a pattern in Indonesian history in which people of Chinese descent become scapegoats in times of national upheaval. The ethnic Chinese minority cannot rid itself of the stereotype of being extremely wealthy related to their business presence and their entrepreneurship, and this image sparks strong reactions in times of crises.

This is the context against which this chapter shall discuss ethnic Chinese entrepreneurship and 'Chineseness' in Indonesia. It shall argue that we can only understand the business activities of ethnic Chinese entrepreneurs in Indonesia if we pay attention to contextual factors, such as the ethnic policies of the government, local cultural contexts, and historical developments.

Chinese-Indonesian business conduct does not stand in isolation but is part of a larger academic debate that continues to intrigue scholars interested in entrepreneurship. The debate revolves around the issue of how to best explain the business success of this ethnic Chinese minority in Southeast Asia. Contested data shows that in the 1990s, the ethnic Chinese in Indonesia (4% of the population) accounted for 50% in GDP; in Thailand they (10% of the population) accounted for 50% in GDP; and 1% accounted for 40% in GDP in the Philippines (Yeung, 2004, p. 13).

Over the years, a large body of literature has emerged that argues specific cultural traits (personal networks, ethnic affinity, Confucian work ethics) enable ethnic Chinese businesses to function successfully both in their new home countries and in terms of business contacts across borders (Redding, 1990). This culturalist approach came under attack for exaggerating the role of culture and intra-ethnic networks, for neglecting business matters (Gomez & Hsiao, 2004), and for the atemporal and acontextual accounts (Ooi & Koning, 2007).

Rather than explaining Chinese networks by referring to cultural values, in other words, Confucian values, it can be argued that "the formation of closely knitted [*sic*] Chinese business networks decades ago emerged out of problems faced by migrants in terms of securing start-up capital, hiring labor and seeking partners" (Ooi, 2007, p. 122). This also means that when these problems fade away, generational attitudes can be expected to change. This is the case for many second- and third-generation Chinese. Gomez and Benton contend that: "migrants' descendants tend to view their identity, and especially their ethnic identity, differently from their migrant forebears" (2004, p. 17).

Hence, this chapter shall address the question of whether there are generational differences between Chinese Indonesian entrepreneurs in the way they conduct their business and use networks. The chapter has an explicit discursive character; it will focus on how the Chinese-Indonesian entrepreneurs who were interviewed narrated their experiences of doing business in Indonesia. This question will then be analyzed from a contextual, embeddedness perspective. Because cultural notions cannot be disconnected from the social context, attaining a historical and contextual perspective is a necessary addition in research that is trying to grasp ethnic identity in entrepreneurship.

## MIXED EMBEDDEDNESS AND GENERATIONS

The approach in this chapter follows what is known as the embeddedness perspective in entrepreneurship studies. This approach has gained momentum and departs from the assertion that entrepreneurs are embedded in social relationships. It has its legacy in the work of Polanyi (1944, 1957), whose substantivist school of thought argued that economic decision making in precapitalist societies was based on social relationships, moral issues, and cultural values as opposed to capitalist societies that behave more 'rationally' because modernization has been about the "dis-embedding of markets and the subordination of society to impersonal economic powers" (Hefner, 1998, p. 9).

Granovetter (1985) reintroduced the idea of embeddedness in entrepreneurship studies by showing that capitalist societies also thrive on social embeddedness. He could not find proof that social categories such as kinship and ethnicity are no longer of importance in the economy of the modern world. His work strengthened the idea that entrepreneurship is a social activity. Being embedded can support the entrepreneur in terms of advice, knowledge, contacts, and information. Such social embeddedness is relevant because it helps the entrepreneur identify the necessary resources for founding an organization (Jack & Anderson, 2002, p. 471).

Kloosterman and Rath (2001) have criticized embeddedness as reintroduced by Granovetter because it omits structural or institutional factors.

Their 'mixed embeddedness' perspective pays equal attention to the entrepreneur—who is embedded in social relations that bring him/her knowledge, contacts, and information and thus potentially allow access to capital, labor, and opportunities—and economic and institutional embeddedness, that is, the rules and regulations in a certain context, urban developments, and the economic and political climate. These are all elements that correspond to opportunity structures and local business traditions.

For research interested in the 'situated' experiences of entrepreneurs, the mixed embeddedness approach is a welcome addition to the field because of its dual embeddedness focus. However, a more dynamic stance can be reached by incorporating a generational approach arguing that motives for starting a business and preferences for specific business practices change throughout subsequent generations (Koning, 2007; Masurel & Nijkamp, 2004).

This paper understands a generation as individuals who share a 'common location in the social and historical process,' in which the latter potentially provides them with overlapping experiences, beliefs, and views. Each new age group can develop new attitudes and modes of thought (Mannheim, 1952, p. 291). This argument is helpful in a context in which the generations are confronted by quite different experiences, for instance, migration or nationalism. Recent research in entrepreneurship studies has discovered the value of a generational approach; it turns out that generational encounters are helpful in understanding processes of identity formation and identification (Down & Reveley, 2004). This offers an appropriate position for exploring how the entrepreneurs in this study use their membership of an older or younger generation as a way to construct their identity as Indonesian entrepreneurs with a Chinese background.

To denote ethnicity, reference is usually made to mutual cultural markers such as language, dialect, custom, religion, some idea of common descent, a shared history, and/or a consciousness of 'sharedness.' More recently, it has been acknowledged, particularly in Eriksen's approach (2002, p. 12), that in order to understand ethnicity, a contextual and relational focus is needed that stipulates the requirement of a relationship and a sense of cultural difference between two groups in order for ethnicity to come about. This relational approach enables an interpretation of ethnic identity according to context, situation, and interaction and subsequently as self-defined, others perceived, and/or state defined; "different places in different times mould different shapes of identity" (Tjhin, 2005, p. 31). As such, it connects identity and generation.

## POSITIONING CHINESE INDONESIANS

The position of Chinese Indonesians must be understood in the context of a long history of contested citizenship and of purposeful ethnic policies by the various regimes, both before and after Indonesia's Independence in 1945.

The Dutch colonial administration had already singled out the Chinese as 'different' and selected them as intermediaries for European enterprises. They were the largest group of immigrant Asians and the most powerful in economic terms. The colonizers assigned the Chinese shares in the lucrative opium trade at the expense of local entrepreneurs, which led to a growing gap between the local population and the Chinese (Hefner, 2001, pp. 17–19). By labeling the different groups as either indigenous or non-indigenous (such as the Chinese), an ethnic divide was also created. This distinction was to be one of the most enduring legacies of the colonial era (ibid.) and continued during and after the formation of the nation-state.

The fierce assimilation policy during the New Order regime of former president Suharto (1966–1989) is an example of this labeling. This Assimilation Program (Program Pembauran) was an attempt to construct a national identity by identifying 'significant others,' namely, the Chinese (Hoon, 2006, p. 151). The systematic 'othering' of the ethnic Chinese in the New Order period created an anti-Chinese rhetoric, which found its expression in many violent attacks. Such identity politics resulted in an either/or position for the ethnic Chinese; "to be completely Indonesian, the Chinese had to give up all their 'Chineseness'" (Hoon, 2006, p. 152). According to Ang (2001), the possibility of a hybrid identity, the more logical outcome of a Chinese migrant's daily life in a non-Chinese environment, was never a real option. The ongoing 'erasure' of Chinese identities (Heryanto, 1998, p. 104) has left its mark on issues of self-identification among the ethnic Chinese groups.

The assimilation policy was aided by regulations that banned all forms of 'Chineseness' from society. Presidential instructions and decrees in 1967 expelled Chinese traditions from the public sphere and required the ethnic Chinese to change their Chinese names to Indonesian ones so that "such citizens shall be assimilated as to avoid any racial exclusiveness and discrimination" (Winarta, 2004, p. 72). The use of Chinese language and characters in newspapers and shops was prohibited, and a law was passed that the ethnic Chinese were required to carry a letter with them showing evidence of their Indonesian citizenship. The elimination of Chinese media, organizations (both political and social), and schools was a dramatic occurrence. Alongside such regulations, the national discourse during much of the New Order contained perceptions about the Chinese as not being true citizens who might turn their back on Indonesia at any time (Freedman, 2000, p. 117).

After the fall of the New Order regime in 1998, interim president Habibie (May 1998 to October 1999) lifted several restrictions on 'Chineseness' and approved the formation of Chinese political parties. Abdurrahman Wahid (October 1999 to July 2001) abolished the law on the manifestation of Chinese cultural and religious expression. Megawati Sukarnoputri (July 2001 to October 2004) issued a decree that made Chinese New Year a national holiday. Notwithstanding this easing of restrictions, some have nonetheless questioned whether there is sufficient political and judicial confidence among the Chinese Indonesians to reclaim their citizenship and legal rights as these still belong to a system controlled by the state, a system that has proven to be unreliable. Furthermore, many of the anti-Chinese sentiments are played out at the lower levels of government, where rules and regulations directly impinge on the daily lives of the Chinese Indonesians (Lindsey & Pausacker, 2005), such as excessive monetary claims made on Chinese-Indonesian entrepreneurs for necessary permits.

Notwithstanding such progress, the ethnic Chinese in Indonesia are still labeled as outsiders, even after generations of settlement in Indonesia and in spite of speaking the national language (Coppel, 2004, p. 20). In discussions focusing on being Chinese in Indonesia, it is clear that the state bureaucracy and instruments of government have been the most important "variables, which have contributed to the 'separateness' of the Chinese in Indonesia, particularly in Java" (Suryadinata, 1993, p. 77).

A final word concerns the study of ethnic Chinese entrepreneurship in Indonesia. It is important to point out that the ethnic Chinese historically were not allowed to occupy civil servant positions or own land (Freedman, 2000). Most ended up as shopkeepers and traders in the private sector of the economy. Politically excluded and in a hostile environment, the Chinese had to establish themselves without much outside support.

It can be concluded that ever since colonial times, the ethnic Chinese in Indonesia have been contested and that their position within the newly built nation-state has been one of exclusion and discrimination. The state has been a dominant player in this "selective creation and manipulation of ethnic identities" (Tan, 2001, p. 952). The regime change in 1998 created more room for expressing Chinese identity, and a revival of Chinese cultural expressions has been witnessed. Whether this also translates into changed business conduct is explored in the following text.

## 'CHINESENESS' AND CHINESE-INDONESIAN BUSINESS CONDUCT

The research position is interpretative, with the larger question being "how men and women give meaning to their life and capture these meanings in written, narrative and oral forms" (Denzin, 1989, p. 10). The data collection consisted mainly of interviews with Chinese Indonesians, combined with observations during social and business meetings. Most interviewees were selected through existing networks or 'snowball' methods.

The research took place in 2004 and 2007 in the city of Yogyakarta, central Java.[1] The older generation consists of people born in the 1940s and 1950s who had witnessed the severe curtailing of their 'Chineseness' with the coming to power of the New Order regime. The group labeled the younger generation includes individuals born just before and during the assimilation policy of the New Order (1960s to 1970s). Yogyakarta is a court city (with a sultan) and the center of high Javanese culture. It has a large ethnic Chinese community, especially in the small- and medium-sized sectors. The 23 semi-structured interviews were conducted as life and business histories of owner-managers.

Those interviewed are descended from southern Chinese (Fujian Province) families and are second- or third-generation Chinese born in Indonesia. They all have businesses that can be labeled small (less than 10 employees) or medium (10 to 100 employees) for which start-up capital was most often derived from family resources. In some cases, the business is a continuation of a family business. Many of the entrepreneurs are involved in more than one business. The majority of the small- and medium-sized enterprises in this study are in retail and services, with some in manufacturing. Examples include motor and car supplies, repair shops, computer sales, printing and publishing, consultancy, and food production and distribution. Whereas the majority of the Chinese in Yogyakarta are in business sectors, there are also quite a few professionals. The following section discusses entrepreneurial business conduct and how it relates to 'Chineseness.'

As expressed by both older and younger generations of entrepreneurs, the preferred business practice for conducting business in Indonesia is 'doing business with other Chinese.' There is a strong discourse on a shared business acumen revolving around trust, personal relationships, referral, and co-ethnic support and business norms that is, and has been for many, the key to setting up a business and running it. The Indonesian context, considered unstable, is not insignificant when it comes to the narratives of their experiences.

> Personal networks are very important. When I seek contact with another Chinese businessman from outside Yogyakarta, we first talk informally, using informal Chinese language. He does not immediately trust me and will try to find references, people who might know me. So, we invest time to reach the right feeling. You can call it trust building. That is business here; we do not work with contracts because we are never sure if these are followed to the letter. If we want to bring a case to court, it never gets resolved and it costs a lot of money. That is Indonesia. (Older-generation entrepreneur)

> When I was asked to join the family business, I did. However, it was not really a success. My mother, who in fact runs the business, felt she became useless because I started to work with computers while she did the bookkeeping by hand. She also disliked the choices I made in management and in recruiting personnel. It took several years before I understood that certain business practices of my mother are quite important; I learned that the Chinese way of doing business always involves relationships, and I learned that one never knows when these come in handy. (Younger-generation entrepreneur)

These personal networks are an important basis for access to capital and goods; the use of these networks is often seen as synonymous with trust and trustworthiness.

> In my days, we used a kind of rotating credit association for start-up capital. I would collect money from my trust group and would pay back the moment my business was doing well. If my business did not go well, I did not have to pay back the money, at least not if I worked hard and did not squander the money. This system changed somewhat over the years, but the idea is the same. The moment the business start-up is conducted, I start paying back through a monthly lottery system. There is no interest. If the business goes bankrupt, those who joined do not protest. But the person who started it will work very hard to return all the money. If the money is kept for other purposes, the trust relationship ends. (Older-generation entrepreneur)

> When I was still working for my father, I got to know many traders. Quite a few of them told me, "If you open your own business, I shall give you some materials to sell, you can pay back later." These owners already trusted me because of my father. This trust has been very important in setting up my own business. (Younger-generation entrepreneur)

A common thread running through the narratives is the idea that 'the Chinese' are better entrepreneurs because they are more business oriented. The interviewees expressed the belief that these differences make it less obvious and less attractive to do business with non-Chinese. Both generations seem to have the same ideas on this.

> In general, Chinese seek other Chinese for businesses. The chance that I start a business with a local is very small. This is because their sense of business is very different. If Chinese people make a profit, they save it in order to open a new store or to invest again, buy new equipment, but also for educational purposes. When needed, there is money. If a new business opportunity comes up, we can react immediately because we do not need to borrow money from others. We do not find this much among local entrepreneurs, and that makes it very difficult to work with them. (Older-generation entrepreneur)

> When there is a soccer match I am pro-Indonesia, while my father supports the Chinese team. In many things I am Indonesian; however, businesswise I guess I have to say that I am more Chinese; Chinese Indonesians are still the better business people. (Younger-generation entrepreneur)

This discourse on being 'the better entrepreneurs' is often linked to migration history.

> Our forefathers migrated from China with nothing. They went everywhere. They started to change what was around them, with hands and head. Also, with trade, one can create richness. (Older-generation entrepreneur)

> The Chinese are very dynamic; they are never satisfied with the way things are. You can either judge this as positive or negative. It is the same to me. This is the way it is. We are not satisfied with a status quo. My parents told me this. This is because the Chinese people here are migrants, people who wanted to change things, people who were brave enough to take many risks, to leave behind everything without knowing if they would be successful. (Younger-generation entrepreneur)

The previous text shows many similarities among the different generations regarding access to capital and goods and with whom to cooperate: both generations prefer to rely on co-ethnics. However, within these similarities a few subtle differences can be detected.

> Chinese businesses try to move ahead with the changing times as well. We started with small shops for daily necessities, but now we open supermarkets. So even though we still have family businesses, we follow the changes and we also start to recruit other people. (Younger-generation entrepreneur)

The previous narratives show quite a number of similarities across the different generations on 'doing business' in Indonesia. The question is how to explain these findings, particularly as the literature (Gomez & Benton, 2004; Masurel & Nijkamp, 2004), points toward generational *differences* in entrepreneurship. Although subtle differences can be detected, the overall discourse under scrutiny here shows a strong focus on intra-ethnic business relationships. This is connected with narratives that the 'Chinese' way of doing business is also the better way of doing business, in particular because the Chinese Indonesians consider themselves to be more business minded (reinvesting profits and saving for new opportunities) than non-Chinese Indonesians. In fact, stereotypical comparisons are made that echo Eriksen's (2002) understanding of ethnicity as it relates to strong 'us versus them' positions in the case of experienced cultural differences. There is the danger of interpreting these findings as support for a culturalist position in the debate on ethnic Chinese business acumen in Southeast Asia. A focus on embeddedness and context, however, helps to circumvent such rash conclusions.

The social embeddedness of Chinese Indonesian entrepreneurs, both young and old, is first and foremost concentrated within Chinese Indonesian networks. Capital, information, goods, and partnerships are derived through intra-ethnic networks and contacts. Being 'outsiders' in a country that they consider theirs can be said to have codetermined such practices; as argued by Coppel (2004, 20), "centuries of settlement in the archipelago are not enough, it seems, to allow ethnic Chinese to call Indonesia 'home.'" This social embeddedness means they can tap into existing ethnic networks. Whereas some entrepreneurship literature would argue that this obstructs further business development (we can think of strong and weak ties arguments), this does not seem to be the case for Chinese Indonesians because of their dominant position in business and entrepreneurship. However, whereas they are strong in the economy, they are politically powerless, which leads to institutional and structural problems. The previous text has shown that Chinese Indonesian entrepreneurs have more difficulty in handling the bureaucracy and local power-holders. This obstructs their businesses with extra rules (and extra money). The few ethnic Chinese businesses that have become conglomerates are the ones that were able to become cronies of the former regime, a position hardly attainable for the majority that owns small businesses.

By broadening the scope to include contextual dimensions, further explanations can be found. First, the nationalist project of the New Order government included the erasure of 'Chineseness' with the support of a forced assimilation program. This has clearly had an impact on feelings about being Chinese, which recurs in business conduct; suppression also brought Chinese Indonesians closer together in business. The fact that younger generation Chinese Indonesian entrepreneurs air a similar business discourse as older generations, albeit combined with a more fluid ethnic identity discourse, implies that the 'outsider' status is still experienced, notwithstanding the recent changes in Indonesia to recognize 'Chineseness.'

Second, the entrepreneurs across the generations judge the sociocultural context as not entrepreneurial enough. They mention that they have difficulty in finding 'business equals' among the local Javanese population because of different business attitudes. Whereas they prefer to reinvest and save profits for new opportunities, they judge their local counterparts as differently minded. As a result, they find it problematic to choose such local entrepreneurs as their partners. This again highlights the juxtaposition of 'us versus them,' and once again, the role of the state cannot be denied.

The aforementioned findings also warn against coming to overly rapid conclusions regarding generational divides; the contextual approach provides a more nuanced and insightful analysis. In the case under scrutiny, the different generations experience similar problematic 'outside' influences that make them cooperate more closely in co-ethnic trusted networks. The shared experiences are discrimination (or negative stereotyping) as an individual (being of Chinese decent and hence not a local), as an entrepreneur by having to 'pay' more than non-Chinese to get business licenses, and as a Chinese Indonesian citizen who encounters unclear rules and regulations (i.e., will the bank provide money for one's business, will the court take one's case seriously). The context in which they live and work is still experienced as 'hostile' as a result of which we detect commonalities across the generations in falling back on tested and successful business practices within the trusted group. However, the younger generation is experimenting with their 'Chineseness,' which, as previously expressed is a particularly entrepreneurial identity; otherwise, they feel and want to be treated as Indonesians. Hence, a generational approach is a very fruitful addition to the study of ethnic entrepreneurship, but this should be studied from a contextual perspective.

## CONCLUSION

This chapter explores the role and meaning of 'Chineseness' in business conduct among different generations of Chinese Indonesian entrepreneurs. The case study consists of younger and older generation entrepreneurs active in small- and medium-sized businesses in Yogyakarta, a central Javanese court town known for its strong retail sector. A discursive and contextual approach was applied to arrive at a more nuanced understanding of ethnicity and entrepreneurial behavior.

The position of the ethnic Chinese born and raised in Indonesia has always been rather insecure, both in material and immaterial terms. During the Dutch colonial period, ethnic Chinese were already singled out as immigrant Asians or foreign Orientals who were bestowed with different rights compared to the indigenous population; and in the formative years of the Indonesian republic, the issue of Indonesian citizenship for the ethnic Chinese was heavily debated. Under the reign of former president Suharto's New Order (1965–1998), Chinese Indonesians were confronted with forced assimilation and discriminative laws that severely restricted their options to express 'Chineseness.'

The case study shows that older and younger generations of Chinese-Indonesian entrepreneurs active in small- and medium-sized companies strongly rely on personal networks that are intra-ethnically based. Although this contradicts several other case studies on ethnic Chinese business acumen in Southeast Asia that stress inter-ethnic networking or studies that point to changing business conduct across the generations, by incorporating the historical, socioeconomic, and sociocultural context, the analysis allows a richer understanding of ethnic Chinese business conduct in Southeast Asia to be gained. However, it does not make much sense to label such business conduct as either culturalist or capitalist; rather, what matters is the provision of contextual knowledge regarding why and how entrepreneurial choices are made.

The conclusion, therefore, is that we can only understand the business activities of ethnic Chinese entrepreneurs in Indonesia if we pay attention to contextual factors such as the ethnic policies of the government and also local cultural contexts and historical developments. At the same time, the findings support a mixed embeddedness perspective that understands entrepreneurship as a social activity while acknowledging the structural and institutional dimension involved.

## NOTES

1. For a more elaborate presentation and discussion of the empirical findings on which this chapter draws, see Koning (2007).

## REFERENCES

Ang, I. (2001). *On not speaking Chinese: Living between Asia and the West.* London: Routledge.
Coppel, C. (2004). Historical impediments to the acceptance of ethnic Chinese in a multicultural Indonesia. In L. Suryadinata (Ed.), *Chinese Indonesians: State policy, monoculture and multiculture* (pp. 17–28). Singapore: Eastern Universities Press.
Denzin, N. (1989). *Interpretive biography.* London: Sage.
Down, S., & Reveley, J. (2004). Generational encounters and the social formation of entrepreneurial identity: "Young guns' and 'old farts." *Organization, 11*(2): 233–250.
Eriksen, T. (2002). *Ethnicity and nationalism: Anthropological perspectives.* London: Pluto.
Freedman, A. (2000). *Political participation and ethnic minorities. Chinese overseas in Malaysia, Indonesia and the United States.* London: Routledge.
Gomez, T., & Hsiao, M. (2004). Introduction: Chinese business research in Southeast Asia. In T. Gomez & M. Hsiao (Eds.), *Chinese business in Southeast Asia: Contesting cultural explanations, researching entrepreneurship* (pp. 131–137). London: Routledge Curzon.
Gomez, T., & Benton, G. (2004). Introduction: De-essentializing capitalism: Chinese enterprise, transnationalism, and identity. In T. Gomez & M. Hsiao (Eds.), *Chinese business in Southeast Asia: Contesting cultural explanations, researching entrepreneurship.* London: Routledge Curzon.
Granovetter, M. (1985). Economic action and social structure: The problem of embeddedness. *American Journal of Sociology, 91*(3): 481–510.
Hefner, R. (1998). Introduction: Society and morality in the new Asian Capitalisms. In R. Hefner (Ed.), *Market cultures: Society and morality in the new Asian capitalisms* (pp. 1–40). Boulder, CO: Westview.
Hefner, R. (2001). Introduction: Multiculturalism and citizenship in Malaysia, Singapore, and Indonesia. In R. Hefner (Ed.), *The Politics of Multiculturalism: Pluralism and Citizenship in Malaysia, Singapore, and Indonesia* (pp. 1–58), Honolulu: University of Hawaii Press.
Heryanto, A. (1998). Ethnic identities and erasure: Chinese Indonesians in public culture. In J. Kahn (Ed.), *Southeast Asian identities: Culture and the politics of representation in Indonesia, Malaysia, Singapore, and Thailand* (pp. 95–114). London: I. B. Tauris.
Hoon, C-Y. (2006). Assimilation, multiculturalism, hybridity: The dilemmas of the ethnic Chinese in post-Suharto Indonesia. *Asian Ethnicity, 7*(2): 149–166.
Jack, S., & Anderson, A. (2002). The effects of embeddedness on the entrepreneurial process. *Journal of Business Venturing, 17,* 467–487.

Kloosterman, R., & Rath, J. (2001). Immigrant entrepreneurs in advanced economies: Mixed embeddedness further explored. *Journal of Ethnic and Migration Studies, 27*(2), 189–201.

Koning, J. (2007). Chineseness and Chinese Indonesian business practices: A generational and discursive enquiry. *East Asia: An International Quarterly, 24*(2), 129–152.

Lindsey, T., & Pausacker, H. (Eds.). (2005). *Chinese Indonesians: Remembering, distorting, forgetting.* Singapore: Institute of Southeast Asian Studies.

Mannheim, K. (1952). The problem of generations. In P. Kecskemeti (Ed.), *Essays on the sociology of knowledge.* London: Routledge and Kegan Paul.

Masurel, E., & Nijkamp, P. (2004). Differences between first-generation and second-generation ethnic start-ups. *Environment and Planning C: Government and Policy, 22,* 721–737.

Ooi, C-S. (2007). Un-packing packaged cultures: Chinese-ness in International Business. *East Asia: An International Quarterly, 24*(2), 111–128.

Ooi, C-S., & Koning, J. (2007). Introduction: The business of identity. *East Asia, 24*(2), 107–110.

Polanyi, K. (1944). *The great transformation.* Boston: Beacon.

Polanyi, K. (1957). *Trade and markets in early empires.* Glencoe, IL: Free Press.

Redding, G. (1990). *The spirit of Chinese capitalism.* Berlin: Walter de Gruyter.

Suryadinata, L. (1993). The state and the Chinese minority in Indonesia. In L. Suryadinata (Ed.), *Chinese Adaptation and Diversity: Essays on Society and Literature in Indonesia, Malaysia and Singapore* (pp. 77–100). Singapore: Singapore University Press.

Tan, E. (2001). From sojourners to citizens: Managing the ethnic Chinese minority in Indonesia and Malaysia. *Ethnic and Racial Studies, 24*(6), 949–978.

Tjhin, C. S. (2005). *Reflections on the identity of the Chinese Indonesians.* Retrieved December 8, 2011 from http://www.csis.or.id/CMS/workingpaper-file/58/wps052.pdf.

Winarta, F. (2004). Racial discrimination in the Indonesian legal system: Ethnic Chinese and nation-building. In L. Suryadinata (Ed.), *Ethnic relations and nation-building in Southeast Asia. The case of the ethnic Chinese* (pp. 66–81). Singapore: ISEAS.

Yeung, H. (2004). *Chinese capitalism in a global era: Towards a hybrid capitalism.* London: Routledge.

# 12 Entrepreneurship, Reverse Migration, and Social Change in a Comparative Perspective

*Heidi Dahles*

## INTRODUCTION

The often long-standing and intensive engagement of exile diasporic communities in their countries of origin produces significant flows of capital, network relations, knowledge and technology, and political support. Researchers have come to assess the significance of such communities for home countries in ambivalent terms. Whereas remittances and philanthropic donations from these communities to home countries are on the positive side of the balance sheet, they are also seen as an engine of 'brain drain,' that is, the loss of human capital that permanently affects the developmental potential of the home country, a loss that cannot be equated by remittances and donations (Agunias, 2006; Maimbo & Ratha, 2005; Naudé, 2007; Newland, 2004). However, the 'classic' brain drain versus remittances equation has come to be replaced by a much more differentiated and complex relationship between countries and their diasporas. The inability to facilitate education and employment in the home country itself results in a sustained state of 'brain waste.' Remittances can be strategically put to use by individuals, households, and agencies to reverse this trend and create conditions that attract diaspora to return—temporarily, permanently or circularly—in order to contribute to development as professionals, experts or aid workers, and as business people and entrepreneurs. In particular, entrepreneurship—with its inherent innovative potential— is expected to contribute significantly to economic growth, development, and social change (Naudé, 2007). This is how 'brain drain' and 'brain waste' may turn into 'brain gain' and 'brain trust' (cf. Agunias, 2006, p. 9). Business-entrepreneurial capital consisting of the built-up business assets, knowledge, skills, and expertise of members of diasporic communities may be rather valuable for (re)building a thriving business community in the home country and, at the same time, contribute to capacity building and social change.

In order to fully assess the potential of returnees for development and social change, I shall move beyond the concept of remittances, which usually implies money transfers and therefore pertains to financial capital only (Maimbo & Ratha, 2005, p. 2). Instead, I will elaborate the concept of remittances as forms of 'capital' at large that come within reach as a consequence of return movements. This is where I turn to the French sociologist Pierre Bourdieu (1977, 1986) who identifies a number of different forms of 'capital' that serve both as material and symbolic resources in human exchanges. The aim of this chapter is to identify, first, the resources—or 'forms of capital'—that returnees bring back to their home countries and, second, the ways in which they generate economic and social change by investing these resources locally by means of entrepreneurial activity. The concept of returnee pertains to migrants and exiles returning to their home countries having lived in a foreign country ('in diaspora') for various reasons. These people may either maintain or forsake their basis in their host countries and return either temporarily or permanently to their home countries. They may also keep up a circular pattern of return and departure (Chapman & Prothero, 1983/1984; Agunias, 2006). Returnees, therefore, are embedded to varying degrees in at least two different societies—their home countries and their host countries—and in addition, maintain ties across borders with people of the same origin living in diaspora in other host countries (cf. Cohen, 1997). It is for this reason that 'context' plays a crucial role in the understanding of the ways in which returnee entrepreneurship emerges, develops, and impacts upon home-country economies. In other words, the embeddedness approach (Granovetter, 2003) to migrant economies advocates the positioning of returnee economic activities in the societal context of both the home and the host countries.

This chapter is based on a comparative literature review on returnee capital investments in countries with large diasporic populations that have come to establish a "reverse or return diaspora within the homeland society itself" (Flores, 2009, p. 3). The comparative approach entails an analysis of similarities and differences across different countries both generating and receiving returnee capital investments and, therefore, implies a sensitivity toward the contextual diversity immanent of the diasporic condition. The database has been established through university library (Picarta and Web of Science) and Google Scholar search and snowball sampling by browsing the bibliographies of recent publications on these themes. There is a considerable amount of literature addressing diaspora and migrant entrepreneurship on the one hand and the returnee economy and reverse diaspora on the other. The former concepts—and similar concepts such as ethnic business networks and transnational entrepreneurship—refer to a huge body of literature addressing migrants' entrepreneurial activities in and between host countries. Only the concepts of remigration, returnee economy, reverse diaspora, and reverse migration refer unambiguously to (economic) activities and the interests of returning migrants or refugees *in their home countries*. These concepts have been used as search terms in the bibliographical research that forms the basis of this chapter.

After the next section, which briefly discusses the strategies applied to obtain data, the chapter proceeds with a critical assessment of the key concepts of (returnee) entrepreneurship, capital, and capital investments. These key concepts will feed into the subsequent literature review focusing on the ways in which different forms of capital are utilized by returnees starting and operating private enterprises in their home countries. The comparative discussion that concludes this chapter assesses the extent to which such capital investments generate social change.

## CAPITAL INVESTMENTS AND ENTREPRENEURSHIP

The concept of embeddedness (cf. Granovetter, 2003; Hamilton, 1996, 2000) has been used by scholars to address the organization of diasporic (Chinese) business firms (Yeung & Olds, p. 15). The embeddedness approach to migrant economies advocates the positioning of migrant and diasporic economic activities in the societal context of both home and the host countries (Flores, 2009; Levitt, 1998, 2001; Portes, 1995). If such activities are viewed only in terms of profit making and if entrepreneurs are defined as "persons who are ingenious and creative in finding ways that add to their own wealth, power and prestige" (Baumol, 1990, p. 987), one may question whether entrepreneurship is an appropriate instrument for social change. Following the definition by Baumol, entrepreneurship is always present in any community or country and may be channeled into activities that are not necessarily productive, as rent-seeking or crime can also add to personal wealth but negatively affect society (Baumol, 1990, pp. 894–895; Naudé, 2007, pp. 3–4). In other words, the significance of returnee entrepreneurs for the development of their home economies can only be assessed if the concept of entrepreneurship is conceptually extended beyond the level of personal profit and is not treated in isolation from issues of community, the production of social values, sense making and life orientations, participation in civil society, business principles guided by social responsibility, alleviation of social problems, and social change (Alvord, Brown, & Letts, 2004 ), thereby pushing the economy into new directions (cf. Swedberg, 2006, pp. 27–29). Entrepreneurship, as an embedded concept (cf. Granovetter, 2003), not only produces, mobilizes, and employs economic capital but also, and perhaps most significant of all, does the same for cultural and social capital in order to innovate, and thus change, society. Defined in terms of 'innovator' and 'agent of social change' (Steyaert & Hjorth, 2006), the concept of entrepreneurship bridges the conceptual gap between the domain of economic performance and different forms of capital.

In order to fully assess the potential of entrepreneurship for providing an injection of innovation and brokering social change, this concept has to be understood in terms of the concrete contributions that entrepreneurship can make to societies. For this purpose, I will differentiate between different forms of capital investments beyond the purely financial input. An attempt will be made to identify capital inputs that enable entrepreneurs to provide local community members with access to social networks, to engage in the production of social value, to participate in civil society and help others to follow suit, to act in a socially responsible manner, and to contribute to the alleviation of social problems. The French sociologist Pierre Bourdieu (1977) identifies a number of different forms of 'capital' that serve as both material and symbolic resources in human exchanges. He distinguishes economic capital (wealth in the narrow sense), social capital (network relations, trust, and credentials), and cultural capital (certified knowledge and expertise acquired through formal education). Social capital and cultural capital generate economic capital; economic capital does not buy social or cultural capital in a simple, direct way (Bourdieu, 1986, p. 252). The concept of social capital—which Bourdieu defines in terms of durable network relations (1986, p. 248)—focuses on membership in formal organizations where people obtain skills such as negotiation, compromise, reciprocity, and establishing contact with people of other groups. At the collective level, social capital is an attribute of social organizations that facilitate coordination and cooperation for mutual benefit (Putnam, 2000). At the individual level, social capital may be established by membership of an age group or an ethnic community, or a community of professionals or business people (Kilduff & Tsai, 2003, p. 26). Although social capital can be exchanged for money, knowledge, jobs, or promotions (Bourdieu, 1986, p. 253), it can be made operational only by securing the cooperation of other actors. Social capital is closely intertwined with the concept of social networks. Cultural capital is accumulated by means of formal education and comprises language proficiency or cultural competence and takes the form of diplomas, certificates, or (academic) titles (Bourdieu, 1986).

In the next section, I will review current literature on returnee entrepreneurs as providers of the diverse forms of capital. A distinction will be made between the economic, social, and cultural capital they inject into their home countries on the one hand and the economic, social, and cultural changes that occur upon the injection of society with such capital on the other.

## RETURNEE ECONOMIES: A LITERATURE REVIEW

Starting in the 1960s, literature on return migration has focused on the economic impact of temporary, permanent, and circular migration on widely differing countries, most of which are situated in the developing world; whereas a number of studies also address European countries such as Italy, Albania, Portugal, and Ireland, which have been major emigration countries throughout the 20th century (cf. Agunias, 2006; Cerase, 1974;

Colton, 1993; Gmelch, 1980; Massey & Espinoza, 1997; McCormick & Wahba, 2001; Thomas-Hope, 1999). The bulk of current literature concentrates on key countries in East and South Asia, namely, China, Taiwan, and India (Agunias, 2006, p. 7). Most of these studies found that entrepreneurship has increased among return migrants, which suggests that migrants become more entrepreneurial through the migration experience (Agunias, 2006, pp. 6–7). There is no consensus, however, on how this enhanced entrepreneurial activity has come about. Basically, these impact studies argue from two diverging perspectives on how migration and the 'diasporic' experience enable return migrants to become entrepreneurs. The first perspective focuses exclusively on *economic capital* and reasons that remittances and accumulated savings brought back from host countries overcome liquidity constraints and hence enable individual migrants and their families to either revitalize existing or set up new enterprises upon their return (Iredale & Guo, n.d.). The second perspective acknowledges that returnees bring back *social and cultural* capital that may engender changing living standards and life orientations and may significantly alter the economic prospects of a community and eventually onset social transformations at large. There is overwhelming evidence that new skills and working experience in a more advanced commercial and technical environment enhances the entrepreneurial potential of migrants on return to their home countries, rather than the level of accumulated savings (cf. Zweig, Fung, & Vanhonacker, 2005a, 2005b for China; cf. McCormick & Wahba, 2001, for an overview of relevant literature).

On the other hand, the evidence also shows that *economic capital* accumulated abroad is more important to low-skilled and illiterate return migrants than to the better educated. Less-educated migrants and those who work in low-skilled jobs in host countries are unable to learn skills that can be utilized for business start-ups in their home countries, as has been shown by McCormick and Wahba (2001) for illiterate Egyptian returnees, by Mahmood (1995) for less-educated Bangladeshi returnees, Agunias (2006) for Filipino migrants, and Ilahi (1999) for Pakistani returnees. Instead, less-educated migrants accumulate savings—economic capital—in the host country, which they usually invest in self-employment or micro- and small-business start-ups upon their return. For once, the dependence of the low-skilled on economic capital illustrates Bourdieu's claim that economic capital cannot be converted into social and/or cultural capital in a simple, straightforward way. This dependence also raises doubts about the contribution to social change accomplished by such investments in self-employment and small businesses. Economists usually point out that return is an expression of failed migration showing that aims have not been reached (cf. Zweig et al., 2005a). Push factors affect low-skilled migrants and in particular those who see their expectations of a career in the host country curtailed. Therefore, it is argued that—as successful migrants have a career abroad—returnees are not among the best talents that a country has to offer. Upon return, they start a business for lack of other opportunities, without the necessary knowledge and experience, and hence with a high failure rate (Zweig et al., 2005b; Agunias, 2006, p. 20). It has also been observed that returnee entrepreneurship contributes to the establishment of survivalist firms (in contrast to high-potential growth firms) and so-called necessity entrepreneurship (in contrast to opportunity entrepreneurship), that is, the informal sector and firms aimed at maintaining lifestyles (Naudé, 2007, p. 5). In the case of Albania, for example, it has been shown (Nicholson, 2001) that microenterprises established or existing micro family businesses maintained by remittances and savings of returnees form a way of subsistence, not a strategy to get rich or develop the Albanian economy.

Success or failure in the host economy as an engine of return migration is regarded as a vital issue pertaining to the entrepreneurial potential of returnees. As a number of researchers point out, success or failure of returnee entrepreneurship is not only a matter of returnees possessing the appropriate resources but also of institutional factors, in particular the migration and return policies in the host and home countries. Higuchi (n.d.) argues that even well-educated Iranian migrants to Japan have been unable to accumulate social and cultural capital because of the low-skilled factory work in which they were employed and because of Japanese immigration laws limiting their period of stay. Germany, having contracted thousands of 'guest workers' from Turkey since the 1960s, has failed to provide any useful training for this category to enable them to acquire new skills; the same applies to Thailand, the Gulf States (with regard to migrant workers from Southeast Asia), and the U.S. (with regard to migrant workers from the Central Americas; Agunias, 2006, p. 13). Conversely, it is also true that home countries that are not prepared for the return of their diasporas and fail to develop return policies produce unemployment and underemployment among their returnees (see Agunias, 2006, p. 13, for the Indian state of Kerala; and Mahmood, 1995 for Bangladesh). As Naudé (2007, pp. 6–7) has pointed out, returnee entrepreneurship can contribute to social change only if governments succeed in creating the conditions for returnee enterprises to grow in such a way that they offer employment. Unless the average firm size is increased and, at the same time, the decline of the number of small and microbusinesses is accelerated, returnee entrepreneurship will remain a source of mere survival. The critical role that home-country governments play in facilitating not only the return of skilled migrants but also of their business start-ups as a part of the return process is aptly illustrated by the Taiwanese case. The Taiwanese government—focusing on highly skilled technicians and scientists—courted its diaspora as a comprehensive source of social and cultural capital that has been strategically employed to support the development of homegrown knowledge-based industries (Chang, 1992; Iredale & Guo, n.d; Newland, 2004).

## OPPORTUNITIES AND THREATS OF
## RETURNEE CAPITAL INVESTMENTS

The long-standing engagement of diaspora communities in their countries and communities of origin produces significant flows of economic capital, networks of social capital, knowledge and technology, and cultural capital in the form of education and certified skills. Increasing numbers of returnees enhance this engagement even further. Capital investments beyond remittances contribute to entrepreneurial activities. Social capital investments provide access to institutions and private companies in host countries that can contribute to social change. Cultural capital investments tap into the (certified) knowledge, skills, and expertise available among members of diaspora communities. One may argue that these forms of capital investment that accrue to entrepreneurial capital consisting of the built-up business assets and experience of diaspora members prove extremely valuable for (re)building a thriving business community in the home country.

Life in diaspora implies far-reaching changes in the migrants' lifestyles; occupational diversity and exposure to new value-systems may result in reluctance to take up their previous lives once they return. New occupations developed in diaspora may yield greater returns than previous economic activities (Kibreab, 1999, p. 154). Small entrepreneurship may be among these new occupations. The assumption that the majority of the returnees would want to return to their previous occupation and lifestyles disregards the considerable degree of social and economic transformation the refugees experience while living under diasporic conditions (ibid., p. 157). A wide array of case studies shows that returnees provide resources that allow them to jump-start local entrepreneurship and join the elite in their respective communities (Portes, Haller, & Guarnizo, 2002; Saxenian, 2002). As has been observed by Kibreab (1999, p. 156), the well-off and more highly skilled returnees in particular engage in diverse forms of entrepreneurship. This category of returnee often sees excellent business opportunities and envisions large profits by bringing information and technology back home. Having access to networks that improve their market position and possessing cultural capital in terms of language proficiency and negotiating skills in foreign business environments makes returnees a powerful force for economic integration in regional and global networks (Yamakawa, Peng, & Deeds, 2008). In the long term, they may contribute to modernizing their home countries' economies through upgrading the quality of domestic and export production (cf. Ma, 2002; Murphy, 2000).

However, there are also obstacles and restrictions involved with the availability of diasporic and/or returnee capital, and there are lacunas in our understanding of the impact that the previously described capital input has in terms of social change. Return migration of skilled professionals and businesspeople can play a major role in transforming economy and society, but it does not lead or drive change. After all, diasporic communities consist of private people or private organizations, and it is not their first and foremost objective to develop their home countries. Their motivation is vested in their families, ancestral obligations, and the expectations to find attractive conditions for business and professional life and to make a profit when investing money. Reverse diaspora as such, left to themselves, cannot be counted upon as a firm basis for social change. If change is under way, then people take a chance (Iredale & Guo, n.d.). There has to be a certain measure of development first before returnees come to accelerate it. As has been shown for Taiwan, for example, the critical condition for making optimal use of the skills offered by highly educated migrants has been a healthy economy. However, there is no clear evidence provided for the claim made by several authors (Chang, 1992; Iredale & Guo, n.d.) that these returnee migrants also had an impact on the gradual democratization of Taiwan. Whereas returnees' economic impact and social and cultural capital investments can be substantiated, their role in social change is much more difficult to assess.

The narrative of innovation of returnees may clash head-on with vested interests, conservative value systems, and a great deal of suspicion toward the 'homecomers' in the home country (cf. also Bovenkerk, 1974; Flores, 2009, pp. 35–37; Gmelch, 1980). Studying the first wave of return migrants from the U.S. to Italy as early as the 1970s, Cerase (1974) pointed out that only a few returnees qualified for the label 'return of innovation' and that these innovators soon experienced great difficulties when implementing their entrepreneurial projects due to opposition in their home communities. Those who succeeded in setting up new ventures were sucked into the system of protection and corruption, whereas those who refused to obey to local rules of the game went bankrupt. A more recent example is provided by Hughes (2004) studying Cambodian returnees from the U.S. who reentered Cambodia with the mission of democratizing and rebuilding the country in collaboration with external agencies. These returnees have come to establish a separate class, a new transnational elite of mobile people holding dual citizenship (Poethig, 2006) and feeling superior in their understanding of a postconflict Cambodian society. As a consequence, Cambodia's reverse diaspora is encountering more and more opposition by those who had stayed behind and lived through civil war. As these examples illustrate, a coincidence of views between diasporas and their communities of origin cannot be taken for granted. Conversely, diasporas are not homogeneous groups. The very fact that diaspora may be located in different host countries and may consist of groups of people who belong to different social classes, ethnic affiliations, or political parties may generate divergent aims for return to the home country.

## CONCLUSION

Entrepreneurship, according to Baumol's definition, is present everywhere, but it is not necessarily of a productive kind. It can be stifling if providing only the means of bare survival. Continuing in this vein, not all returnee entrepreneurship is beneficial to the home country in terms of development and social change. Returning diaspora bring along (often diverging) economic and political agendas. They may play a crucial role in the rebuilding of the economy and establishing successful business start-ups and may rise to power as business leaders capable of directing their home countries into a stable and prosperous future.

Institutional embeddedness is a crucial factor in stimulating and channeling returnees and their capital investments in home countries. In order for returnee entrepreneurship to blossom, more than just basic facilities are required. The governments of Taiwan, China, Korea, India in Asia; Uruguay, El Salvador, and Mexico in the Americas; and Ethiopia and South Africa in Africa established programs and agencies that coordinate, facilitate, and reward returnees who contribute to the development of their economies (Agunias, 2006, pp. 22–24). Governments may also stimulate diaspora to return to their home countries to invest, start up business, or take up leadership positions, as the case of Taiwan illustrates. However, it is still to be seen to what extent such support for returnees does not remain confined to the economic sphere but extends into the educational and social domains.

What are the chances, then, for social change emanating from returnees in general and returnee entrepreneurs in particular? If defining entrepreneurship in terms of those economic activities that produce, mobilize, and employ—besides economic capital in terms of Schumpeterian entrepreneurship—cultural, political, and social capital in order to innovate and thus transform society, economic activities that are directed purely at profit maximization in a linear growth scenario are excluded. Instead, entrepreneurship involves a change of attitudes and behavior of those involved in productive activities. In the knowledge-based sectors of innovative technologies, sourcing, product cycles, and market trends are critical for the successful operation of enterprises. The case of Taiwan shows how this change of attitude results in the growing integration of the national economy in patterns of cross-regional collaboration. The emerging collaborative networks cannot be understood purely as market transactions linking independent firms based on 'mutual interest.' Instead, the economic ties are dependent upon a shared culture that fosters openness and cooperation between producers in geographically distant regions. Taiwan's late-industrializing firms could not only benefit from the institutional embeddedness in the local developmental state but also from transnational embeddedness into the overseas Chinese technical community. Eventually, the embeddedness in transnational ties is expected to affect the political culture of the home country as may be illustrated by the eventual transformation of the developmental Taiwanese state. Conversely, for scholars to offer an adequate understanding of returnee economies, the lesson learned is to base their economic assessment in a comprehensive contextual analysis.

## REFERENCES

Agunias, D. R. (2006). *From a zero-sum to a win-win scenario? Literature review on Circular Migration.* Washington, DC: Migration Policy Institute.

Alvord, S. H., Brown, L. D., & Letts, C. W. (2004). Social entrepreneurship and societal transformation. *Journal of Applied Behavioural Science, 40*(3), 260–282.

Baumol, W. J. (1990). Entrepreneurship: Productive, unproductive and destructive. *Journal of Political Economy, 98*(5), 893–921.

Bourdieu, P. (1977). *Outline of a theory of practice.* Cambridge: Cambridge University Press.

Bourdieu, P. (1986). Forms of Capital. In J. E. Richardson (Ed.), *Handbook of theory of research for the sociology of education* (pp. 241–258). New York: Greenwood.

Bovenkerk, F. (1974). *The sociology of return migration: A bibliographic essay.* The Hague: Martinus Nijhof.

Cerase, F. (1974). Expectations and reality: A case study of return migration from the United States to Southern Italy. *International Migration Review, 8*(2), 245–262.

Chang, S. L. (1992). *Taiwan's brain drain and its reversal.* Taipei: Lucky Bookstore.

Chapman, M., & Prothero, R. M. (1983/1984). Themes on circulation in the third world. *International Migration Review, 17*(4), 597–632.

Cohen, R. (1997). *Global diasporas: An introduction.* London: UCL.

Colton, N. (1993). Homeward bound: Yemeni return migration. *International Migration Review, 27*(4), 873–886.

Flores, J. (2009). *The diaspora strikes back: Caribeño tales of learning and turning.* New York: Routledge.

Gmelch, G. (1980). Return migration. *Annual Review of Anthropology, 9,* 135–159.

Granovetter, M. (2003). The economic sociology of firms and entrepreneurs. In R. Swedberg (Ed.), *Entrepreneurship: The social science view* (pp. 244–275). Oxford: Oxford University Press.

Hamilton, G. G. (Ed.). (1996). *Asian business networks.* Berlin: Walter de Gruyter.

Hamilton, G. G. (2000). Reciprocity and control: The organization of Chinese family-owned conglomerates. In H. W. Yeung & K. Olds (Eds.), *Globalization of Chinese business firms* (pp. 55–74). Houndmills: Macmillan.

Higuchi, N. (n.d.). Remittances, investments and social mobility among Bangladeshi and Iranian returnees from Japan. Unpublished paper.

Hughes, C. (2004). Democracy, culture and the politics of gate-keeping in Cambodia: The transnation goes home. In B. S. A. Yeoh & K. Willis (Eds.), *State/nation/transnation: Perspectives on transnationalism in the Asia-Pacific* (pp. 197–217). London: Routledge.

Ilahi, N. (1999). Return migration and occupational change. *Review of Development Economics, 3,* 170–186.

Iredale R., & Guo, F. (n.d.). *The transforming role of skilled and business returnees: Taiwan, China and Bangladesh.* Australia: Centre for Asia Pacific Social Transformation Studies, University of Wollongong.

Kibreab, G. (1999). The consequences of non-participatory planning: Lessons from a livestock provision project to returnees in Eritrea. *Journal of Refugee Studies, 12*(2), 135–160.

Kilduff, M., & Tsai, W. (2003). *Social networks and organizations.* London: Sage.

Levitt, P. (1998). Social remittances: Migration-driven local-level forms of cultural diffusion. *International Migration Review, 32*(4), 926–948.
Levitt, P. (2001). *The transnational villagers.* Berkeley: University of California Press.
Ma, Z. (2002). Social-capital mobilization and income returns to entrepreneurship: The case of return migration in rural China. *Environment and Planning, 34*(10), 1763–1784.
Mahmood, P. A. (1995). Emigration dynamics in Bangladesh. *International Migration, 33*(3/4), 699–726.
Maimbo, S. M., & Ratha, D. (Eds.). (2005). *Remittances, development impact and future prospects.* Washington, DC: World Bank.
Massey, D., & Espinosa, K. (1997). What's driving Mexico-US Migration? A theoretical, empirical, and policy analysis. *American Journal of Sociology, 102*(4), 939–1000.
McCormick, B., & Wahba, J. (2001). Overseas work experience, savings and entrepreneurship amongst return migrants to LDCS. *Scottish Journal of Political Economy, 48*(2), 164–178.
Murphy, R. (2000). Return migration, entrepreneurship and local state corporatism in rural China: The experience of two counties in south Jiangxi. *Journal of Contemporary China, 9*(24), 231–247.
Naudé, W. (2007). *Peace, prosperity, and pro-growth entrepreneurship.* Helsinki: United Nations University-WIDER.
Newland, K. (2004). Beyond remittances: The role of diaspora in poverty reduction in their Countries of Origin; A scoping study by the migration policy Institute for the Department of International Development. Washington, DC: Migration Policy Institute.
Nicholson, B. (2001). From migrant to micro entrepreneur: Do-it-yourself development in Albania. *South-East Europe Review, 3*, 39–42.
Poethig, K. (2006). Sitting between two chairs: Cambodia's dual citizenship debate. In L. C.-P. Ollier & T. Winter (Eds.), *Expressions of Cambodia: The politics of tradition, identity, and change* (pp. 73–85). London: Routledge.
Portes, A. (1995). *The economic sociology of immigration: Essays on networks, ethnicity and entrepreneurship.* New York: Russel Sage Foundation.
Portes, A., Haller, W., & Guarnizo, L. E. (2002). Transnational entrepreneurs: An alternative form of immigrant economic adaptation. *American Sociological Review, 67*(2), 278–298.
Putnam, R. D. (2000). *Bowling alone: The collapse and revival of American community.* New York: Simon and Schuster.
Saxenian, A. (2002). *Local and global networks of immigrants in Silicon Valley.* San Francisco: Public Policy Institute of California.
Steyaert, C., & Hjorth, D. (Eds.). (2006). *Entrepreneurship as social change: A third movements in entrepreneurship book.* Cheltenham: Edward Elgar.
Swedberg, R. (2006). Social entrepreneurship: The view of the young Schumpeter. In C. Steyaert & D. Hjorth (Eds). *Entrepreneurship as social change: A third movements in entrepreneurship book* (pp. 21–34). Cheltenham: Edward Elgar.
Thomas-Hope, E. (1999). Return migration to Jamaica and its development potential. *International Migration, 37*(1), 183–203.
Yamakawa, Y., Peng, M. W., & Deeds, D. L. (2008). What drives new ventures to internationalize from emerging to developed economies? Entrepreneurship Theory & Practice, 32(1), 59–82.
Yeung, H. W.-Ch., & Olds, K. (Eds.). (2000). *Globalization of Chinese business firms.* Houndmills: Macmillan Press.
Zweig, D., Fung, C. S., & Vanhonacker, W. (2005a). Rewards of technology: Explaining China's reverse migration. Paper presented at the conference *People*

*on the Move: The Transnational Flow of Chinese Human Capital*, Hong Kong University of Science and Technology, October 20–22, 2005.

Zweig, D., Vanhonacker, W., Fung. C. S., & Rosen, S. (2005b). Reverse migration and regional integration: Entrepreneurs and scientists in the PRC. Paper prepared for the conference *Remaking Economic Strengths in East Asia: Dealing with the Repercussions of Increased Interdependence*, Institute of East Asian Studies, University of California, Berkeley, April 8–9, 2005.

# 13 Mennonite Community-Based Entrepreneurship in Belize, Central America

*Carel Roessingh*

## INTRODUCTION

Belize is a small multiethnic nation located in Central America with 300,000 inhabitants (Belizean Government, 2007). Since 1958 there have been several Mennonite settlements in this country. As a particularly religious community, the entrepreneurial activities of these Mennonites provide an interesting field of study when it comes to the ways in which they organize their community-based enterprises within the specific societal context. This chapter addresses the social capital of the Mennonites of Springfield in the Cayo District in Belize. The Mennonites have their origins in the Anabaptist wing of the Protestant Reformation in Western Europe during the first half of the 16th century (Hedberg, 2007; Redekop, 1989; Roessingh & Plasil, 2009). Both culturally and with regard to their religion, the Mennonites are primarily inward focused. They have their own schools and speak a language called 'Low German' (Hedberg, 2007; Loewen, 1993; Roessingh & Plasil, 2006). Contrary to the fact that most Mennonites live more or less on the edges of society, they have nonetheless been able to establish a strong and stable economic position within Belize. For instance, since their migration from Mexico to Belize in 1958, the more modern settlements have transformed into a more complex economic system with commercial agriculture and agribusiness (Loewen, 2006; Sawatzky, 1971). Simultaneously, the Mennonites in small conservative settlements, such as Springfield, live in very isolated areas and depend on subsistence agriculture, logging, and small-scale craftsmanship (Roessingh & Plasil, 2009). In Belize, the Mennonites represent reliability and, for that reason, Belizeans like to do business with them (Roessingh & Schoonderwoerd, 2005). The same applies to the Springfield Mennonites, who rely on their community-based entrepreneurship. For instance, more and more restaurant owners in the Cayo District buy their groceries in Springfield. The way these Mennonites produce their crops symbolizes eco-horticulture.

This chapter focuses on social capital and community-based entrepreneurship and how these concepts have manifested in the ways the Springfield Mennonites handle their business relations with the outside world.

## SOCIAL CAPITAL AND COMMUNITY-BASED
## ENTREPRENEURSHIP: A THEORETICAL FRAME

Social capital is a heavily debated concept (Bourdieu, 1977, 1989; Martes & Rodriguez, 2004; Putnam, 1995). Woolcock defines social capital as "the information, trust, and norms of reciprocity inhering in one's social networks" (1998, p. 153). His emphasis on mutually exchangeable information and trust is especially interesting when it comes to the importance of reciprocity within social networks. Bourdieu places this interdependence within a social world in which all humans can be divided into smaller worlds, or fields (Bourdieu, 1977, 1989). This can be networks or configurations of relationships between positions that are defined by their situation in a structure of different kinds of power (Brouns, 1993). A field functions as a battlefield, in which people 'fight' with each other using different kinds of tools or capital (Roessingh & Mol, 2007). People use their capital in the social arena to acquire power in a certain field.

Portes and Sensenbrenner (1993, pp. 1323–1325) distinguish four resources of social capital that appear as an aspect of 'common good,' namely, value introjection, reciprocity transaction, bounded solidarity, and enforceable trust. As we will argue in the following, these four resources play a role in the Mennonite settlement of Springfield in the Cayo District of Belize and, more specifically, in the field of religion and entrepreneurship.

Mennonites can bring about value introjection (getting their community to adhere to their beliefs and values) through the influence of the church. Transaction reciprocity is visible in the ways that the different settlement inhabitants and congregations/communities support each other and provide each other with jobs and other means. With respect to bounded solidarity, the Mennonites are a migrant group in Belize that is considered as a 'them' group by other ethnic groups, which stimulates the development of ethnic ties within the Mennonite settlement, alongside religious ties. The Mennonites also have a strong awareness of their own history, which adds to intragroup solidarity. The communal 'us' feeling gives rise to internal enforceable trust, which is controlled by church regulations and a strong social cohesion.

When talking about the concept of social capital among the Mennonites, it is important to also consider the issue of community-based entrepreneurship as this concept is closely related. Anderson, Honig, and Peredo define community-based entrepreneurship as "a community acting corporately as both entrepreneur and enterprise in pursuit of the common good" (2006, p. 77). In this course of action, enterprises make use of the social structures that exist in a settlement. The social structures within a settlement are very important for the building and functioning of an organization. The concept of community-based entrepreneurship in this chapter is related to social capital because of the importance of social networks, which reflect in the use of 'common goods' within the community. Peredo and Chrisman

(2006) argue that the kind of entrepreneurship that is based on social capital and community culture will transform the community into an enterprise. Within this argument, it is also important to shape clarity about the markers on which the community-based entrepreneurship is rooted.

It is significant to note that Mennonites are seen as an ethnic group. In practice, Mennonite ethnicity turns out to be a dual concept (Roessingh, 2007). Most of the Mennonites retain their Canadian citizenship alongside their Belizean citizenship (Quiring, 2003). Anderson et al. (2006) reveal the traits of ethnic entrepreneurship, starting with the fact that ethnic entrepreneurship always concerns immigrants. According to Light (2004), immigrants and ethnic minorities bring strong resources, such as social capital, to their new living area to empower their self-employment. Ethnic entrepreneurship typically engages enterprise development at the individual or family level.

The Mennonites are known for their business mindset and their strong economic position in the country. The amount of social capital present in their business environment is an important aspect of doing business (Smits, 2007). The entrepreneur receives significant advantages from social capital that allow persons or organizations to enhance access to required openings and changes (Ryman, 2004). The Mennonites' social capital is part of the core of their existence, which is based on the themes *Ordnung* and *Gelassenheit*, both deeply embedded in the Mennonite lives. *Ordnung* encompasses the norms and values that regulate the Mennonites' everyday lives and can be translated as 'discipline.' *Gelassenheit* can be seen as a trait with which Mennonites deliver themselves to the will of God. With *Gelassenheit* they submit to God's will and his demand to live a modest and introverted life (Mol, 2005).

This chapter demonstrates how these resources of social capital affect their community-based entrepreneurship by describing the case study of the Mennonites of Springfield in the Cayo District of western Belize. The data presented in this chapter are the result of several periods of ethnographic research conducted in Belize between 2002 and 2008.

## THE SETTLEMENT OF SPRINGFIELD

The road to Springfield is dusty, bumpy, and unpaved. The road becomes a cart track upon entering the village. Springfield is a small settlement that was founded because of the land shortage in the Barton Creek area in the Cayo District. Family ties connect the Upper Barton Creek Mennonites and Springfield Mennonites. This connection is a result of the population growth of Upper Barton Creek and internal migration of Lower Barton Creek families (Schneider, 1990). Quite simply, there was nowhere for Upper Barton Creek to expand, the occasional small parcel notwithstanding. With so many youth coming of age and young couples in need of land, it became necessary to find new farming land (Nippert, 1994). The Mennonites of Springfield, Upper Barton Creek, and Pine Hill (in the Toledo District) are conservative in their lifestyle.

> Their reasons for migrating to this quite isolated area are many and varied, but they are basically conservative and dislike association with other Mennonites in Belize, Mexico and Canada who have become too worldly. (Everitt, 1983, p. 89)

The Mennonites of Springfield use horse and buggy and horse-drawn wagons. The small farms lie scattered between the hillsides of the Maya Mountains over an area of 1,432 acres. The houses are small and modest, and the fields are more like horticultural land. In contrast with some other Mennonite settlements, Springfield looks tranquil. The settlement counts approximately 150 inhabitants in 23 families (Lentjes, Plasil, & Roessingh, 2009). The bishop, minister, and deacon have much influence in the community and the church. They are the ideological, religious, and secular leaders. The school council is the other organizational body. This council is responsible for executive activities, such as the conservation of the wooden school and church building, and also the maintenance of the road in and around the community. The school council is also the organization that maintains contact with the government and institutions of the 'outside world,' such as wholesale buyers of their agricultural products (Lentjes et al., 2009).

The Springfield Mennonites do not use machinery or electricity. Everything in this settlement is based on strict rules that enforce plainness, modesty, and interpretation of the scriptures. Horsepower drives the sawmill in Springfield, which is owned by the people of the community. All transport is by horse-drawn wagons. The Springfield Mennonites make their living via small-scale farming and agriculture. The main crops are beans, corn, cane, potatoes, peanuts, and melons. The Mennonites cultivate honey and fruit trees for the market. Most of the farmers have livestock, such as cows, pigs, and chickens. Their entrepreneurial activities are based on small-scale trade with outsiders. The Springfield Mennonites sell some of their products, such as fruit and honey, at the nearest market in Belmopan, the capital of Belize.

Aside from some religion-based exchanges with Mennonite groups in Paraguay and Bolivia, as well as with very conservative groups in North America, this community has no substantial transnational network rooted in entrepreneurial exchanges. Many families presently living in Upper Barton Creek and Springfield have their roots in other Mennonite groups in Belize. Because of the ideological and religious differences on the interpretation of the scriptures and how this interpretation is put into practice, however, there is no strong link based on these kinship relations. The deacon of Springfield said that he did not recognize the Mennonites of Spanish

Lookout, another Mennonite settlement in the Cayo District of Belize, as Mennonites because they are too worldly. On the other hand, Spanish Lookout is a settlement where there is always a shortage of workers, so when someone from Springfield is in need of a temporary job, he or she can take advantage of these family ties. Being a member of lager Mennonite 'family' and being a distant relative is a guarantee of work.

## COMMUNITY-BASED ENTREPRENEURSHIP IN SPRINGFIELD

Most families in Springfield obtain their livelihoods via agriculture. According to their ideology, this is how man should make a living: plant, grow, and harvest his own crop. This is how Jesus wanted them to live. All Mennonite settlements are still generally oriented toward agriculture with some small businesses very often related to this. Tilling the soil and harvesting its fruits is part of the hard and simple life that the Springfield Mennonites strive to lead. However, some people do engage in some small-scale businesses to make a living or to supplement their income from agriculture. One could divide the businesses of Springfield into four categories: agriculture, handicraft, retail trade, and their local market.

### Agriculture

For the Springfield Mennonites, agriculture is the form of life that is most appropriate according to the Bible. Whereas women pay for their sins with the pain they suffer during labor, men must do penance by working the land with their own hands: "by the sweat of your brow you will eat your food until you return to the ground, since from it you were taken; for dust you are and to dust you will return" (Genesis 3:18–20, King James Bible). Therefore the Mennonites of Springfield refuse to use any kind of modern technology that would ease the hard work on the fields. It is mainly the men and boys who work on the land; the women and girls help only during planting and harvest. They then generally do the easier tasks and leave the heavy and demanding work to the men.

The products of the harvest then meet different needs. A great deal is kept as seeds for the next season. Some crops are used for consumption in the family, mainly corn, peanuts, beans, melons, sugarcane, and potatoes. Products such as lettuce, cauliflower, ox heart cabbage, carrots, potatoes, melons, and sugarcane are sold on the market in Belmopan or at the market building in the settlement. Most of the farmers of Springfield work the land for their own needs, but nowadays there are also those who work for a small profit on the market. One respondent described his work thus: "We live like the birds, collect enough food to live for a day. But even if we do not look too far into the future, we have to make sure that we plant the corn a few months before we need it."

Next to the fields where crops are grown, most families also have a little vegetable and herb garden, which is mainly taken care of by the women. There they grow herbs, lettuce, beetroot, carrots, and radishes mainly for family consumption. Most families grow some fruit trees, mainly for their own consumption but also for the market. This activity is often led by the eldest sons of the house to teach them to take responsibility from a very young age. Within Springfield there is one exception to the general 'fruit-tree practice.' Three boys, Daniel, Peter, and Benjamin, raise fruit trees just for the market. They want to raise money to be able to buy land and start families. They give their trees to Jacob, who sells them at the market in Belmopan, and if he runs out, he advises potential buyers to come to Springfield. They also have a sign on the way to Springfield that advertises their fruit trees. These fruit trees are known on the Belizean market for their high quality and are therefore much in demand. Some of the villagers also keep bees for honey production. Paul sells his honey to Jacob, who in turn sells it on the market of Belmopan.

Most families also keep livestock, such as cows, pigs, horses, and chickens. These are generally for the family's own consumption and use. Horses are necessary for work on the fields and as a means of transportation. Chickens provide eggs and consume garbage, and they are sometimes slaughtered for a special occasion. Other products that find their way to the local market of Belmopan are homemade cheese and butter. Today, farmers in Springfield are increasing the number of cows and pigs they own because there is an increasing demand by traders to buy their animals. They also sell slaughtered animals to a butcher in the area. The Springfield farmers have realized that the need for meat is growing, so they are currently busy building a little slaughterhouse to serve their customers more directly.

## Local Market Building

In 2007 the Springfield Mennonites constructed a market building in the center of their settlement near the sawmill, the church, and the school. Because they mainly grow products such as carrots, potatoes, lettuce, cauliflower, ox heart cabbage, and various beans on a small scale, which can be harvested by hand, it is relatively easy for them to take their products to the market. The market generates much attention from the surrounding settlements. Business people who buy these popular products are mainly middlemen working for the tourist industry, among others. In turn, these middlemen sell the products to restaurants and other businesses. Twice a week on market days, this usually rather isolated settlement bustles with activity. Vans and pickup trucks drive in and out while the Springfield Mennonites (the men, women, and older children) are busy packing and selling products.

As business in the settlement is prospering, some of the villagers even employ workers from outside. One Mestizo family has built their house at the entrance to Springfield. The owner of the house is working for one of the farmers of Springfield. The worker has a driver's license so he is able to drive a pickup truck with goods to nearby markets. It becomes clear that agriculture is the main economic activity in Springfield. However, others also work as small-scale craftsmen or in retail. They produce lamellas for blinds, buggy parts, and ovens, for example. The retail trade consists of four shops in the community and one individual who has a market stand in Belmopan. Overall, the Mennonites have successfully established themselves within the economic system in Belize through the development of their community-based enterprises. However, their particular social and religious background constitutes both the reason for their success as well as a potential risk.

## TERROR IN THE VALLEY

Over the years, Mennonite settlements in Belize have become subject to robberies on a fairly regular basis. Mainly because of their image as successful entrepreneurs who make quite a lot of money, in combination with their relatively isolated position in society and their reputation as nonresistant and peaceful, the Mennonites are an easy target for robberies and attacks on individuals, families, or the entire community.

Robbers—the *banditos*—sometimes focus their attacks on individuals at times when they are busy working outside the settlement. In these cases, the *banditos* purposefully kidnap someone and ask for ransom money. During attacks aimed at families and households, *banditos* come to the settlement at night and knock on the door. When the door is opened, they forcefully enter the house, hold the family under fire with shotguns, and demand money. Sometimes they also take a family member hostage in order to demand ransom money.

Apart from these personal attacks, thieves are known to steal cattle from the Mennonites. These developments have led the Belizean government to establish a police station in Spanish Lookout, despite the reserved attitude of the Spanish Lookout Village Committee. One of the reasons for the government establishing police protection in Spanish Lookout might be the high number of enterprises and commercial activities in the area, which gives the community an important economic and societal position.

In contrast to Spanish Lookout, Springfield is an almost entirely self-supporting enclave without electricity or running water, which gives the settlement an atmosphere of peace and quiet. The Mennonites in Springfield are vulnerable; they live in an isolated manner, and there are no telephones to contact any of the villages in their vicinity. What is more, the settlement is completely surrounded by the jungle, which provides an easy escape for the *banditos* after a robbery. However, the Mennonites in Springfield also use the cover of the jungle for their own purposes. If there is an attack and the villagers have sufficient time to respond, the women and children flea into the jungle while the men stay behind. Two such incidents in Springfield are set out in the following. The first is an example of an attack on the entire settlement. The second story tells of an incident whereby the *banditos* aimed their attacks at the most isolated households in the community, located at the end of the road through the village.

## Incident One: They Came From the Jungle

It is May 2004. Slowly but steadily, the temperature rises and the first heavy rainfall of the season has announced itself. Around 4:00 in the afternoon, Isaac, one of the Mennonites working on his farmland, notices five men coming out of the jungle. The men, carrying shotguns, walk toward the houses of Springfield. Without hesitation, Isaac runs home and warns his wife. He sends his eldest son to the houses that are situated closest to the jungle. In no time, most of the households have been warned, and the women and children move toward a part of the jungle farthest from where the *banditos* have been witnessed in the jungle. This is where they will hide for the duration of the attack.

The men gather together in a group and they walk toward the attackers while reciting various Bible texts. The attackers threateningly wave their shotguns and demand money. The Mennonite men continue to murmur their biblical utterances while they take position around the attackers in a half-circle. The attackers seem to be taken off guard by this situation. Because their threats do not seem to lead them anywhere, one of the attackers shoots a dog and announces that the next victim will be a Mennonite. The Mennonite men persevere in their monotonous murmur and refuse to give way. Perhaps this behavior makes the *banditos* nervous for they suddenly retreat into the jungle, without money, leaving a terrified community behind.

## Incident Two: And Shots Were Fired

It is January 2006. The dry season is at its height. The temperature is quite chilly by Belizean standards. It is getting toward the end of the day and the sun is slowly starting to set when four figures are spotted in the twilight, walking from the jungle toward Johan's farmyard. Johan summons his family to move into the house immediately. The attackers start shooting and one of Johan's sons is hit. The family barricades the front door and withdraws to the upper floor of the wooden house. The entrance to the second floor is also barricaded and the family, comprising two parents and the nine remaining children, hide in the sleeping quarters. The wounded son is bleeding heavily, but his condition does not seem life threatening. Johan leads his family in prayer, and they patiently wait to see what will happen.

Meanwhile, the attackers force their way into the house through the barricaded door. They hastily search the room for money or other valuables but find nothing. In their frustration they try to force the entrance to the second floor, but without luck. When they realize that they will not succeed in opening the door to the upper part of the house they gather all kinds of inflammable material and place it in front of the door. They hope to smoke the family out by setting fire to this.

The gunshots and noise have warned a large part of the settlement, and a group of men proceed toward Johan's house. As before, the determination and persistence of the Mennonites proves to have a significant influence on the situation. The attackers finally retreat into the jungle, again without any money. Luckily, Johan's wounded son has sustained only minor injuries.

The situations described in these two stories indicate the urgency for the Springfield Mennonites to come up with strategies to defend themselves. One of the strategies consists of keeping as little money in the village as possible. The use of fake money and taking all earnings to the bank as soon as possible makes them a less attractive target for robberies. They have also created a warning system with large bells in the village to announce any attackers and warn the whole settlement as well as neighboring villages. Many of the families also keep horns and other instruments at home so that they can make a great deal of noise when they are attacked. As was clear from the second incident, this is a useful strategy for warning other villagers to come to the rescue. If all this fails, the Mennonites resort to other strategies such as barricading the doors and hiding out in their houses or in the jungle.

## CONCLUSION

In this chapter I described the Mennonites as an ethnic group in Belize that is focused on community-based entrepreneurship. The Mennonites are immigrants in Belize, who concentrate on their own community and make use of their own resources. Community members have built the businesses and, with the help of community members, the organizations in Springfield can function effectively. Every enterprise in Springfield is committed to the community.

Social capital plays an important role in the entrepreneurial activities of Springfield. By making use of their social capital, entrepreneurs can increase their activities with support from their friends, family, and community members. Most businesspeople involve their offspring in their work, and new employees are usually members of the immediate family or are related to the same ethnic grapevine (Kraybill & Nolt, 1995).

Redekop, Ainlay, Siemans (1995) state that the Mennonite society is based on a network of personal connections. Over the years, the Mennonites have developed a strong set of values and beliefs that focus on living in harmony and supporting fellow believers through mutual aid (Ryman, 2004). Elements of social capital such as trust, goodwill, and mutual aid contribute to the productive Mennonite lifestyle. Cultural resources such as an energetic work ethic, managerial skills, frugality, strong kinship networks, and large stable family units also facilitate the Mennonites in expanding their entrepreneurial activities (Kraybill & Nolt, 1995). Mennonites are known for their hard work, their sincere attitude, and their quality goods and services that generate opportunities for broader economic possibilities (Ryman, 2004). As their local market expanded, the need for more assistance from community members was required in order to expand. This also impacts on the daily life of the Mennonites in the community. The four resources of social capital that were introduced by Portes and Sensenbrenner (1993) play an intriguing role herein and appear in an intertwined, almost indistinguishable form in relation to the concept of community-based entrepreneurship. The rules of *ordnung* outline the norms and value imperatives with regard to the community members acting collectively but, simultaneously, their entrepreneurship also indicates reciprocity transactions on an individual level.

The case study also illustrates that bounded solidarity, such as a shared history and communal basic assumptions, is an important, rooted aspect of their community-based entrepreneurship. Bounded solidarity and enforceable trust increase the social capital within the community but also impact upon how outsiders interpret their settlement. Community members are identified as familiar, creating a bond of interpersonal trust and understanding. The social arena in which the Springfield Mennonites are established is based on a network of shared perspectives and resources that can support an entrepreneur in his business activities. Trust and reciprocity are evidently strongly present in the entrepreneurial activities of these Mennonites. Their community-based entrepreneurship is based on a shared history, strong family bonds, and overarching religious principles. And of course these strong family bonds and religious principles are also the foundations for their community-based and collective stand against the terror from outside.

It can be concluded from this case study that the community-based entrepreneurship among the Springfield Mennonites is strongly based on their shared social capital. This is the basic foundation for the existence of their community and their ability to protect and maintain their way of life. However, this strong community value simultaneously limits opportunities for individual actors to expand their entrepreneurial activities beyond the boundaries of the Springfield community. Furthermore, their social isolation and reputation for being peaceful and nonresistant corresponds to an increased risk of being terrorized. Despite these risks, the Mennonites have succeeded in maintaining their successful entrepreneurial position in the Cayo District of western Belize.

# REFERENCES

Anderson, R., Honig, B., & Peredo, A. (2006). Communities in the global economy: Where social and indigenous entrepreneurship meet. In C. Steyaert & D. Hjorth (Eds.), *Entrepreneurship as social change: A third movement in entrepreneurship book* (pp. 56–78). Cheltenham: Edward Elgar.

Belizean Government (2007). Retrieved 08/12/2007 from http://www.governmentofbelize. gov.bz.

Bourdieu, P. (1977). *Outline of a theory of practice.* Cambridge: Cambridge University Press.

Bourdieu, P. (1989). Social space and symbolic power. *Sociological Theory,* 7(1), 14–26.

Brouns, M. (1993). *De homo economicus als winkeldochter: Theorieën over arbeid, macht en sekse.* Amsterdam: SUA.

Everitt, J. (1983). Mennonites in Belize. *Journal of Cultural Geography,* 3(2), 82–93.

Hedberg, A. S. (2007). *Outside the world: Cohesion and deviation among old colony Mennonites in Bolivia.* Uppsala: Uppsala University Libary.

Kraybill, D. B., & Nolt, S. M. (1995). *Amish enterprise: From plows to profits.* Baltimore: Johns Hopkins University Press.

Lentjes, L., Plasil, T., & Roessingh, C. (2009). The heavenly valley: Small-scale farmers and entrepreneurs in Springfield. In C. Roessingh & T. Plasil (Eds.), *Between horse and buggy and four-wheel drive: Change and diversity among Mennonite settlements in Belize, Central America* (pp. 149–169). Amsterdam: VU University Press.

Light, I. (2004). The ethnic ownership economy. In C. H. Stiles & C. S. Galbraith (Eds.), *International research in the business disciplines: Vol. 4. Ethnic entrepreneurship: Structure and process* (pp. 3–44). Amsterdam: Elsevier.

Loewen, R. (1993). *Family, church and market: A Mennonite community in the Old and New Worlds, 1850–1930.* Urbana: University of Illinois Press.

Loewen, R. (2006). *Diaspora in the countryside: Two Mennonite communities and mid-twentieth-century rural disjuncture.* Toronto: University of Toronto Press.

Martes, A. C., & Rodrigues, C. L. (2004). Church membership, social capital, and entrepreneurship in Brazilian communities in the U.S. In C. H. Stiles & C. S. Galbraith (Eds.), *International research in the business disciplines: Vol. 4. Ethnic entrepreneurship: Structure and process* (pp. 171–201). Amsterdam: Elsevier.

Mol, L. (2005). *Over working ladies en general managers of household affairs. Processen van continuïteit en verandering op de arbeidsmarkt voor Mennonietenvrouwen in Spanish Lookout, Belize.* Masters thesis, Vrije Universiteit Amsterdam.

Nippert, D. J. (1994). *Agricultural colonization: The Mennonites of Upper Barton Creek, Belize.* Master's thesis, University of Memphis, TN.

Peredo, A. M., & Chrisman, J. J. (2006). Towards a theory of community-based enterprise. *Academy of Management Review,* 31(2), 309–328.

Portes, A., & Sensenbrenner, J. (1993). Embeddedness and migration: Notes on the social determinants of economic action. *American Journal of Sociology,* 98(6), 1320–1351.

Putman, R. D. (1995). Bowling alone: America's declining social capital. *Journal of Democracy,* 6(1), 65–78.

Quiring, D. M. (2003). *The Mennonite old colony vision: Under siege in Mexico and the Canadian connection.* Steinbach: Crossway.

Redekop, C. (1989). *Mennonite society.* Baltimore: Johns Hopkins University Press.
Redekop, C., Ainlay, S. C., & Siemans, R. (1995). *Mennonite entrepreneurs.* Baltimore: Johns Hopkins University Press.
Ritchie, J., & Lewis, J. (2003). *Qualitative research practice: A guide for social science students and researchers.* London: Sage.
Roessingh, C. (2007). Mennonite communities in Belize. *International Journal of Business and Globalisation, 1*(1), 107–124.
Roessingh, C., & Mol, L. (2007). Working ladies: Mennonite women in the enterprises of Spanish Lookout, Belize. *International Journal of Entrepreneurship & Small Business, 5*(3/4), 241–256.
Roessingh, C., & Plasil, T. (Eds.) (2009). Between horse and buggy and four-wheel drive: Change and diversity among Mennonite settlements in Belize, Central America. Amsterdam: VU University Press.
Roessingh C., & Plasil, T. (2006). From collective body to individual mind: Changes in leadership and attitudes in an old colony Mennonite community in Northern Belize. *Journal of Mennonite Studies, 24*, 57–74.
Roessingh, C., & Schoonderwoerd, A. (2005) Traditional farmers or modern businessmen? Religious differentiation and entrepreneurship in a Kleine Gemeinde Mennonite community in Belize. *Journal of Developmental Entrepreneurship, 10*(1), 65–77.
Ryman, J. A. (2004). Are you at peace with God and you neighbour? Cultural resources and restraints on Mennonite entrepreneurship. In C. H. Stiles & C. S. Galbraith (Eds.), *International Research in the Business Disciplines: Vol. 4. Ethnic entrepreneurship: Structure and process* (pp. 203–217). Amsterdam: Elsevier.
Sawatzky, H. L. (1971). *They sought a country: Mennonite colonization in Mexico.* Berkeley: University of California Press.
Schneider, H. (1990). *Tradition und veränderung in Belize (Mittel Amerika): Ein soziologischer vergleich der gemeiden san ignacio und Upper Barton Creek.* Diploma thesis, Latinamerika-Institut der Freien Universität Berlin.
Smits, K. (2007). *A taste of Mennonite businesses: Mennonite entrepreneurship and self-employment in Blue Creek, Belize.* Master's thesis, Vrije Universiteit Amsterdam.
Stake, R. E. (2003). Case studies. In N. K. Denzin & Y. S. Lincoln (Eds.), *Strategies of Qualitative Inquiry* (pp. 134–164). Thousand Oakes, CA: Sage.
Woodcock, M. (1998). Social capital and economic development: Towards a theoretical synthesis and political framework. *Theory and Society, 27*, 151–208.

# 14 Entrepreneurship and Culture

*Roy Thurik and Marcus Dejardin*

## INTRODUCTION

It is well known that the level of entrepreneurial activity, for instance as expressed as the percentage of owner/managers of businesses relative to the labor force, differs widely across countries (Van Stel, 2005). This variation is related to differences in levels of economic development and also to diverging demographic, cultural, and institutional characteristics (Blanchflower, 2000; Wennekers, 2006). There is evidence of a U-shaped relationship between the level of business ownership (self-employment) and per capita income (Carree, Van Stel, Thurik, & Wennekers, 2002; Wennekers, Van Stel, Carree, & Thurik, 2010). Recent research within the framework of the Global Entrepreneurship Monitor (GEM) using the rate of nascent entrepreneurship or the prevalence of young enterprises shows the same phenomenon (Suddle, Beugelsdijk, & Wennekers, 2010; Van Stel, Carree, & Thurik, 2005; Wennekers, Van Stel, Thurik, & Reynolds, 2005). The meaning of this U shape is much disputed because it is merely a stylized fact awaiting an explanation using the double causal relationship between entrepreneurship (indicated by business ownership rates, self-employment rates, or nascent entrepreneurship rates) and the level of economic development (Thurik, Carree, Van Stel, & Audretsch, 2008). Nascent entrepreneurship also reveals a wide-ranging diversity across nations and even regions. An explanation for this variation is needed as many governments attach high hopes to the positive effect of entrepreneurship on economic growth and, as a consequence, try to promote new business start-ups.

Whereas a number of individually relevant determinants of entrepreneurship have been widely explored (Grilo & Thurik, 2008; Parker, 2009), differences across countries remain unexplored. There is a general feeling that whereas intertemporal differences can be attributed to economic effects such as per capita income and to technological developments, contemporaneous differences are of a mainly institutional or cultural nature. In other words, the relative stability of differences in entrepreneurial activity across countries suggests that factors other than economic ones are at play (Freytag & Thurik, 2010). Cultural factors, as a subset of stable contextual factors, may play a role. In this chapter we give examples of various theories on the relationship between cultural values and entrepreneurship, providing both a conceptual basis and an empirical test.

## CULTURAL VALUES AND ENTREPRENEURIAL BEHAVIOR

As we explain in the following, there is no generally accepted interpretation of culture as a determinant of entrepreneurship. Neither is there a generally accepted definition for entrepreneurship (for an overview, see Wennekers & Thurik, 1999). In the chapter at hand, we adopt a pragmatic approach by equating entrepreneurship, business ownership, and self-employment and thus understand an entrepreneur to be the owner/manager of either an unincorporated or an incorporated business.

Because extensive research at the individual level of analysis shows a link between values, beliefs, and behavior, it is plausible that the differences in national culture in which these values and beliefs are embedded may influence a wide range of behaviors, including the decision to become self-employed rather than to work for others (Mueller & Thomas, 2000). Using this logic, several studies have explored the relationship between various aspects of culture and entrepreneurial behavior across cultures (Autio, Pathak, & Wennberg, 2010; Busenitz, Gomez, & Spencer, 2000; Lee & Peterson, 2000; McGrath & MacMillan, 1992; Mueller & Thomas, 2000; Stephan & Uhlaner, 2010). The remainder of this section initially introduces four schools of thought, related to culture, that may explain entrepreneurial prevalence. We then try to relate these to the notion of push-versus-pull factors as influences on entrepreneurship.

The aggregate psychological traits perspective explains differences in rates of entrepreneurial activity as follows: If there are more people with entrepreneurial values in a country, then there will be an increased number of people displaying entrepreneurial behaviors (Davidsson, 1995).

Inglehart (1990, 1997, 2003) uses the concept of postmaterialism to explain observed changes in values in modern societies. More generally, it describes the transformation in many countries from a culture dominated by materialistic-oriented individuals to a society in which an increasing proportion of the population favors nonmaterialistic life goals over materialistic ones. In the following, it is argued that a society that is more post-materialist is likely to be less entrepreneurial. This concept comes close to the aggregate psychological trait perspective but rather than refer to a value or a treat, it describes how a society should behave. Its operationalization is complex and heterogeneous.

The social legitimation or moral approval of entrepreneurship focuses on the impact of social norms and institutions on society at large (Etzioni, 1987). This view claims that greater rates of entrepreneurship are found in societies where the entrepreneur is endowed with higher social status, the educational system pays attention to entrepreneurship, and more tax incentives exist to encourage business start-ups. This results in a higher demand for and supply of entrepreneurship (Etzioni, 1987). Although the direction of the predictions are the same for the social legitimation and aggregated psychological traits perspectives, the explanations differ. Thus, in the social legitimation view, the effect is due to institutional and cultural influences; whereas in the aggregated psychological traits view, the effect is due to the aggregated effects of individual characteristics. For instance, in the social legitimation view, more individuals value entrepreneurship as a result of the higher social status conferred on entrepreneurs in certain societies; whereas in the aggregated psychological traits view, the average person simply indicates that he holds entrepreneurs in high esteem. Although the theoretical explanations may differ, it may be difficult, especially at the macro level, to empirically test which of these explanations is correct as cultural indices are drawn from aggregating responses by individuals.

The dissatisfaction perspective is an entirely different approach when compared to the first three approaches. As we argue in our dissatisfaction section, this macro-level explanation for entrepreneurship assumes that variation in entrepreneurship is based upon differences in values and beliefs between the population as a whole and potential entrepreneurs. Thus, in a predominantly nonentrepreneurial culture, a clash of values between groups may drive would-be entrepreneurs into self-employment (Baum et al., 1993, p. 505). The predicted relationship between the cultural indicators and entrepreneurship according to the dissatisfaction hypothesis is thus the opposite of that which might be expected according to the aggregate psychological trait or social legitimation views.

Applicable to both economic and cultural factors is the notion of supply, or push, and demand, or pull, factors for business start-up and entrepreneurship in general (Thurik et al., 2008; Stephan & Uhlaner, 2010). Pull factors relate to the expectation of being better off as an entrepreneur. Thus, individuals are often attracted to entrepreneurship with the expectation that it will provide greater material and/or nonmaterial benefits. Push factors take into account the conflict between one's current state and one's desired state. Push factors are often associated with some level of dissatisfaction. It is not easy to classify the four schools of thought according to the push or pull view, although postmaterialism seems to lean toward pull factors, whereas dissatisfaction adopts more of a push 'flavor.' This difficulty in classifying cultural elements in a supply versus demand view—as is standard procedure in economic modeling—is one reason combining cultural and economic variables to explain entrepreneurship is substantially underdeveloped (Thurik, 2009).

The remainder of this chapter proceeds as follows: The postmaterialism approach is illustrated in the section based upon Uhlaner and Thurik (2007). Following that, the dissatisfaction approach is illustrated based upon Noorderhaven, Thurik, Wennekers, and Van Stel (2004). Finally, the aggregate psychological traits approach is illustrated by research on uncertainty avoidance based upon Wennekers, Thurik, Van Stel, and Noorderhaven (2007). We do not present evidence of the social legitimation or moral approval of entrepreneurship approaches here. These can be found in the literature on institutions and entrepreneurship (Baumol,

1990; Busenitz et al, 2000; Djankov, La Porta, Lopez-de-Silanes, & Shleifer, 2002; Bowen & De Clercq, 2008; Freytag & Thurik, 2010; Henrekson & Sanandaji, 2010).

## POSTMATERIALISM AND ENTREPRENEURSHIP

Although less frequently used in macroeconomic research as a predictor of economic activity than the cultural indices developed by Hofstede (1980), Inglehart's (1990, 1997, 2003) work on postmaterialism as a cultural attribute is well established. Inglehart uses the concept of postmaterialism to help explain observed changes in values in modern societies. More generally, the postmaterialism hypothesis describes the transformation in many countries from a culture dominated by materialistic-oriented individuals to a society where an increasing proportion of the population favors nonmaterialistic life goals over materialistic ones.

The hypothesis of postmaterialism is based on two subhypotheses, that of socialization and that of scarcity. The socialization hypothesis assumes that one's values reflect, to a great extent, the prevailing circumstances during the formative years. The scarcity hypothesis assumes that an individual's priorities reflect their socioeconomic circumstances; they therefore attach the greatest value to relatively scarce goods (Inglehart, 1990, 1997). Taken together, these two hypotheses imply that, as a consequence of the unprecedented prosperity and the absence of war in Western countries since 1945, younger birth cohorts attach less importance to economic and physical security (materialistic values) than older birth cohorts who experienced poverty (and/or other ravages associated with war) in their early years. Instead, younger birth cohorts ascribe a higher priority to nonmaterial goals such as esteem, self-realization, and quality of life (postmaterialist values), often referred to in psychology literature as Maslow's 'higher-order needs' (Maslow, 1954).

In his research, Inglehart's (1990) findings support the conclusion that the primary reason for the shift toward postmaterialism is intergenerational replacement, not changes in values to individuals within their own life-spans. A consequence of this shift is a declining emphasis on economic growth in these countries, together with an increasing emphasis on the protection of the environment and the quality of life. Other research on postmaterialism shows that, in countries with a prevailing postmaterialist climate, the emphasis on income attainment is less significant than in materialistic countries (De Graaf, 1988), supporting Inglehart's description of postmaterialist cultures as 'economic underachievers.' More recent research shows that the trend toward postmaterialism may be declining (Van Deth, 1995). Regardless of direction, the bulk of the research shows that these values are very slow to change within particular cultures. Furthermore, as noted in the introduction to this chapter, research by Inglehart

(1990) supports the view that postmaterialism is only partly influenced by economic climate.

## Testing the Influence of Postmaterialism on Entrepreneurship

Nonmaterial motives for entrepreneurs notwithstanding, Uhlaner and Thurik (2007) conclude that (a) material gains are central or crucial to entrepreneurship; and (b) because those gains, by definition, are of less value to postmaterialist individuals, a society that is more postmaterialist is likely to be less entrepreneurial. They use data from different sources, including the Global Entrepreneurship Monitor (GEM), World Value Surveys, and the World Development Indicators database of the World Bank. The measure for postmaterialism is based upon Inglehart's four-item postmaterialism index (Inter-University Consortium for Political and Social Research, 1994). The measures for entrepreneurship are total entrepreneurial activity measured as a combination of nascent entrepreneurship (the percentage of people in the age group of 18 to 64 years who are actively engaged in the start-up process) or new business formation (those owning and managing a business less than 42 months old expressed in percentage of adults in the same age group). Twenty-seven countries had complete data, including Argentina, Belgium, Brazil, Canada, Chile, China, Denmark, Finland, France, Germany (Western), Hungary, India, Ireland, Italy, Japan, Korea, Mexico, Norway, Poland, South Africa, Slovenia, Spain, Sweden, Switzerland, the Netherlands, the United Kingdom, and the United States.

The results of Uhlaner and Thurik (2007) confirm the importance of postmaterialism when explaining total entrepreneurial activity in general and new business formation in particular. The negative relationship between postmaterialism and entrepreneurship is also evident when controls are used. However, a certain lack of stability within the findings suggests rather complex interrelationships between the controls and postmaterialism. One possibility is that postmaterialism mediates the relationship between per capita income and total entrepreneurial activity, consistent with Inglehart's conclusions that economic climate drives social change, rather than the reverse (Inglehart, 1990).

## DISSATISFACTION AND ENTREPRENEURSHIP

Various types of dissatisfaction are used in microstudies of entrepreneurship. Brockhaus (1980) states that dissatisfaction with previous work experience is closely related to the 'entrepreneurial decision.' He finds that self-employed individuals tend to be relatively highly dissatisfied with the previous work itself, with supervision, and with opportunities for promotion (but more satisfied with actual pay). Shapero and Sokol assert that "research data show that individuals are much more likely to take action upon negative information rather than positive, and the data on company formations support that conclusion" (1982, p. 79). In their final model, both pull and push factors contribute to the start-up of a business, but negative 'displacements' such as forced emigration, being fired, and being bored or angered predominate. Dyer (1994, p. 10) cites several other studies showing that people are more likely to start their own enterprises when they face a lack of opportunities for viable careers in existing organizations.

This fits with what psychology tells us about motivation. Individuals with a high sense of self-efficacy, in particular, are activated by self-dis-satisfaction, that is, when they do not attain their goals. This spurs efforts to align outcomes with their value standards (Bandura & Cervone, 1983). Vroom infers from his model "that job satisfaction should be related to the strength of the force on the person to remain in his job" or, in other words, "that job satisfaction and turnover are negatively related to one another" (1982, p. 175). Consequently, it is no surprise that dissatisfaction is one of the most important predictors of job mobility (Vroom, 1982). Hence, at the level of the individual, various kinds of dissatisfaction are conducive to job mobility and the propensity to become self-employed.

It is tempting to generalize these findings at the country level. However, a positive correlation between dissatisfaction and self-employment at the country level may also originate from self-employed people being relatively dissatisfied with their lives. This reversed causality, self-employment caus-ing low satisfaction, is ruled out by ample empirical evidence, however. In many studies (Benz & Frey, 2008a, 2008b; Blanchflower & Oswald, 1998; Bradley & Roberts, 2004) the job satisfaction of the self-employed is, on average, found to be higher than, or at least equal to, that of salaried employees. These studies report that the self-employed (and entrepreneurs, as a subgroup of the self-employed) have higher work satisfaction than the employed. This seems to be the case despite longer work hours, poorer working conditions, heightened job stress, and higher risk (Bradley & Rob-erts, 2004). Apparently, these are compensated by other factors such as autonomy and the possibility of becoming wealthy. Given the strong posi-tive correlation between dissatisfaction and self-employment at the country level, it is likely that the 'push' effect of actual dissatisfaction on the number of business start-ups is enhanced by the 'pull,' or demonstration, effect of the self-employed being relatively satisfied with their businesses, boosting the anticipated satisfaction of entrepreneurship.

## Testing the Influence of Dissatisfaction on Entrepreneurship

Noorderhaven et al. (2004) conclude that higher levels of dissatisfaction with life in a country is conducive to higher rates of self-employment, whereas higher levels of prosperity lead to lower rates of self-employment. The dependent variable is the number of self-employed (excluding agricul-ture, hunting, forestry, and fishing) divided by the total labor force of a country. Labor income share, unemployment, earning differentials, female labor participation, and population density are used as controls. Data are used from various sources, such as Compendia 2000.2 (EIM), OECD Labour Force Statistics, OECD National Accounts, Eurobarometer, and so on. An unbalanced panel of 48 observations (15 European countries in 1976, 1984, 1990, and 1998) is available for testing. The conclusion of this exercise is that countries with relatively more people who are dissatisfied with the society they live in and/or who have a lower overall life satisfaction have a higher proportion of self-employed. This conclusion is robust when controlling for other explanatory variables. In addition to the positive influence of dissatisfaction, a negative influence of the level of economic development is found. The fact that nations with a higher average level of dissatisfaction have a higher proportion of self-employed individuals should not be taken as a sign that the average self-employed individual is more dissatisfied than the average wage-employed individual. The conclusion to be drawn is that if more people in a country feel dissatisfied with their life and with the way democracy works, this increases the chance that they will seek self-employment. Those who do so tend to improve their life and job satisfaction over those who do not (Hofstede, 1998).

## UNCERTAINTY AVOIDANCE AND ENTREPRENEURSHIP

Attitudes, such as risk aversion, pertain to individuals and may vary widely within groups. At the level of nations, cultural traits related to these individual psychological traits may be distinguished. Empirically, these traits may be derived as mean, modal, or extreme values of individual observations or through a direct analysis of 'ecological data' (pertaining to national practices and achievements). Cultural traits—or aggregated psychological traits—represent a nation's 'mental programs' that are developed in socialization processes in the family in early childhood and reinforced in schools and organizations (Hofstede, 2001, p. xix). Accordingly, cultural traits may differ between societies.

A cultural trait strongly associated with individual attitudes toward risk and uncertainty is 'uncertainty avoidance.' According to Hofstede, uncertainty avoidance relates to the extent to which societies tolerate ambiguity (2001, p. 146). A culture is characterized by high uncertainty avoidance when its members feel threatened by uncertain or unknown situations. People in these cultures "look for structure in their organizations, institutions and relationships, which makes events clearly interpretable and predictable" (ibid., p. 148). In countries with lower uncertainty avoidance "not only familiar but also unfamiliar risks are accepted, such as changing jobs and starting activities for which there are no rules" (ibid, p. 148). Low uncertainty avoidance thus implies a "willingness to enter into unknown ventures" (ibid., p. 164). Hofstede operationalizes uncertainty avoidance using three survey questions about whether employees feel "company rules should not be broken even when the employee thinks it is in the company's best interests" (ibid., p. 148), about their personal expected job stability, and about how often they feel nervous or tense at work.

## Testing the Influence of Uncertainty Avoidance

Wennekers et al. (2007) have tested the direct and the indirect contribution of uncertainty avoidance to the variance in business ownership across nations and over time. They use several controls, such as level of economic development, share of services, relative earnings of self-employed, unemployment, social security entitlements, income disparity, financial variables, and demographic characteristics. A panel data set is constructed for 21 OECD countries for 1976, 1990, and 2004. Many different data sources are used, the uncertainty avoidance data are from Hofstede (2001), and the entrepreneurship variable is the percentage of business owners in the labor force.

A positive *direct* influence of uncertainty avoidance on business ownership rates has been found indicating that, in the years 1976 through 2004, a climate of high uncertainty avoidance in existing firms and organizations may have pushed enterprising individuals toward self-employment (in line with Baum et al., 1993). These findings also show that a personal trait (risk aversion) and its cultural counterpart (uncertainty avoidance) may have a diverging impact on entrepreneurship. Repeating the regressions in three separate sample years confirms these results for 1976 and 1990. However, for 2004, the main outcome is that uncertainty avoidance no longer has any direct influence on business ownership. The interpretation of Wennekers et al. (2007) is that the advent of the entrepreneurial economy (Audretsch & Thurik, 2001) has created pull factors mobilizing the relatively abundant supply of potential entrepreneurial capital in countries with low uncertainty avoidance. Evidence is also found for a negative *indirect* influence of uncertainty avoidance through a moderating effect on the influence of per capita income on business ownership. In low uncertainty avoidance countries, the negative influence of per capita income on the rate of business ownership is clearly smaller than in high uncertainty-avoidance countries. In a group of 8 high uncertainty-avoidance countries, a relatively strong negative relationship between GDP per capita and the level of business ownership suggests that rising opportunity costs of entrepreneurship are the dominant perception in this cultural environment. On the other hand, in a group of 13 low uncertainty-avoidance countries, the relatively weak negative relationship between business ownership and per capita income suggests that rising opportunities are a countervailing force in an environment of low uncertainty avoidance.

## CONCLUSION

The notion of patterns of values that shape human behavior is common to different definitions of culture (Hofstede, 1980; Kroeber & Parsons, 1958). Sometimes the view is taken that cultural values are typically determined early in life (Hofstede, 1980) and tend to endure over time (Hofstede, 1980; Mueller & Thomas, 2000). Other researchers assume that although certain values may prevail in a particular culture at a moment in time, shifts may take place over time, from generation to generation, particularly in societies undergoing radical industrial transformation. For instance, Inglehart examines the shift among Americans and Western Europeans toward postmaterialism between 1970 and 1988 (Inglehart, 1990). Even if these shifts take place, they are expected to move slowly. Hence, it should come as no surprise for scholars examining the context of entrepreneurial activities that cultural values are candidates for explaining persistent differences between levels of entrepreneurship between countries. This chapter aims to show how theories such as the postmaterialism approach, the dissatisfaction approach, and the aggregate psychological traits approach may help in contrasting and explaining the relationship between cultural values and entrepreneurship. Examples of all three theories are given including a conceptual framework and a basic empirical test.

Despite increasing empirical interest for the topic of the influence of culture on entrepreneurship (Acs & Szerb, 2010; Autio et al., 2010; Freytag & Thurik, 2010; Henrekson & Sanandaji, 2010; Stephan & Uhlaner, 2010), the limitations of the recent exercises on the relationship between cultural values and entrepreneurship remain clear. Although more and more individual data are used, the low number of available aggregate data points makes a serious test of which cultural variables have an effect very difficult. This is frustrating given the richness of ideas about the cultural influences on the level of entrepreneurship. This frustration is bound to persist for three reasons. First, cultural shifts move very slowly when they takes place, so a time dimension will not easily contribute to the number of data points. Second, schools of thought about the meaning and content of cultural variables come with their own independent data sets that usually have different constraints, and a lack of overlap hampers a fair testing exercise. Third, cultural variables are difficult to classify in the usual supply versus demand set-up of economic models (Thurik, 2009). Despite these limitations, there is general agreement that when explaining levels of entrepreneurship, we cannot simply state that culture is the residue when economic variables and regulator arrangements have had their say (Bowen & De Clercq, 2008; Djankov et al., 2002; Van Stel, Storey, & Thurik, 2007).

## ACKNOWLEDGMENTS

The present chapter attempts to combine the ideas and results of earlier papers, such as Noorderhaven et al. (2004); Uhlaner and Thurik (2007); Wennekers, Thurik, et al. (2007); and Freytag and Thurik (2007, 2010). Assistance by Adam Lederer, Marco van Gelderen, Frank Janssen, Erik Swets, Lorraine Uhlaner, and Sander Wennekers is gratefully acknowledged. This chapter is written in cooperation with the research program

SCALES, carried out by EIM/Panteia and financed by the Dutch Ministry of Economic Affairs. It benefitted from visits by Marcus Dejardin and Roy Thurik to CRECIS (Centre for Research in Entrepreneurial Change and Innovative Strategies), Louvain School of Management, to EM-Lyon, and to CREM, UFR Sciences Economiques et de Gestion, Université de Caen Basse-Normandie.

# REFERENCES

Acs, Z. J., & Szerb, L. (2010). The link between culture and entrepreneurship: Universal values, institutional characteristics and individual features. Paper presented at the GEM scientific conference, Imperial College London, September 30 – October 2.

Audretsch, D. B., & Thurik, A. R. (2001). What is new about the new economy: Sources of growth in the managed and entrepreneurial economies. *Industrial and Corporate Change, 10*(1), 267–315.

Autio, E., Pathak, S., & Wennberg, K. (2010). Culture's consequences for entrepreneurial behaviours. Paper presented at the GEM scientific conference, Imperial College London, September 30 – October 2.

Bandura, A., & Cervone, D. (1983). Self-evaluative and self-efficacy mechanisms governing the motivational effects of goal systems. *Journal of Personality and Social Psychology, 45*(5), 1017–1028.

Baum, J. R., Olian, J. D., Erez, M., Schnell, E. R., Smith, K. G., Sims, H. P., Scully, J. S., & Smith, K. A. (1993). Nationality and work role interactions: A cultural contrast of Israeli and US entrepreneurs' versus managers' needs. *Journal of Business Venturing, 8*(6), 499–512.

Benz, M., & Frey, B. S. (2008a). Being independent is a great thing: Subjective evaluations of self-employment and hierarchy. *Economica, 75*, 362–383.

Benz, M., & Frey, B.S. (2008b). The value of doing what you like: Evidence from the self-employed in 23 countries. *Journal of Economic Behavior and Organization, 68*, 445–455.

Blanchflower, D. G. (2000). Self-employment in OECD countries. *Labor Economics, 7*(5), 471–505.

Blanchflower, D. G., & Oswald, A. J. (1998). What makes an entrepreneur? *Journal of Labor Economics, 16*(1), 26–60.

Baumol, W. J. (1990). Entrepreneurship: Productive, unproductive, and destructive. *Journal of Political Economy, 98*(5), 893–921.

Bowen, H. P., & De Clercq, D. (2008). Institutional context and the allocation of entrepreneurial effort. *Journal of International Business Studies, 39*(4), 747–767.

Bradley, D. E., & Roberts, J. A. (2004). Self-employment and job satisfaction: Investigating the role of self-efficacy, depression, and seniority. *Journal of Small Business Management, 42*(1), 37–58.

Brockhaus, R. H. (1980). The effect of job dissatisfaction on the decision to start a business. *Journal of Small Business Management, 18*(1), 37–43.

Busenitz, L. W., Gomez, C., & Spencer, J. W. (2000). Country institutional profiles: Unlocking entrepreneurial phenomena. *Academy of Management Journal, 43*(5), 994–1003.

Carree, M. A., Van Stel, A. J., Thurik, A. R., & Wennekers, A. R. M. (2002). Economic development and business ownership: An analysis using data of 23 OECD countries in the period 1976–1996. *Small Business Economics, 19*(3), 271–290.

Davidsson, P. (1995). Culture, structure and regional levels of entrepreneurship. *Entrepreneurship and Regional Development,* 7(1), 41–62.

De Graaf, N. D. (1988). *Postmaterialism and the stratification process: An international comparison.* Utrecht: ISOR.

Djankov, S., La Porta, R., Lopez-de-Silanes F., & Shleifer, A. (2002). The regulation of entry. *Quarterly Journal of Economics, 117*(1), 1–35.

Dyer, W. G. (1994). Toward a theory of entrepreneurial careers. *Entrepreneurship Theory and Practice, 19*(2), 7–21.

Etzioni, A. (1987). Entrepreneurship, adaptation and legitimation. *Journal of Economic Behavior and Organization, 8*(2), 175–189.

Freytag, A., & Thurik, A. R. (2007). Entrepreneurship and its determinants in a cross-country setting. *Journal of Evolutionary Economics, 17*(2), 117–131.

Freytag, A., & Thurik, A. R. (2010). *Entrepreneurship and culture.* New York: Springer.

Grilo, I., & Thurik, A.R. (2008). Determinants of entrepreneurial engagement levels in Europe and the US. *Industrial and Corporate Change, 17*(6), 1113–1145.

Henrekson, M., & Sanandaji, T. (2010). *The interaction of entrepreneurship and institutions.* IFN Working Paper No. 830, Research Institute of Industrial Economics, Stockholm.

Hofstede, G. (1980). *Culture's consequences: International differences in work-related values.* Cross-Cultural Research and Methodology Series 5. Newbury Park, CA: Sage.

Hofstede, G. (1998). *Entrepreneurship in Europe.* Maastricht/House of Europe: Schuman Lecture, Studium Generale.

Hofstede, G. (2001). *Culture's consequences: Comparing values, behaviors, institutions and organizations across nations.* 2nd edition. Thousand Oaks, CA: Sage.

Inglehart, R. (1990). *Culture shift in advanced industrial society.* Princeton, NJ: Princeton University Press.

Inglehart, R. (1997). *Modernization and post-modernization: Cultural, economic and political change in 43 societies.* Princeton, NJ: Princeton University Press.

Inglehart, R. (2003). *Human values and social change: Findings from the values surveys.* Leiden: Brill.

Inter-University Consortium for Political and Social Research (1994). *World values survey 1981–1984 and 1990–1993* (codebook). Ann Arbor, MI: Author.

Kroeber, A. L., & Parsons, T. (1958). The concepts of culture and of social system. *American Sociological Review, 23*(5), 582–583.

Lee, S. M., & Peterson, S. J. (2000). Culture, entrepreneurial orientation, and global competitiveness. *Journal of World Business, 35*(4), 401–416.

Maslow, A. (1954). *Motivation and personality.* New York: Harper and Row.

McGrath, R. G., & MacMillan, I. C. (1992). More like each other than anyone else? A cross-cultural study of entrepreneurial perceptions. *Journal of Business Venturing, 7*(5), 419–429.

Mueller, S. L., & Thomas, A. S. (2000). Culture and entrepreneurial potential: A nine country study of locus of control and innovativeness. *Journal of Business Venturing, 16*(1), 51–75.

Noorderhaven, N. G., Thurik, A. R., Wennekers, A. R. M., & Van Stel, A. (2004). The role of dissatisfaction and per capita income in explaining self-employment across 15 European countries. *Entrepreneurship Theory and Practice, 28*(5), 447–466.

Parker, S. C. (2009). *The economics of entrepreneurship.* Cambridge: Cambridge University Press.

Shapero, A., & Sokol, L. (1982). The social dimensions of entrepreneurship. In C. A. Kent, D. L. Sexton, & K. H. Vesper (Eds.), *Encyclopedia of Entrepreneurship* (pp. 72–90). Englewood Cliffs, NJ: Prentice-Hall.

Stephan, U., & Uhlaner, L. M. (2010). Performance-based vs socially supportive culture: A cross-national study of descriptive norms and entrepreneurship. *Journal of International Business Studies, 41*(8), 347–1364.

Suddle, K., Beugelsdijk, Sj., & Wennekers, S. (2010). Entrepreneurial culture and its effect on the rate of nascent entrepreneurship. In A. Freitag and R. Thurik (Eds), *Entrepreneurship and culture* (pp. 227-244). New York: Springer.

Thurik, A. R. (2009). Entreprenomics: Entrepreneurship, economic growth and policy. In Z. J. Acs, D. B. Audretsch, & R. Strom (Eds.), *Entrepreneurship, Growth and Public Policy* (pp. 219–249). Cambridge: Cambridge University Press.

Thurik, A. R., Carree, M. A., Van Stel, A., & Audretsch, D. B. (2008). Does self-employment reduce unemployment? *Journal of Business Venturing, 23*(6), 673–686.

Uhlaner, L. M., & Thurik, A. R. (2007). Post-materialism: A cultural factor influencing total entrepreneurial activity across nations. *Journal of Evolutionary Economics, 17*(2), 161–185.

Van Deth, J. W. (1995). De stabiliteit van oude en nieuwe politieke oriëntaties. In J. J. M. Van Holsteyn & B. Niemoller (Eds.), *De Nederlandse Kiezer.* Leiden: DWSO.

Van Stel, A. (2005). Compendia: Harmonizing business ownership data across countries and over time. *International Entrepreneurship and Management Journal, 1*(1), 105–123.

Van Stel, A., Carree M. A., & Thurik, A. R. (2005). The effect of entrepreneurial activity on national economic growth. *Small Business Economics, 24*(3), 311–321.

Van Stel, A., Storey, D., & Thurik, A. R. (2007). The effect of business regulations on nascent to young business entrepreneurship. *Small Business Economics, 28*(2–3), 171–186.

Vroom, V. H. (1982). *Work and motivation.* Malabar, FL: Robert E. Krieger.

Wennekers, A. R. M. (2006). *Entrepreneurship at country level: Economic and non-economic determinants.* PhD thesis, Erasmus Research Institute of Management (ERIM), Rotterdam.

Wennekers, A. R. M., & Thurik, A. R. (1999). Linking entrepreneurship and economic growth. *Small Business Economics, 13*(1), 27–55.

Wennekers, A. R. M., Thurik, A. R., Van Stel, A. J., & Noorderhaven, N. (2007). Uncertainty avoidance and the rate of business ownership across 21 OECD countries, 1976–2004. *Journal of Evolutionary Economics, 17*(2), 133–160.

Wennekers, A. R. M., Van Stel, A. J., Carree, M. A., & Thurik, A. R. (2010). The relation between entrepreneurship and economic development: Is it U-shaped? *Foundations and Trends in Entrepreneurship, 6*(3), 167–237.

Wennekers, A. R. M., Van Stel, A. J., Thurik, A. R., & Reynolds, P. (2005). Nascent entrepreneurship and the level of economic development. *Small Business Economics, 24*(3), 293–309.

## Part VI

# Descriptions of Context

## 15 The New Dutch Economy
### 'New and Colorful Entrepreneurship'

*Karima Kourtit & Peter Nijkamp*

### INTRODUCTION: 'NEW ECONOMY'

The modern global economy and the development of today's business environment has in recent years brought cultural diversity as well as creative and innovative activities into a new focus, namely, the 'new economy.' Creativity, innovation, and entrepreneurship are often mentioned in current literature as critical success factors that spur economic development and growth.

It is often argued that the emergence of the 'new paradigm' of creativity, innovation, and entrepreneurship (Matheson, 2006) is mainly due to Florida's (2002, 2003, 2004) and Scott's (2000) seminal work on the creative industries (CIs) in modern cities. This new paradigm has prompted a trend for a creative, open, and globalizing world and economy that includes social, cultural, and creative urban environmental factors (Matheson, 2006). These forces are open, diverse, and dynamic (Florida, 2003; Peck, 2005). This leads to a new 'urban imperative': Modern cities are being forced to turn into heterogeneous settlements with unprecedented innovative, creative, and cultural diversity, which are all competitive assets that can improve socioeconomic performance to shape a spectacular new and diverse urban design and lifestyle for accelerated economic growth.

Cultural diversity fosters creativity, and innovation contributes to entrepreneurship, enhances productivity, and promotes economic growth. The results of many studies demonstrate that diversity is associated with increased sales revenue, more customers, greater market share, and greater relative profits for many firms. Cultural diversity also contributes to productivity, job creation, and economic growth in many countries; it also provides useful resources to the CIs and stimulates new ideas and cross-cultural cooperation for cultural production, and therefore fosters social cohesion.

Because it is linked to creative activities, diversity offers a major source of competitiveness for multicultural cities; it assists the cities' efforts to boost their international profile, attracting investments and a well-educated, creative workforce and therefore contributes to the improvement of the creative capacities of cities and regions. Through their agglomeration, modern cities offer advantages (i.e., local identity, an open and attractive urban 'milieu' or atmosphere, new business initiatives, and access to financial and social capital and networks) in which a broad array of business opportunities for creative cultures, self-employment opportunities and small- and medium-sized enterprises (SMEs) in particular, may play a central role in creating a new urban vitality.

In general, the economic importance of the SME sector in the Netherlands is formidable (European Commission, 2010a). The SME sector accounts for almost 99% of all business in the Netherlands, employs 4.2 million people, and is responsible for approximately 58% of the jobs on the labor market. Its estimated annual turnover is approximately €750 billion. Assuming there are 824,000 SME firms in the Netherlands, we may estimate that the average employment generated by 1 SME firm in the Netherlands is five persons and average turnover is approximately €900,000. Nowadays, new trends show a rise in migrant businesses, in particular within the CIs. This will be the focus of this chapter in the context of entrepreneurship.

The sociocultural 'pluriformity' approach aims to determine the various impulses that stimulate many different ethnic groups to become engaged in the CIs, especially in the context of entrepreneurship, by deploying urban space as an action platform and mobilizing all resources. This approach can significantly contribute to the economy by increasing the economic and cultural diversity of a city and reducing unemployment among immigrants (in the 'multicultural melting pot' of cities).

## NEW ENTREPRENEURSHIP

Entrepreneurship has emerged as a significant organizational form and one of the most important and dynamic forces shaping the changes in the global economic and social landscape throughout the world (Wennekers, Van Stel, Thurik, & Reynolds, 2005). In the last decade, however, in the spirit of innovation theory of global competition and economic dynamics, we have observed a revival of interest in the economics of entrepreneurship, with a strong emphasis on its microeconomic foundation and on applied econometric and statistical work.

Entrepreneurship and innovation are two closely connected phenomena that are responsible for a nation, region, or city's economic growth and culture. They lead to new forms of productivity and act as the engine of continued prosperity. Entrepreneurship is often found in the SME sector and therefore also offers new opportunities for immigrants with a business-oriented attitude. They are known as 'ethnic' or 'migrant' entrepreneurs, hence the term 'new entrepreneurship.' Ethnic entrepreneurship, which includes business owners, start-ups, or takeovers originating from non-Western countries including first- and second-generation (CSB by Statistics Netherlands) ethnic entrepreneurs, has become an essential dimension of migrant or ethnic minorities' presence in modern cities, is raising the living standards of ethnic groups, and is an important aspect of modern urban life and economy. New entrepreneurs form a significant part of the SME sector in our modern cities and have become a source of new economic opportunities for regions and cities. Structural factors (i.e., social exclusion and discrimination, poor access to markets, and high unemployment) and cultural factors (i.e., specific values, skills, and cultural features including internal solidarity and loyalty, flexibility, personal motivation, a strong work ethic, informal network contacts with people from the same ethnic group, and flexible financing arrangements) or a blend of these factors all influence the step toward ethnic entrepreneurship.

But it should be recognized that in various cases, significant opportunities for and the barriers to ethnic entrepreneurship do still exist (e.g., language and cultural barriers, skill levels, etc.). A valid and intriguing question is: What are the critical success or performance conditions for migrant entrepreneurs in the (large) urban areas? (see, e.g., Bates, Jackson, & Johnson, 2007). This calls for further empirical research. Various studies on ethnic entrepreneurship still focus mainly on the first generation ethnic entrepreneurs who are more concentrated in the traditional sectors (i.e., clothing, hotels, and catering sectors). Thus, only a limited number of studies focus on the nontraditional sectors in which the new generation of ethnic entrepreneurs are now beginning to operate. From this point, we will focus on the new generation in the creative industries in the four largest cities in the Netherlands.

To this end, we will describe the results of a Dutch case study on one of the three largest ethnic groups that has had the sharpest rise in absolute numbers of non-Western entrepreneurs and a relatively high birthrate, namely, the higher-educated young Moroccan entrepreneurs in the CIs concentrated in the four largest Dutch modern cities (the so-called the 'G4'): Amsterdam, Rotterdam, The Hague, and Utrecht. This will have implications for various stakeholders, such as other ethnic entrepreneurs, policy makers, and business investors, in this dynamic and promising business environment.

## ETHNIC ENTREPRENEURS

New entrepreneurship contributes to the development of integration and the great diversity in entrepreneurship in our modern social economy (EIM, 2006). It has emerged as one of the most challenging and rapidly expanding sectors among ethnic minorities and migrants, and it has become a popular broader concept, explained within the demand-supply relationship (goods and services) as what customers want to buy and their geographical concentration and what immigrants can provide, their response to specific demands for (ethnic) products and services, in a modernizing multicultural society and open economy (Van Light & Bonacich, 1988; Waldinger, McEvoy, & Aldrich, 1990).

Migrant minorities usually appear to be a highly motivated and qualified entrepreneurial group. A growing migrant economy creates a virtuous circle:

Business success gives rise to a distinctive motivational structure and breeds a community-wide orientation toward entrepreneurship. In general, immigrants are more likely to be self-employed than similarly skilled native-born workers, and in many countries self-employment rates of immigrants exceed those of the native-born. Whereas assimilation has a positive impact on self-employment probabilities (Borjas, 1986), the level of education and the period since immigration are important determinants of self-employment (Fairlie & Meyer, 1996).

The increase in and importance of ethnic entrepreneurship has recently prompted policy and research interest regarding migrant business in Europe. This new phenomenon is also increasingly being recognized in the Netherlands as an interesting focus for a city's SME policy. They operate in interesting niches and form a positive stimulus for creative business-making in modern cities.

In the past, self-employment has been a source of economic survival (the so-called 'lifeboat economics', which refers to Garrett Hardin's Lifeboat Ethics, 1974a,b) for immigrants and ethnic minority groups. Historically, migrants often had a specific and isolated position: 'the stranger is the trader' (a possible solution to their unemployment situation, by improving their working conditions, while also escaping from discrimination, integration and emancipation problems). Nowadays we observe an overwhelming impact of specific migrant groups on the regional and local economy in many host countries. New trends in ethnic/migrant entrepreneurship and their growth strategies in the Netherlands tend to show a rise in second-generation migrant entrepreneurs in the CIs instead of focusing on traditional sectors, where the first generation is operating. They are also progressing more than ever before in education and in the workforce (Cormack & Niessen, 2002).

In general, ethnic entrepreneurs are often entrepreneurs who see new opportunities in areas where other people do not. When native entrepreneurs move away from the older urban neighborhoods, ethnic entrepreneurs are inclined to take over their businesses in those areas. It is therefore clear that in addition to economic effects, ethnic entrepreneurs can also make a critical contribution to the improvement of the social climate of specific neighborhoods.

## MIGRANT (ETHNIC) ENTREPRENEURSHIP IN THE NETHERLANDS

Over the past decades, ethnic entrepreneurship has become a prominent feature of business life in the major cities of the Netherlands. Not only do these businesses create employment with their increasing share in self-employment, particularly for immigrant employees, but they also strengthen the urban social economy. Urban diversity is of great importance here. In the city, entrepreneurs can share facilities and benefit from the combined knowledge and expertise of one another. Diversity will lead to new and

Table 15.1 Development of the Number of Firms in the Netherlands, 2000–2007

| Year | Native entrepreneurs | Ethnic entrepreneurs | Western ethnic entrepreneurs | | | | | Non-Western ethnic entrepreneurs | | | | | Total |
|---|---|---|---|---|---|---|---|---|---|---|---|---|---|
| | | | Total Western ethnic entrepreneurs (first and second generation) | First generation | First generation (%) | Second generation | Second generation (%) | Total non-Western ethnic entrepreneurs (first and second generation) | First generation | First generation (%) | Second generation | Second generation (%) | |
| 2000 | 843 | 114 | 76 | 27 | 24 | 49 | 43 | 39 | 34 | 30 | 5 | 4 | 957 |
| 2001 | 849 | 121 | 77 | 28 | 23 | 50 | 41 | 44 | 38 | 31 | 6 | 5 | 970 |
| 2002 | 846 | 123 | 77 | 28 | 23 | 49 | 40 | 46 | 39 | 32 | 6 | 5 | 969 |
| 2003 | 845 | 125 | 78 | 28 | 22 | 50 | 40 | 48 | 41 | 33 | 6 | 5 | 971 |
| 2004 | 825 | 123 | 75 | 27 | 22 | 48 | 39 | 48 | 41 | 33 | 7 | 6 | 948 |
| 2005 | 842 | 127 | 77 | 28 | 22 | 50 | 39 | 50 | 42 | 33 | 8 | 6 | 969 |
| 2006 | 899 | 140 | 85 | 32 | 23 | 53 | 38 | 56 | 46 | 33 | 10 | 7 | 1,039 |
| 2007 | 935 | 152 | 90 | 35 | 23 | 55 | 36 | 61 | 50 | 33 | 11 | 7 | 1,088 |
| 2008* | 942 | 159 | - | - | - | - | - | - | - | - | - | - | 1,100 |
| 2009* | 933 | 155 | - | - | - | - | - | - | - | - | - | - | 1,087 |

Note. *Estimates. Adapted from EIM (2010).

innovative combinations, which in turn will attract new companies. Ethnic entrepreneurs can therefore help to set up this differentiated economy and contribute to its further growth as a result of their diversity.

## Development of the Number of Entrepreneurs in the Netherlands

The economic value of entrepreneurship can be recognized after starting up and hiring employees. In recent years, entrepreneurship has substantially increased among people of different migrant minority groups in the Netherlands. One out of five new businesses in the Netherlands is set up by a migrant entrepreneur. This group often works in the service sector and frequently delivers high-quality products. Ethnic entrepreneurs in the Netherlands can be categorized in two groups: Western immigrants originating from Europe (excluding Turkey), North America, Japan, Oceania, and Indonesia; and non-Western immigrants originating from Africa, Asia, South and Central America, and Turkey (i.e., not including Japan and Indonesia; EIM, 2007). The total number of businesses in the Netherlands continued to grow from 957,000 to 969,000 (843,000 native entrepreneurs, 76,000 Western entrepreneurs, 39,000 non-Western entrepreneurs) in the period 2000 to 2007 (see Table 15.1).

Table 15.1 shows that in the last decade, the number of non-Western ethnic firms has considerably increased. In particular, firms owned by the second generation have doubled from 5,000 firms in 2000 to 11,000 firms in 2007. This indicates that in the course of five years, there has been an increase of more than 50% in the second generation of ethnic entrepreneurs. They traditionally belong to large migrant groups of ethnic entrepreneurs from Morocco, Turkey, Suriname, the Antilles, and Aruba. The share of ethnic entrepreneurs of the first generation in the total number of entrepreneurs increased from 15% to 25% in the period from 2000 to 2009. The total number of ethnic entrepreneurs in the Netherlands continued to grow from 114,000 to 152,000 in the period from 2000 to 2007 (see table 15.1), mainly due to growth in the number of non-Western ethnic entrepreneurs. In 2007 more than 60,000 non-Western migrant entrepreneurs (first and second generation) started an enterprise in the Netherlands; this equates to 22,000 enterprises more than in 2000.

Table 15.2 shows that the largest group of both first- and second-generation immigrant entrepreneurs in the Netherlands originates from Turkey, with 12,300 Turkish firms in 2004, followed by Suriname, with 7,700 Surinamese firms in 2004, both groups are largely concentrated in Dutch urban areas. In the period from 1999 to 2004, the number of Moroccan entrepreneurs increased by 61%, the sharpest rise of any immigrant entrepreneurs, particularly within the younger generation. The number of Turkish and Antillean entrepreneurs also greatly increased in that period by 56% and 47%, respectively, and the number of Chinese and Surinamers grew by 32% and 27%, respectively (EIM, 2007).

*Table 15.2*  Number of Entrepreneurs (x 1,000) Specified by Country of Origin, First and Second Generation, 1999–2004

| Year | Turkey | Morocco | Netherlands/Antilles | Suriname | China/Hong Kong |
|------|--------|---------|----------------------|----------|-----------------|
| 1999 | 7.9 | 2.8 | 1.5 | 6.4 | 5.3 |
| 2000 | 9.2 | 3.3 | 1.8 | 7.1 | 5.7 |
| 2001 | 11.0 | 4.0 | 2.0 | 7.8 | 6.2 |
| 2002 | 11.5 | 4.3 | 2.1 | 7.9 | 6.2 |
| 2003 | 11.9 | 4.4 | 2.2 | 8.0 | 6.6 |
| 2004 | 11.8 | 4.6 | 2.1 | 7.7 | 7.0 |

*Note.* From EIM (2007).

## Distribution of Migrant Entrepreneurs in the Netherlands

Non-Western ethnic entrepreneurs are active in branches different than those in which native entrepreneurs work. Ethnic entrepreneurs, particularly first-generation immigrants, distinguish themselves by having a larger share than native-born, Surinamese or Antilleans entrepreneurs in traditional sectors: travel, clothing, hotel, and catering sectors are still most popular (Waldinger, 1996; EIM, 2007). However, the distribution of migrant entrepreneurs in the Netherlands has changed over a long period.

Table 15.3 shows that in the business world, there is a clear shift in migrant entrepreneurship of non-Western immigrants toward producer services in the service sector compared with 10 years ago. The share of non-Western migrant entrepreneurs in the retail, hotel, and catering industries has decreased in the last decade. This applies to all migrant groups, although there are some differences between the migrant groups concerned. When we look at the Turkish group, it is clear that the share of entrepreneurs working in the service sector is higher than the average. Moroccan and Antillean entrepreneurs have a lesser share in the retail sector. Chinese entrepreneurs have the highest share of entrepreneurs in this sector (EIM, 2004).

On the other hand, a growing number of second-generation migrant entrepreneurs have moved toward new sectors and have become more active in the CIs. This is a new trend in migrant entrepreneurship. The younger generation is more open and is seeking new opportunities outside the traditional sectors and geographical areas, that is, an external market orientation beyond their own ethnic group that might offer better opportunities to serve target groups outside the Moroccan niche. They are attracted to new business sectors, such as ICT, marketing, accountancy, global trade, real estate, consultancy, and leisure and recreation management agencies.

Thus, they want to expand into high-volume trade by engaging with indigenous entrepreneurs and other ethnic groups. Among the foreign entrepreneurs, the position of the second generation is much better

Table 15.3 Development of Sectoral Division, 2000–2007 (in %)

| Sectors | Native entrepreneurs | | Ethnic entrepreneurs | | Non-Western ethnic entrepreneurs | | | | Western ethnic entrepreneurs | | | | Total | |
|---|---|---|---|---|---|---|---|---|---|---|---|---|---|---|
| | | | | | First generation | | Second generation | | First generation | | Second generation | | | |
| | 2000 | 2007 | 2000 | 2007 | 2000 | 2007 | 2000 | 2007 | 2000 | 2007 | 2000 | 2007 | 2000 | 2007 |
| Agriculture/fishery | 17 | 13 | 3 | 3 | 2 | 2 | 2 | 1 | 2 | 3 | 5 | 3 | 16 | 11 |
| Energy/industry | 6 | 5 | 5 | 4 | 4 | 4 | 4 | 3 | 6 | 4 | 6 | 5 | 6 | 5 |
| Construction | 9 | 11 | 6 | 9 | 4 | 4 | 6 | 9 | 5 | 13 | 7 | 8 | 9 | 11 |
| Trade | 23 | 19 | 22 | 19 | 25 | 25 | 21 | 20 | 20 | 16 | 21 | 17 | 23 | 19 |
| Catering | 5 | 4 | 15 | 12 | 33 | 33 | 13 | 10 | 11 | 7 | 6 | 4 | 6 | 5 |
| Transport and communication | 5 | 4 | 4 | 4 | 4 | 4 | 6 | 8 | 4 | 3 | 5 | 3 | 5 | 4 |
| Financial institution | 2 | 2 | 2 | 4 | 1 | 1 | 2 | 3 | 2 | 3 | 3 | 6 | 2 | 6 |
| Business services | 17 | 22 | 21 | 23 | 14 | 14 | 23 | 25 | 25 | 26 | 24 | 29 | 18 | 22 |
| Health care/education/government | 7 | 7 | 9 | 9 | 7 | 6 | 6 | 9 | 11 | 10 | 11 | 10 | 7 | 7 |
| Other services | 9 | 10 | 11 | 12 | 7 | 7 | 15 | 13 | 14 | 15 | 12 | 13 | 9 | 10 |
| Total | 100 | 100 | 100 | 100 | 100 | 100 | 100 | 100 | 100 | 100 | 100 | 100 | 100 | 100 |

*Note.* Adapted from EIM (2010).

than that of the first generation because they have been educated in the Netherlands and also participate more intensively in Dutch society. This means they experience fewer barriers and problems than first-generation foreign entrepreneurs.

## The Geographical Business Location

For a long time, large Dutch urban and city areas have been places of settlement for major migrant groups of different national and cultural origins because of their agglomeration advantages (i.e., better business environment and availability of employment). This has now become an important strategic activity of modern cities (i.e., 'urban imperative'). Today, almost 9% of ethnic entrepreneurs (21% Western ethnic and 39% non-Western ethnic entrepreneurs) are concentrated in one particular city of the G4 in the Netherlands: Amsterdam. The number of ethnic entrepreneurs in the G4 increased much more than the number of indigenous entrepreneurs. Almost one in three entrepreneurs in the cities of Amsterdam, The Hague, and Rotterdam have an ethnic background, whereas in Utrecht less than one in four entrepreneurs was involved in ethnic entrepreneurial activities. However, the number of non-Western entrepreneurs was higher than the number of Western entrepreneurs, and the sharpest rise was particularly evident among second-generation non-Western entrepreneurs.

First-generation entrepreneurs are more concentrated in the ethnic enclaves in Rotterdam, The Hague, and Utrecht—where average house values are lower than in other districts—than the higher-educated young ethnic second and third generations. Most of these enterprises are small businesses, mainly oriented toward their own ethnic niche markets, that are characterized by low barriers to entry in terms of required capital and educational qualifications, an informal nature, less-formal ownership, small-scale production, high labor intensity, and low added value.

The development of the distribution of entrepreneurs in these metropolitan, industrial, and rural locations—which are characterized by a high degree of dynamism, knowledge, and creativity—changes and enhances the image of these areas as a major attraction force and strategy for economic growth. Thus, migrant entrepreneurship is a growing market that brings 'the world' into the neighborhood.

## CASE STUDY

Today, Moroccan entrepreneurs show the sharpest rise in terms of absolute numbers of all non-Western entrepreneurs. They also have a relatively high birthrate in the Netherlands. Many Moroccan entrepreneurs appear to have small businesses and are relatively young and active in small (ethnic) niches; however, they do not always have the expertise or know the right people to make the big step toward an external market orientation (break-out strategies).

The question we investigate is: What are the critical success or performance conditions for ethnic entrepreneurs?

## Young Moroccan Entrepreneurs in the Creative Sectors

To trace the opportunities for and barriers to these ethnic entrepreneurs, we recently conducted an in-depth field survey of a limited set of 24 ethnic entrepreneurs of Moroccan origin (8 females and 16 males). These were selected from a group of creative and innovative ethnic entrepreneurs in the G4 with a focus on their personal and business characteristics and on their motivation and driving forces, all of which could explain their entrepreneurship and business performance.

## Personal Characteristics: Age, Birthplace, and Education

The average age of the entrepreneurs of Moroccan origin who participated in the research is between 35 and 39 years; most are married and have children. The majority of the Moroccan entrepreneurs were born in Morocco and came to the Netherlands at the age of 12 or younger, where they achieved their educational qualifications: a high level of vocational education (HBO), university education (WO), or postdoctorate level. They speak both Dutch and English fluently. This group has mastered the language of the host country better than the first generation, is more highly qualified, and is better acquainted with the local labor market.

Depending on their age on arrival to the Netherlands (being younger than 12 years, the border between primary and secondary education) and their educational achievements in the Netherlands, the majority of the entrepreneurs fall into the second-generation category (see also Veenman, 1996; Masurel & Nijkamp, 2004).

## Motivation and Driving Forces

The majority of Moroccan entrepreneurs were students before they started their own business and because of their educational backgrounds were also partly active as entrepreneurs in a similar sector during their studies. However, this constituted more of a hobby, an interest which they pursued in their spare time. Thus, their experiences of entrepreneurs through their studies and employment motivated them to start their own businesses in similar sectors (i.e., because of market opportunities, sustainability, specialization, and high demand in that sector), mainly as a result of a desire to be independent and 'be their own bosses.' This shows that unemployment had not pushed the majority to become self-employed as a means of economic survival.

The majority of Moroccan entrepreneurs had no business plan or an inadequate business plan for the purposes of starting up their own business (lack of entrepreneurial qualifications). However, they used their own capital and experience, with some information from family and relatives, after first carefully analyzing market prospects. This demonstrates that these entrepreneurs are quite independent of their family or friends.

## Business Characteristics: Foundation Year and Enterprise Activities

Moroccan businesses are relatively young. The individuals concerned started their own small businesses after 2006 (a few go back to 2001), mostly as sole owners with less than five employees, within the ICT, consultancy, and research sectors. It is very interesting to observe that some Moroccan entrepreneurship goes back to 2001.

## Strategic Business Performance: Financial and Nonfinancial Advantages

Moroccan entrepreneurs experienced a positive development in their business performance results in 2008. They experienced both financial improvements (i.e., increase in sales and profit) and nonfinancial improvements (i.e., more innovative and high-quality products at a competitive price, better organization quality, good strategic marketing/promotion, and priority for sustainable development).

In order to stay ahead and remain competitive under various conditions, they have become very critical and use more formal practices. They regularly adapt their organizational growth strategies in response to market and economic conditions. This formal approach increases the focus on the management of the business which not only reflects today's increasingly diverse and dynamic business environment and also helps them monitor the firm's strategic response to this complexity.

## Composition of Employees: Customers, Employees, Sector

Moroccan entrepreneurs are not dependent on customers and labor from their own ethnic group in their business environment because they do not offer specifically ethnic products or services. This applies particularly to entrepreneurs in the ICT sector, where their products and services are not related to the needs of a particular ethnic group. The share of Moroccan clients is quite low, and the majority of the entrepreneurs mentioned that they preferred to hire skilled and ambitious employees without focusing on their ethnic backgrounds.

## Participation in Social Networks

The majority of the entrepreneurs make extensive use of their own social networks within their own ethnic groups through friendship and shared community of origin in their destination areas on a local level. These networks are used, among other things, for information, promotions, shared experiences, recruitment of cheap and loyal labor, cooperation, advice on the amount of crucial resources for their desired growth strategies, ownership of multiple businesses, and the expansion of their own network.

## CONCLUSION

The Netherlands is a remarkable example of an ethnically colorful country with strong multiculturalism, where migrant enterprises enrich society and people appreciate the added value of cultural differences. The rise of migrant entrepreneurship, in general, appears to have had a favorable effect on the economy of the Netherlands. Migrant entrepreneurship reflects different cultures and open-ended capacities for economic growth creation in cities and contributes to economic diversity. Different migrant groups and cultures can show a range of characteristics in terms of their driving force, motivation, performance, and the conditions for success.

An overall evaluation of immigrant entrepreneurship in the Netherlands highlights the changing trends of recent years. The new trends have emerged as (a) a new orientation to nontraditional sectors; (b) sectoral change in immigrant entrepreneurship, especially toward producer services; (c) an increasing number of second-generation immigrant entrepreneurs; and (d) an interest in the creative industry as a new market for innovative migrant entrepreneurs.

In general, second-generation Moroccan entrepreneurs are well educated and integrated in the Dutch community (i.e., they are very familiar with Dutch culture and speak the language fluently). Their excellent previous study and work experience in similar types of businesses, coupled with innovative and positive entrepreneurial attitude and motivation, means they have the ability to be involved in all areas of business activities and think from different perspectives in order to achieve their organizational objectives and innovations without adverse personal and financial consequences.

Thus, they have not faced extreme problems in terms of running their businesses that could impede growth and success in a challenging and dynamic business environment. However, they do have to tackle other problems (e.g., confusing and complex tax structure and overregulation) that are also commonly experienced by native Dutch entrepreneurs.

The most important variables, such as pronounced motivation, enthusiasm, and persistence; a strong reputation for the organization; the high quality of customized services; the ability to speak several languages; and higher result orientation all contribute to their success, improving the quality of management and processes and enabling the achievement of successful organizational results.

However, the majority of these entrepreneurs still make extensive use of the local, informal social networks with which they have a strong common interest (based on a sense of trust, tolerance, hope, and norms of reciprocity among the entrepreneurs). They see these informal networks as an important and central source of 'social capital' (see also Massey, 1988), which may confine their desire to grow their entrepreneurship solely within their 'melting pot' communities. Nevertheless, in the long run, the lack of formal commitments and expectations will result in a failure to meet the members' needs. This will not help to bridge the gaps that exist between the various ethnic entrepreneurs in their local social network and other formal networks, institutions, or groups in Dutch society (on local, regional, and national levels). Isolation, therefore, limits the formulation and implementation of breakout strategies. However, migrants are proud, work hard, offer good service, have loyal customers, and are always open to new markets.

Given the trends and growing importance of 'new and colorful entrepreneurship,' there is practical value in being able to identify their entrepreneurial characteristics. Insight into the entrepreneurial behavior of migrants is necessary to develop an urban business culture in which migrants are no longer a source of problems but are rather a source of great socioeconomic opportunities for both the migrant groups concerned and urban vitality. Strategic information will also be necessary for the development of a promising urban policy and will bring to light the kind of policy strategies that encourage the participation of traditionally less-privileged groups and improve their business performance potential. This has implications for various stakeholders such as other ethnic entrepreneurs, policy makers, and business investors in this dynamic and promising business environment.

## REFERENCES

Bates, T., Jackson, W. E., III, & Johnson, J. H., Jr. (2007). Introduction to the special issue on advancing research on minority entrepreneurship. *Annals of the American Academy of Political Science and Social Science, 613*, 10–17.

Borjas, G. J. (1986). The self-employment experience of immigrants. *Journal of Human Resources, 21*(4), 485–506.

Cormack, J., & Niessen, J. (2002). Supplier diversity: The case of immigrant and ethnic minority enterprises. Background paper prepared for the Transatlantic Round Table on Supplier Diversity, Brussels, 15 January 2002..

EIM (2004). *Monitor etnisch ondernemerschap 2004.* Onderzoek voor Bedrijf & Beleid, Zoetermeer: Ministerie van Economische Zaken.

EIM. (2006). *Internationale Benchmark Ondernemerschap 2005.* Zoetermeer: EIM Business and Policy Research.

EIM. (2007). *Global Entrepreneurship Monitor 2007.* Zoetermeer: The Netherlands Ministry of Economic Affairs.

EIM. (2010). Monitor vrouwelijk en etnisch ondernemerschap. Zoetermeer: The Netherlands Ministry of Economic Affairs.

European Commission (2010a). *European SMEs under Pressure – Annual Report on EU Small and Medium-sized enterprise 2009.* [http://ec.europa.eu/enterprise/policies/sme/facts-figures-analysis/performancereview/pdf/dgentr_annual_report2010_100511.pdf]

Fairlie, R. W., & Meyer, B. D. (1996). Ethnic and racial self-employment: Differences and possible explanations. *Journal of Human Resources, 31*(4), 757–793.

Florida, R. (2002). *The rise of the creative class.* New York: Basic.

Florida, R. (2003). Entrepreneurship, creativity and regional economic growth. In D. M. Hart, (Ed.), *The emergency of entrepreneurship policy.* Cambridge: Cambridge University Press.

Florida, R. (2004). *The flight of the creative class.* New York: Basic.

Hardin, G. (1974a). *Living on a lifeboat.* Bioscience, 24, 561-568.

Hardin, G. (1974b). *Lifeboat ethics: the case against helping the poor.* Psychology Today,8, 38-43.

Marshall, A. (1920). *Principles of economics.* London: Macmillan.

Massey, D. S. (1988). Economic development and international migration in comparative perspective. *Population and Development Review,* 14, 383–413.

Masurel, E., & Nijkamp, P. (2004). Differences between first-generation and second-generation ethnic start-ups: Implications for a new support policy. *Environment and Planning C: Government and Policy,* 22(5), 721–737.

Matheson, B. (2006). A culture of creativity: Design education and the creative industries. *Journal of Management Development,* 25(1), 55–64.

Peck, J. (2005). Struggling with the creative class. *International Journal of Urban and Regional Research,* 29(4), 740–770.

Scott, A. (2000). *The cultural economy of cities.* London: Sage.

Van Delft, H., Gorter, C., and Nijkamp, P. (2000). In search of ethnic entrepreneurship opportunities in the city: A comparative policy study. *Environment and Planning: Government and Policy,* 18, 429–451.

Van Light, I., & Bonacich, E. (1988). *Immigrant entrepreneurs: Koreans in Los Angeles.* Los Angeles: University of California Press.

Veenman, J. (1996). Keren de kansen? De tweede-generatie allochtonen in Nederland. Assen: Van Gorcum.

Waldinger, R. D. (1996). Still the promised city? African-Americans and new immigrants in postindustrial New York. Cambridge, MA: Harvard University Press.

Waldinger, R., McEvoy, D., &. Aldrich, H. (1990). Spatial dimensions of opportunity structures. In R. Waldinger, H. Aldrich, & R. Ward (Eds.), *Ethnic entrepreneurs: Immigrant business in industrial societies* (pp. 106–130). London: Sage.

Wennekers, S., Van Stel, A., Thurik, R., & Reynolds, P. (2005). Nascent entrepreneurship and the level of economic development. *Small Business Economics,* 24, 293–309.

# 16 Entrepreneurial Competences in the Creative Sector

## Empirical Evidence From Dutch Dance Teachers

*Enno Masurel & Sentini Grunberg*

## INTRODUCTION

The creative sector is one of the most important sectors today. Although this sector cannot be described in any detail here, a number of characteristics distinguish the people who represent this sector, such as individual creativity, skills, and talents. Furthermore, projects that follow each other in terms of time also characterizes the creative sector. Teaching dance constitutes one subsector of the creative sector. In this subsector we recognize the individual creativity that the dance teacher uses in his/her contact with the class, the necessary use of skills and talents in order to provide successful dance classes and participation in sequential projects.

This chapter focuses on the self-perceived importance of various generic entrepreneurial competences for dance teachers. It assesses the importance of these competences in the context of a creative industry. After a thorough review of the literature, six generic entrepreneurial competences were distinguished: need for achievement, self-efficacy, creativity, opportunity identification, risk-taking propensity, and proper management. On the basis of this literature study, a questionnaire was compiled with four propositions typifying each of the six competences. This questionnaire was completed by a group of Dutch dance teachers, and this process is described in the section on fieldwork. The results of the fieldwork are then presented and discussed. The chapter ends with conclusions and recommendations.

## ENTREPRENEURIAL COMPETENCES

Before we start to examine the six most important entrepreneurial competences, the question 'Who or what is an entrepreneur?' should be answered, as entrepreneurship comes in many forms (see, e.g., Austin, Stevenson, & Wei-Skillern, 2006; Gartner, 1989; and Westhead, Ucbasaran, & Wright, 2005). We decided to use a broad approach to entrepreneurship in this instance. This broad approach is a combination of the approaches developed by Shane and Venkataraman (2000) and Alvarez and Barney (2007).

In our view, entrepreneurship stands for the discovery, creation, and the exploitation of profitable opportunities. 'Discovery' refers to existing opportunities, and 'creation' to new opportunities. 'Exploitation' means effectively extracting value from these opportunities. 'Profitable' means that the opportunities have potential to deliver value. 'Opportunities' are the central element in our definition of entrepreneurship and can be seen as favorable situations that lead to something positive. In our list of entrepreneurial competences, we shall see that the identification of opportunities plays an important role.

In his seminal work, Schumpeter (1934) credited the entrepreneur with an important role in economic development: The entrepreneur is the innovator, and innovation is the strategic impulse to economic development. However, in the role of innovator, the entrepreneur meets difficulties that involve uncertainty: One lacks proper input for decision making because one has to take unknown paths; one feels reluctant to do something new; the environment reacts against the entrepreneur for doing something new. Certain people, nevertheless, do want to become entrepreneurs, and Schumpeter (1934) identified three reasons: the dream of founding a 'private kingdom' (which can be based on an endless variety of motives from spiritual ambition to mere snobbery); the will to conquer (the impulse to fight, to prove oneself superior to others, to succeed for the sake of succeeding); and the joy of creating (to get things done or simply to exercise one's energy and creative abilities).

Three aspects of entrepreneurship should be taken into account for this paper: Entrepreneurship is dealt with as an activity, not just for (small) business owners; many combinations of discovery, creation, and exploitation are possible; and profitability involves creating societal value, not necessarily only economic value (profits) but possibly also social value and ecological value. The latter indicates the importance of sustainable entrepreneurship. This can be defined as leading the organization in making balanced choices between profit, people, and planet (Masurel, 2007).

Many entrepreneurial competences can be detected in the literature (see in particular Shane, Locke, & Collins, 2003). We have deliberately chosen not discuss the differences and similarities between competences, motivations, success factors, and so on here. We regard competences as personal abilities to perform well as an entrepreneur. Based on a thorough literature review (which deliberately also covered older sources), the following six competences were found to be the most outstanding in having a positive influence on successful entrepreneurship, in the sense of enabling individuals to discover, create, and exploit profitable opportunities:

1. Need for achievement: the personal commitment of an individual to succeed in reaching a certain position (see, e.g., Hansemark, 2003; Lee & Tsang, 2001; McClelland, 1961).

2. Self-efficacy: the personal belief of an individual that set goals will be met (see, e.g., Bandura, 1993; Chen, Greene, & Crick, 1998; Hmieleski & Corbett, 2008; Kickul, Gundry, Barbosa, & Whitcanack, 2009).
3. Creativity: the ability of an individual to make something new out of nothing (see, e.g., S. Y. Lee, Florida, & Acs, 2004; Ward, 2004).
4. Opportunity identification: the ability of an individual to discover existing favorable circumstances and/or create new favorable circumstances (see, e.g., Gaglio & Katz, 2001; Puhakka, 2007; Stearns & Hills, 1996; Ucbasaran, Westhead, & Wright, 2009).
5. Risk-taking propensity: the ability of an individual to cope with the possibility of negative outcomes (see, e.g., Begley & Boyd, 1987; Douglas & Shepherd, 2000; Stearns & Hills, 1996; Stewart, Watson, J. C. Carland, & J. W. Carland, 1998).
6. Proper management: the ability of an individual to make the right decisions in order to reach his goals (see, e.g., J. W. Carland, Hoy, Boulton, & J. C. Carland, 1984; Ireland, Hitt, & Sirmon, 2003).

We are aware that these six competences are not mutually exclusive and that in a number of instances they even overlap. Other competences may also be considered (see, e.g., Shane et al., 2003). Each competence was measured with four relevant propositions (see the appendix).

## FIELDWORK: THE DUTCH DANCE TEACHERS

In his seminal work on the creative sector, Florida (2002) attributes three characteristics to people who operate in the creative class: creativity, autonomy, and flexibility. He lists a number of sectors that belong to the creative class, such as education, music, entertainment, and health care. One of the most popular definitions of creative industries today is provided by the UK Department for Culture, Media, and Sport (DCMS, 1998): "Those activities which have their origin in individual creativity, skill and talent and which have the potential for wealth and job creation through the generation and exploitation of intellectual property." Furthermore, working in projects that follow each other in time also characterizes the creative sector (e.g., in the form of campaigns; see Moeran, 2009). It is, however, beyond the scope of this paper to have an extensive discussion about the exact content of the creative sector.

Without a doubt, teaching dance involves individual creativity, skills, and talent. The fact that the dance teacher has to interact intensely with his/her class means that creativity is of the utmost importance. Dance classes are organized as sequential projects, which is also one of the characteristics of the creative sector.

The latter part of the definition by DCMS (1998) is focused on traditional aspects of entrepreneurship (wealth and job creation, intellectual property).

Today, the emphasis of entrepreneurship can also be placed on welfare aspects and sustainability. This emphasis particularly applies to teaching dance as this activity combines education, music, entertainment, and often health aspects (directly or indirectly). Dancing requires movement and therefore involves health aspects that have become even more important in recent times due to the increasing societal problem of obesity. All in all, this makes dance teachers (as representatives of the creative sector) perfectly suitable for investigation in terms of their entrepreneurial aspects.

According to Braaksma, De Jong, and Stam (2005), 15.0% of all private firms in the Netherlands belong to the creative sector. There is a sliding scale in relation to size: 69.5% are run by self-employed people without personnel (versus 53.6% overall in the private sector); 25.8% employ between 1 and 9 people (versus 37.6% overall); 4.3% employ between 10 and 99 people (versus 8.1% overall), and 0.4% employ 100 people or more (versus 0.7% overall). This shows that entrepreneurs representing the creative sector operate in relatively small units.

The arts sector is the core of the creative sector as defined by Braaksma et al. (2005) and encompasses both expressive and performing arts. This definition is in line with Florida (2002) and DCMS (1998). Arts occupy 18.8% of the Dutch creative sector, and dancing schools are part of the performing arts. Note that the term 'dancing school' (organization) is used in Braaksma et al. (2005), whereas the actual dance teacher (individual) is the subject of this chapter. Because our definition of entrepreneurship focuses on the activity, we chose to focus on the individual rather than the organization.

The exact market share of dancing schools or dance teachers in Dutch arts is not known. Additionally, it can be noted that the sector of teaching dance in the Netherlands is not clearly delineated. We therefore describe teaching dance in terms of its activities. To give a proper dance class, music must be chosen and the choreography must be prepared. To do this, it is important to know certain facts about the participants, such as their ages, their level of dancing ability, and the reasons they want to participate in this activity (i.e., the difference between a class for individuals who view dancing as a recreational activity and one for individuals who wish to pursue a professional dance career). In most cases, dance classes are divided into three parts: the class starts with a warm-up, the choreography is taught, and the class ends with a cooling-down session. A variety of modules are taught in dancing classes including sports, ballroom, Latin, street dance, kids, and wheelchair (FDO, 2010). The popular TV programs *Dancing With the Stars, So You Think You Can Dance* (in the Netherlands), and *Strictly Come Dancing* (in the United Kingdom) have increased the popularity of dancing and were also a consequence of its increasing popularity.

For our fieldwork among dance teachers in the Netherlands, several dance educational institutes, centers for the arts, sector organizations, dancing schools, and freelance dance teachers were approached by us via phone and e-mail. Our main request was that they present the hyperlink to our online questionnaire on their website or e-mail the hyperlink to the dance teachers known by them. This questionnaire contained the propositions about the six entrepreneurial competences plus questions about the demographics and the activities of the respondents. Ultimately, 103 dance teachers participated. The questionnaire was online for approximately five weeks (April 2009 to May 2009). After the questionnaire, respondents were given the option to participate in an in-depth interview. Not all the respondents completed the questionnaire in full. Therefore, we chose to work with the maximum number of respondents per item or combination of items, instead of identifying a subgroup of respondents who had answered all questions, in order to reach the highest level of reliability.

Of the respondents, 85.4% are female and 14.6% are male. At the time of answering the questionnaire, 44.2% of the respondents were under 30 years of age and 55.8% of the respondents were age 30 or older. 60.8% of the respondents had been a dance teacher for less than 10 years; 25.8% of the respondents had a university of applied sciences diploma for teaching dance, whereas 36.5% had no such diploma at all; 3.5% of the respondents had a diploma at an intermediate vocational level, 7.1% had a certificate, and 27.1% had another diploma in the field of teaching dance. Our respondents teach many different dance styles. It is significant that the majority of the respondents (22.6%) described their dance styles by choosing the 'other' category. This is probably a mix of existing dance styles, put together in a creative way by the dance teacher and/or on request by the class. Furthermore, seven different styles were mentioned: hip-hop/street dance (20.1%), jazz (17.6%), ballet (13.2%), modern (11.9%), salsa/Latin (6.9%), traditional dance/folk dance (4.4%), and ballroom (3.1%). Note that respondents were allowed to give more than one answer to the question regarding what kind of dance style they teach (on average 2.6 different dance styles were taught per teacher). Most dance teachers operate locally (19.5%) or regionally (53.7%), whereas the remainder (26.9%) operate nationally. It was found that the subsector of dance teachers in the Netherlands is mainly (but not exclusively) female, young, diverse, and local/regional.

In 2008, 90.2% of the respondents were active as dance teachers. Of all lessons given in 2008, 55.4% were given on a freelance basis, 25.8% in an employer/employee relationship, and 18.8% of all lessons were given under another regime (presumably mostly for free). Also in 2008, 67.6% of the respondents earned part of their income from teaching dance on a freelance basis, and 48.5% earned their full income as a dance teacher on a freelance basis. Less than half of the respondents (47.6%) had a so-called VAR declaration that is issued by the Dutch Tax Department to self-employed people without personnel. Slightly more than half of the respondents (53.0%) were registered with a subscription to the Chamber of Commerce. Only 7.5% of the respondents were also employers of other dance teachers, and 11.5%

of the respondents also supervised other dance teachers who worked for them as freelancers. So we see that self-employment without personnel is an important phenomena in the world of Dutch dance teachers.

## RESULTS

Our literature review revealed that the six main, general entrepreneurial competences are: need for achievement, self-efficacy, creativity, opportunity identification, risk-taking propensity, and proper management. Before we take a look at what the dance teachers themselves say about the entrepreneurial competences that best describe their personal situations, we will detail expert opinions on this subject.

The first expert (organization) we consulted was Kunstenaars&Co (see also the acknowledgement in this paper). Kunstenaars&Co has developed an online test for professionals in the creative sector (or as they call them, artists) to benchmark their entrepreneurial competences (i.e., to determine which are sufficiently developed and which need development). This test concerns 10 entrepreneurial competences:

1. Strong sense of one's identity
2. Reflection on one's own activities
3. Ability to develop artistic knowledge and skills
4. Perseverance
5. Communication
6. Collaboration with others
7. Customer orientation
8. Planning and organizing
9. Ability to get into the market
10. Societal engagement

We see that a number of the entrepreneurial competences we derived from the literature study are also included in the entrepreneurial competences identified by Kunstenaars and Company: the need for achievement corresponds to perseverance; self-efficacy corresponds to a strong sense of one's identity, customer orientation, and an ability to get into the market; proper management corresponds to reflection on one's own activities and planning and organizing. This means two of the competences from our literature study are not directly covered by the competences that have been identified by Kunstenaars: risk-taking propensity and creativity. These differences between the literature survey and the insights of Kunstenaars and Company may be the result of having different ideas about entrepreneurial competences and due to the fact that Kunstenaars&Co deals specifically with what they call 'artists' in the creative sector, whereas the literature review contained general information on entrepreneurs.

Next, six experts were interviewed to investigate which entrepreneurial competences these experts recognize in dance teachers specifically. Two of the experts were from the field of entrepreneurship and four experts were from the field of dance. The expert interviews had a qualitative approach. The experts emphasized that entrepreneurial dance teachers know their market and consequently know where their customers are (in line with the general competence of opportunity identification); they are aware of their own qualities and know how to sell their services (in line with need for achievement); they pay attention to the organizational aspects of their profession (in line with proper management); and they have the courage to step out of their comfort zone and dare to take risks (in line with risk-taking propensity and self-efficacy). The expert interviews demonstrated, somewhat unexpectedly, that creativity (one of the entrepreneurial competences from our literature study) is not particularly important to dance teachers. Again, the explanation for the difference from the literature review may be that the literature contained general information on entrepreneurs, whereas the experts were asked to deal with dance teachers specifically. Both the expert interviews and the list by Kunstenaars&Co more or less denied the importance of creativity or simply took it for granted.

Nevertheless, we continued our analysis using the six main entrepreneurial competences. All six entrepreneurial competences from our literature study were translated into four propositions. The respondents were then asked to indicate to what extent these propositions described their personal situation. The answers were presented on a 5-point Likert scale, split into 'fully disagree' (score 1), 'disagree' (score 2), 'neither disagree nor agree' (score 3), 'agree' (score 4), and 'fully agree' (score 5).

In table 16.1 the averages and standard deviations concerning the six entrepreneurial competences derived from our literature review are presented. First, we observe (in the third column) that all competences show a rather low standard deviation, which indicates that it is possible to work with the averages. We used the one-tail test (where $p < .05$) for the differences between the competences.

Looking at the averages (see the second column) it transpires that, in the eyes of the dance teachers themselves, self-efficacy best describes their personal situation (with a score of 3.91 on a range from 1 to 5). The score on this competence is significantly higher than the scores on all other five competences (see the fourth column). Then we have proper management, with a score of 3.55. This competence does not score significantly higher than need for achievement, but it does score significantly higher than the remaining three competences (see the fifth column). Need for achievement comes in at third place (score 3.48); it does not score significantly higher than opportunity identification but does score substantially higher than the remaining two competences (see the sixth column). Opportunity identification comes in fourth place (score 3.36) but does not score significantly higher than the remaining two competences (see the seventh column).

*Table 16.1*  Entrepreneurial Competences of Dutch Dance Teachers

| Competences | Mean | SD | S.E. | P.M. | nACH | O.I. | R.T.P. | CR. |
|---|---|---|---|---|---|---|---|---|
| Self-efficacy | 3.91 | 0.91 | - | | | | | |
| Proper management | 3.55 | 1.11 | 0.00* | - | | | | |
| Need for achievement | 3.48 | 1.21 | 0.00* | 0.15 | - | | | |
| Opportunity identification | 3.36 | 1.22 | 0.00* | 0.01* | 0.06 | - | | |
| Risk-taking propensity | 3.35 | 1.06 | 0.00* | 0.09* | 0.03* | 0.46 | - | |
| Creativity | 3.33 | 1.06 | 0.00* | 0.00* | 0.01* | 0.39 | 0.42 | - |

Note. *Significant at 5% level.

Risk-taking propensity (score 3.35) takes fifth place but does not score significantly higher than the final competence, creativity (score 3.33; see the eighth column).

## DISCUSSION

Hence, on the one hand, we see that the entrepreneurial competences from our literature review all apply to this subsector of the creative sector (dance teachers), as the scores are all above neutral (> 3.0). On the other hand, we also see a sequence of entrepreneurial competences that are apparently typical for Dutch dance teachers, which typifies the specific effect of the context in which they are operating. Note again, this is based on the perception of the dance teachers themselves, in terms of to what extent the competences best describe their personal situation.

Self-efficacy is seen as the competence that best describes their personal situation. This may be because the environment in which the dance teachers operate is constantly changing. Each dance lesson can be seen as an event in itself, and each has to be planned ahead with the participants (and often with the physical environment) in mind. Two scores in particular look very typical: the second place of proper management (high) and the last place of creativity (low). The combination of creative professionals in general, and dance teachers specifically, and the entrepreneurial competence proper management is not obvious at first sight: Creative professionals and dance teachers are not specifically known for their managerial skills. However, planning, preparation, administration, and renewal apply perfectly well to dance teachers, in their own opinion. This may be because we are talking about small business units with administrations that are easily managed. Or could we be dealing with a certain prejudice against the creative sector?

Furthermore, one would expect that creativity merits a higher score than the last place it currently has because creativity would seem to be a core aspect of teaching dance. The ability to inspire the class and the choreography in a physical environment calls for creative solutions. However, the last place of creativity does confirm the aforementioned list by Kunstenaars&Co and the expert interviews, which even suggested the absence of creativity entirely. Perception may play an important role here, both by the experts and by the dance teachers themselves, as the role of creativity in the daily work of dance teachers cannot be denied. Apparently, being creative is so normal for dance teachers that they do not see it as really describing their personal situation; they seem to take it for granted. So in a sense, they would seem to underestimate the innovative character of their work. Need for achievement, opportunity identification, and risk-taking propensity have scores in the middle of the range, and this is not particularly surprising.

## CONCLUSION

Teaching dance is one illustrative subsector of the increasingly important creative sector. Nevertheless, hardly anything is known about the entrepreneurial competences of professionals in the creative sector in general and about the entrepreneurial competences of dance teachers specifically. This chapter has shed light on this underresearched subject. After a thorough literature review, six generic entrepreneurial competences were derived, namely, need for achievement, self-efficacy, creativity, opportunity identification, risk-taking propensity, and proper management. All six competences were each expressed in terms of 4 propositions, and these 24 propositions were included in a questionnaire, along with questions about personal and professional characteristics. A group of Dutch dance teachers then answered this questionnaire, indicating what best described their personal situation. In this way we were able to determine the importance of these competencies in the context of the dance-teaching subsector. The first finding from the fieldwork was that the subsector of dance teachers is mainly female, young, diverse, and local/regional. Furthermore, self-employment without personnel appeared to be an important characteristic of dance teachers.

All six entrepreneurial competences apply to this subsector of the creative sector, in the eyes of the dance teachers who responded. The competence self-efficacy scored significantly above the rest. Next came proper management and need for achievement. The lowest scores were obtained by opportunity identification, risk taking, and creativity (in descending order). The high score of proper management and the low score of creativity are most eye-catching. Planning, preparation, administration, and renewal apply very well to the dance teachers, in their own opinions. This could be related to the small scale on which they operate, with administrations that are easily managed, or could have more to do with a certain prejudice against the creative sector. Perception may play an important role in the low score on creativity, as creativity is so 'normal' for dance teachers that they take it for granted and do not see it as describing their personal situation. This low score on creativity, however, was confirmed by the expert interviews.

These conclusions demand additional research on the reasons behind this ranking of entrepreneurial competences in the subsector of dance teachers. The difference between self-perception and external observation may also be considered as a future research subject. Furthermore, similar research could be undertaken in other subsectors of the creative sector to find out whether (or not) dance teachers and other professionals are special cases and subsequently assess the influence of context. The latter research could also form the basis of a tailor-made tool for different groups of entrepreneurs within the creative sector.

## ACKNOWLEDGMENT

This research project was made possible by Kunstenaars&Co, the Dutch organization that stimulates and supports artists and cultural organizations in terms of professionalism and development toward improved economic results.

## REFERENCES

Alvarez, S. A., & Barney, J. B. (2007). Discovery and creation: Alternative theories of entrepreneurial action. *Strategic Entrepreneurship Journal, 1*(1), 11–26.

Austin, J., Stevenson, H., & Wei-Skillern, J. (2006). Social and commercial entrepreneurship: Same, different or both? *Entrepreneurship Theory and Practice, 30*(1), 1–22.

Bandura, A. (1993). Perceived self-efficacy in cognitive development and functioning. *Educational Psychologist, 28*(2), 117–148.

Begley, T. M., & Boyd, D. P. (1987). Psychological characteristics associated with performance in entrepreneurial firms and smaller businesses. *Journal of Business Venturing, 2*(1), 79–93.

Braaksma, R.M., J.P.J. de Jong, and E. Stam (2005) Creatieve bedrijvigheid in Nederland: Structuur, ontwikkeling en innovatie, Zoetermeer: EIM. [Creative activity in the Netherlands: Structure, development and innovation]

Carland, J. W., Hoy, F., Boulton, W., & Carland J. C. (1984). Differentiating entrepreneurs from small business owners: A conceptualization. *Academy of Management Journal, 9*(2), 354–359.

Chen, C. C., Greene, P. G., & Crick, A. (1998). Does entrepreneurial self-efficacy distinguish entrepreneurs from managers? *Journal of Business Venturing, 13*(4), 295–316.

DCMS (1998). *Creative industries mapping document.* Department of Culture, Media and Sport. Retrieved from: http://www.culture.gov.uk/creative/creative_industries.html. (June 2009)

Douglas, E. Y., & Shepherd, D. A. (2000). Entrepreneurship as a utility maximizing response. *Journal of Business Venturing, 15*(3), 231–251.

FDO (2010). Retrieved from: http://www.dansleraar.com (Feburary 2010)

Florida, R. (2002). *The rise of the creative class*. New York: Basic.

Gaglio, C. M., & Katz, J. A. (2001). The psychological basis of opportunity identification: Entrepreneurial alertness. *Small Business Economics, 16*(2), 95–111.

Gartner, W. B. (1989). 'Who is an entrepreneur?' is the wrong question. *Entrepreneurship Theory and Practice, 13*(1), 47–67.

Hansemark, O. C. (2003). Need for achievement, locus of control and the prediction of business start-ups: A longitudinal study. *Journal of Economic Psychology, 24*(3), 301–319.

Hmieleski, K. M., & Corbett, A. C. (2008). The contrasting interaction effects of improvisational behavior with entrepreneurial self-efficacy on new venture performance and entrepreneur work satisfaction. *Journal of Business Venturing, 23*(4), 482–496.

Ireland, R. D., Hitt, M. A., & Sirmon, D. G. (2003). A model of strategic entrepreneurship: The constructs and its dimensions. *Journal of Management, 29*(6), 963–989.

Kickul, J., Gundry, L. K., Barbosa, S. D., & Whitcanack, L. (2009). Intuition versus analysis? Testing different models of cognitive style on entrepreneurial self-efficacy and the new venture creation process. *Entrepreneurship Theory and Practice, 33*(2), 439–453.

Lee, D. Y., & Tsang, E. W. K. (2001). The effects of entrepreneurial personality background and network activities on venture growth. *Journal of Management Studies, 38*(4), 583–602.

Lee, S. Y., Florida, R., & Acs, Z. J. (2004). Creativity and entrepreneurship: A regional analysis of new firm formation. *Regional Studies Association, 38*(8), 879–891.

McClelland, D. C. (1961). *The achieving society*. Princeton, NJ: Van Nostrand.

Masurel, E. (2007). Why SMEs invest in environmental measures: Sustainability evidence from small and medium-sized printing firms. *Business Strategy and the Environment, 16*(3), 190–201.

Moeran, B. (2009). The organization of creativity in Japanese advertising production. *Human Relations, 62*(7), 963–985.

Puhakka, V. (2007). Effects of opportunity discovery strategies of entrepreneurs on performance of new ventures. *Journal of Entrepreneurship, 16*(1), 19–51.

Schumpeter, J. A. (1934). *The theory of economic development*. Cambridge, MA: Harvard University Press.

Shane, S., Locke, E. A., & Collins, C. J. (2003). Entrepreneurial motivation. *Human Resource Management Review, 13*(2), 257–279.

Shane, S., & Venkataraman, S. (2000). The promise of entrepreneurship as a field of research. *Academy of Management Review, 25*(1), 217–226.

Stearns, T. M, & Hills, G. E. (1996). Entrepreneurship and new firm development: A definitional introduction. *Journal of Business Research, 36*(1), 1–4.

Stewart, W. H., Watson, W. E., Carland, J. C., & Carland, J. W. (1998). A proclivity for entrepreneurship: A comparison of entrepreneurs, small business owners, and corporate managers. *Journal of Business Venturing, 14*(2), 189–214.

Ucbasaran, D., Westhead, P., & Wright, M. (2009). The extent and nature of opportunity identification by experienced entrepreneurs. *Journal of Business Venturing, 24*(2), 99–115.

Ward, T. B. (2004). Cognition, creativity and entrepreneurship. *Journal of Business Venturing, 19*(2), 173–188.

Westhead, P., Ucbasaran, D., & Wright, M. (2005). Decisions, actions, and performance: Do novice, serial, and portfolio entrepreneurs differ? *Journal of Small Business Management, 43*(4), 393–417.

APPENDIX

## Questions on the Entrepreneurial Competences

All six entrepreneurial competences from our literature study were each translated into four propositions. The respondents were asked to tick the answer that best described their personal situation on a 5-point Likert scale. This included 'fully disagree' (score 1), 'disagree' (score 2), 'neither disagree nor agree' (score 3), 'agree' (score 4), and 'fully agree' (score 5).

### 1. Need for achievement

I am dissatisfied when I have not reached my targets.
I feel motivated to make a difference in society.
Even if I am told something is impossible, I will succeed.
I think it is terrible when I don't succeed in things that are important for me.

### 2. Self-efficacy

When I get what I want, it is mostly because I worked hard for it.
My life is mainly determined by my own actions.
I am able to reach most goals I have set myself.
I often give others the initiative to start new projects.

### 3. Creativity

I often improvise choreography on the spot.
I am able to convert problems into opportunities.
When my agenda is full and another assignment comes in, I still accept it.
I often think about new ways to handle problems.

### 4. Proper management

I plan things far ahead.
Before I start an assignment I think broadly about the relation between hours and income.
I keep financial records.
I set new targets regularly.

### 5. Risk-taking propensity

I do not step into a situation if I cannot judge the end result.
I tolerate unexpected changes.

I don't like to make decisions in uncertain situations.
If I want to achieve something in which I have to invest money, I will
  do it.

### 6. *Opportunity identification*

I do not really look for new target groups to whom I can offer my
  lessons.
When a dance style is popular, I will not adapt it quickly.
I am constantly looking for original ways to give my dance lessons.
I am often looking for new places in which to offer my dance
  lessons.

# 17 Entrepreneurship and Science-Based Venturing

## The Case of Vaccine Development

*Esther Pronker, Ab Osterhaus, Eric Claassen, and Willem Hulsink*

## INTRODUCTION

A major challenge in every science- and technology-driven industry is the continuous development of novel products, concepts, and designs based on new scientific achievements. It requires a bridging of the gap between the organizations that conduct fundamental and applied research (universities, academic hospitals, research institutes, and industrial research departments) and those that develop them (existing and newly created companies). Apart from the generation of new knowledge and its effective transfer to business and society (i.e., commercializing scientific discoveries), science-based venturing includes distinctive roles that have to be taken by scientists, entrepreneurs, and small and large businesses.

This chapter addresses the phenomenon of science-based venturing in a biomedical field. It outlines the academic and business context that shapes research on viral infectious diseases and the development of vaccines and the strategic interaction between universities, small and young firms, and established companies. Fuelled by a series of scientific breakthroughs in the second half of the 20th century, the life-sciences sector has rapidly expanded and has successfully developed itself into an engine of economic growth. Moreover, considering technology push (new scientific breakthroughs, e.g., from stem cell research), market pull (aging population, quality of life) and business need (new products to sustain and boost turnover in the pharmaceutical and biotechnology industries), the life-sciences sector promises to develop even further in the decades ahead of us.

The societal and economic value of research, development, and the diffusion of preventive vaccines goes beyond measurement, and the effective application of immunization strategies cannot be ignored. In the words of Andrew (2001, 2206): "It is undeniable that the use of vaccines has prevented more premature deaths, permanent disability and suffering, in all regions of the world, than any other medical discovery or intervention." Immunization strategies are considered highly effective in targeting a plethora of external pathogens and also having the potential to prevent or even cure chronic infections, allergic conditions, autoimmune diseases, and cancer

(Andre, 2002). The effectiveness of this intervention can be attributed to the fact that it employs the host's own immune system to attain protection. This feature is inherent to the technology and distinguishes vaccines from other pharmaceutical products. Among the various techniques available for immunization, active vaccination is the most common. Given their impact on public health, vaccines form an inevitable part of our future. Currently, more than 900 international vaccine projects are underway internationally, each requiring an investment in the order of U.S. $200 to U.S. $900 million. It has been estimated that each vaccine development project takes about 10 years to complete from preclinical phase to approval, and no more than 22% will attain market approval (Struck, 1996).

This chapter aims to explore the different roles scientists, entrepreneurs, and managers of small and large firms play in advancing the health and life sciences, and applies this with a special focus on vaccine development. We provide a general description of the academic and business context to illustrate the holistic and complex nature of drug development, as well as the distinctive roles that scientists, entrepreneurs, and small and large firms play in the chain of activities from discovery to market. The chapter is divided into two main sections. It begins with a theoretical explanation of science-based venturing and knowledge transfer, including historical accounts of Louis Pasteur and Fritz Hoffmann, to delineate the division between the roles of inventor and entrepreneur. It then zooms in on the captivating world of the vaccine research and development value chain and concludes by defining the current state of vaccine development and the actors and issues that influence it.

## SCIENCE-BASED VENTURING: ENTREPRENEURSHIP, KNOWLEDGE TRANSFER, AND INNOVATION

The three building blocks of science-based venturing are invention, knowledge transfer, and entrepreneurship. In this section we will focus on the different roles that can be distinguished in bringing new ideas to the market: the role of researchers, the role of liaison officers and other transfer professionals, and the contribution of entrepreneurs and their small or large firms. Starting with the profiles of academic inventors, Stokes (1997) came up with a clear and useful 2 x 2 matrix through which he mapped the efforts of scientists. This included they type of research they do (i.e., basic research, more applied R&D, or both) and the extent to which scientists take the interests of users, sponsors, and other stakeholders (us) into account while carrying out their research (from no involvement to user-inspired basic research to pure applied research). By mapping the scientists' considerations of us (yes/no) and the quest for fundamental basic research understanding (yes/no), Stokes generated four quadrants: from basic research that is performed without any thought being given to practical ends (an example is the physicist Niels Bohr), to user-oriented basic research capturing the benefits from new scientific knowledge and applying them effectively (a clear case of this is Louis Pasteur), to pure applied research that hops from one experimental project to another (Thomas Edison). The 2 x 2 matrix is completed by the 'bird-watching' quadrant in which no real question for fundamental understanding is present and where a (potential) consideration of use is absent, that is, watching birds just for the fun of it. Basic research is directed toward a more complete understanding of nature; it embarks upon the unknown, attempting to enlarge the realm of the possible. Applied research concerns itself with the elaboration and application of the 'known' and aims to convert the possible into the actual by systematically adapting research findings into useful materials, methods, and processes. Pasteur combined the extreme poles of the research spectrum by doing basic research and laboratory work in the domains of crystallography, biochemistry, and immunology with real-world utility potential (i.e., by developing preventive vaccines), but he never lost sight of the desire to advance scientific understanding.

For new knowledge to be effective and for the efforts of scientists and inventors to have an impact, the gap between knowledge generation and its application in the market place or society must be bridged. For that purpose, a working relationship between inventors and researchers on the one hand and entrepreneurs, established firms, and consumer (patient) groups on the other has to established. Knowledge transfer involves the development of an idea from a (public or private) laboratory into a commercial product, in this case involving the transfer of people, knowledge, know-how, and practices from a university or research establishment to industry and society. The key mechanisms in technology transfer are cooperative extension and outreach to business and society on one side and patenting, licensing, and spin-off creation on the other (Postlewait, Parker, & Zilberman, 1993). Whereas the former focuses on the development and dissemination of publicly available technologies (notably in the agricultural domain), the latter is aimed at making money from the inventions of public or corporate researchers through the sale of patents, licensing, and royalty payments, and equity in spin-off companies. In the former case, there is a strong belief in the free dissemination of knowledge, for instance, through publishing, consulting, and collaboration between university and industry scientists, and the idea of appropriating and commercializing intellectual property is opposed. In the latter case, alternatively, private gains from academic research are sought and secrecy requirements to protect proprietary information are met; the university starts licensing its intellectual property rights (IPR) in exchange for cash, (future) sponsored research, or equity (i.e., taking shares in new ventures).

Smith and Miner (1983) developed a typology of entrepreneurs and their businesses on the basis of the motivations and the management styles of the business owners and the types of firm they establish and run. Initially, they identified the 'craftsman' and the 'opportunistic entrepreneur,' as well as the organizational vehicles with which they are associated and the respective rigid and adaptive firm structures. The craftsman is characterized by limited education and training, low social awareness, difficulty interacting in the social environment, and a short-term perspective. The opportunistic entrepreneur is the polar opposite, having a broad education, high social involvement, the confidence in his or her ability to deal with the social environment, and an orientation toward the future. Smith and Miner (1983), together with Bracker (1992), later identified a third category, the inventor-entrepreneur, who focuses on obtaining patents and making new products. Whereas the craftsman is in the business of making a better product and the opportunistic entrepreneur is trying to build a better company, the inventor-entrepreneur lives to invent; his or her sole purpose in doing business is to discover new things, obtain patents, and generate new products.

Successful innovation requires a collective effort in bringing together people, ideas, and objects that were previously separate, and also when it comes to effective networking among heterogeneous ties spanning various markets and technologies. One successful strategy is combining what they already know and recombining existing ideas and practices from other industries and innovators (Hargadon, 2003). Edison, for instance, owed his success not so much to his ability to build something out of nothing but rather to the way he managed to exploit his network, borrow the ideas of others, and incorporate and recombine them in his breakthrough innovations. Edison is an example of a technology broker, someone who links otherwise disconnected communities in an attempt to maximize their range of connections. By doing so, a technology broker is in a better position to be the first to see how people, ideas, and objects from one world may provide valuable solutions in another.

## VACCINE DEVELOPMENT IN THE 19TH CENTURY: THE SCIENTIST AND THE ENTREPRENEUR

The emerging biomedical industry in the 19th century was shaped by scientists such as Louis Pasteur and entrepreneurs such as Fritz Hoffmann. Some of the smaller businesses turned themselves into large pharmaceutical companies (e.g., Hoffmann-La Roche) and created a value chain running from invention/discovery to actual testing and the usage of medical treatments.

### Louis Pasteur

Whereas some scientists like Bohr, Darwin, and Einstein saw science and politics as rather separate spheres and never engaged much in combining their scientific and technological activities with education and/or selling it to the larger public, the microbiologist Pasteur saw science, politics, and technology as one tightly woven whole. He combined his dedication to science with aggressive self-promotion and a strong defense against critics, stating that his work had a real impact on society (Latour, 1988; Robbins, 2001). Although Pasteur was involved in some commercial activities during his career (he did patent but did not establish a firm), he showed truly entrepreneurial behavior though his fundraising activities and the fact that he addressed the needs of sick people, farmers, and the beer and wine industry directly. Furthermore, together with others, Pasteur established a new private research institution that carries his name.

In the early days of Pasteur's research career, his focus was on crystallizing chemical structures, a technique that subsequently proved to be of major importance in alcoholic fermentation and drug design processes. After having read about beverage contamination, his research moved away from crystals and shifted toward the role of microorganisms in fermentation, with special reference to wine and beer, before carrying out his well-known studies into infectious diseases in animals and humans (e.g., anthrax and rabies). His research was triggered by a curiosity to solve specific scientific puzzles concerning microbes or germs as agents of fermentation but also as agents of disease. He was also driven to articulate the needs and solve the problems of farmers, textile manufacturers, veterinarians, beer brewers, wine growers, doctors, and their patients.

At the Ecole Normale Superieure, Pasteur put together an extensive and multidisciplinary research team that sought to develop vaccines for chicken cholera, rabies, anthrax, and a score of other diseases. For this purpose, he mobilized the necessary financial resources and obtained funds from the national government and agricultural societies. As an academic researcher, Pasteur had an aggressive concern for his scholarly contributions and intellectual property and, to a large extent, he succeeded in keeping the method by which he had produced his vaccines private (Geison, 1995). Pasteur had also taken out several patents for his methods of manufacturing and preserving wine, vinegar, and beer, and for the vaccines against anthrax and other livestock diseases. He used the royalties from these patents to fund more of his research and build up a pension scheme. Although he had an interest in patenting his methods, treatments, and preventive vaccines, Pasteur was not motivated to commercialize his scientific discoveries and treatments any further, for instance, by manufacturing and selling vaccines himself or through a new company in which he would have a substantial share (Geison, 1995).

Pasteur was able to link his work on microbes to the interests of clients and stakeholders, using his microbiology laboratory and public demonstrations of the anthrax and rabies vaccines to fuse the interests of the stakeholders with his own drive to advance science and uncover the truth. For Pasteur, this would have been the ultimate source of the power a scientist has over society, in line with Latour's (1983) paraphrasing of Archimedes: "Give me a laboratory and I will raise the world" (p. 141). In 1888 a grand research center in Paris was founded as a center for education and research on infectious diseases. Initially, this Pasteur Institute relied upon private donations from all over the world and the royalties from Pasteur's patents, but at a later stage, when the patent revenues declined, the institute became increasingly dependent on state support (Geison, 1995).

## Fritz Hoffmann-La Roche

Unlike Pasteur, who gave us the method of pasteurization (preventing wine and beer from spoiling), a number of preventive vaccines, and a large and internationally well-known research institute in his name, Fritz Hoffmann's fame and recognition lies in the fact that he established an internationally top-ranking life-sciences company and made a fortune during his entrepreneurial career (Wanner, 1968). His family had made its fortune in textile manufacturing and trading and provided him the necessary contacts and financial support he needed at the beginning of his business career. Without any formal training in pharmacology, Hoffmann entered the pharmaceutical industry in 1893 when he joined the pharmaceutical merchant Droguerie. Much to the surprise of the Droguerie's owners and managers, Hoffmann, together with his colleague Carl Traub, spotted an opportunity for in-house development of drugs and expressed their interest in buying out the company's laboratory. In 1894, Hoffmann, Traub, and Company was established; Hoffmann took care of manufacturing and selling a small range of pharmaceutical and chemical products, his father supplied the majority of the start-up capital, and Traub provided the patents.

A few years later, Traub and Hoffmann agreed to break up their business. With financial support from his family, Hoffmann effectively managed to take over and relaunched it as Hoffmann-La Roche and Company in 1898. Hoffmann modernized the business by extending small-batch manufacturing into mass-scale industrial production, pursuing a proactive sales policy (by simultaneously targeting the larger public, chemists, and doctors), and establishing a network of sales agents and distributors throughout Europe and the United States. In early 1900, the company started to shift its research strategy from extracting natural products to synthesizing compounds. Hoffman-La Roche's products were already internationally available; the cough syrup Sirolin, Tubunic, and the flu treatment for the 1918 epidemic sold particularly well. To obtain more money to recover from World War I and proactively invest in R&D, innovation, and geographical expansion, Hoffmann-La Roche went public in 1919. In the same year, Hoffmann retired from the company's board due to ill health, and he passed away one year later. In the 1920 and 1930s the company had started with the large-scale production of various vitamin preparations and by the 1950s and 1960s had begun introducing tranquilizers, such as Valium and Rohypnol.

Whereas Pasteur was more of an inventor/scientist, Hoffmann was an innovator/entrepreneur who explored and exploited opportunities: He put new discoveries into practical use and brought his pharmaceutical products to the market. Hoffmann was particularly interested in product promotion and paid attention to the whole value chain, from encouraging research and looking into the patentability of a discovery to transforming the invention into a market innovation, producing and packaging it, and advertising and selling it to pharmacists. He also established an international network of businesses supplying the raw materials needed and the relevant sales contacts for his end products. Moreover, he can be considered a pioneer in large-scale manufacturing through standardizing packaging and preserving batch quality.

## TODAY'S VALUE CHAIN FOR VACCINE DEVELOPMENT

After discussing the distinctive scientific profiles and different entrepreneurial styles and providing two illustrative cases showing what it means to be an inventor and entrepreneur in the health and life sciences, this second section describes the context of vaccine development in current times. First, the concept of the vaccine development chain is described, introducing several contextual factors that potentially influence the cost and length of product development. Vaccines can be distinguished from other pharmaceutical products on the basis of the inherent feature of the intervention technology: It employs the host's own immune system to attain protection. Second, the value chain of vaccine drug development is evaluated with the actual and potential contributions from scientists, entrepreneurs, and firms in mind: What are/could be their roles in advancing, promoting, and commercializing effective treatments for infectious diseases?

To start, one has to understand the importance of the technology within the vaccine value chain. Epidemiology is the study of factors that influence the spread and control of diseases. It is a macrolevel factor in light of the fact that viral infectious diseases are not geographically isolated and their spread is difficult to predict. The influenza epidemic is a perfect example of this. Influenza is a seasonal viral infection that spreads and causes local epidemics during the colder months of the year—autumn, winter, and spring. It has been estimated that during such a seasonal outbreak, 5% to 20% of the population can be infected, and a substantial percentage of these people develop influenza and stay at home for an average of 3 to 5 days (Keech & Beardsworth, 2008). In most cases, the body's own immune system is capable of clearing the virus; however, certain severe and sometimes lethal manifestations and complications can arise, particularly in high-risk groups. These groups include the very young, elderly, and immune-compromised individuals (Lagacé-Wiens, Rubinstein, & Gumel, 2010).

The societal burden of seasonal influenza is measured in terms of its financial impact, caused by issues such as patient and caretaker absenteeism and a significantly increased demand on medical resources. As a result, in the Unites States alone the annual economic impact of influenza epidemics can reach U.S. $87 billion (Keech & Beardsworth, 2008). This figure is significantly reduced through introducing influenza vaccines and other antiviral compounds. In case of an influenza pandemic, fighting the infection becomes an internationally coordinated event by the World Health Organization (WHO). The latest pandemic originated in Mexico during the first half of 2009, and the economic burden for this country alone was estimated at U.S. $57 million a day (Lagacé-Wiens et al., 2010). The H1N1 virus, which causes swine influenza (called the Mexican flu in some countries), was considered harmful because, in addition to the classic high-risk groups, individuals with no increased risk developed serious complications and died from the infection. In case of a pandemic threat, it is crucial that the pharmaceutical industry responds quickly and provides an accurate vaccine product for immunization. When it comes to designing a vaccine against a pandemic threat, WHO collaborating centers provide reference seed viruses. These are subsequently used by the pharmaceutical industry for production of the vaccine. Fierce competition arises as each firm wants to be the first in the market with the vaccine product. In the European Union, the most important vaccine producers during the pandemic vaccination campaign were GSK and Novartis producing Pandemrix and Focetria, respectively. The pharmaceutical value chain unifies all pharmaceutical and biotechnological product research and development, including vaccines, as a common factor. Once a target compound has been identified, it enters a linear development path that eventually results in a commercial product. Development consists of a series of chronological phases governed by national and international legislation (see table 17.1).

Since Edward Jenner's cowpox immunization days, the process of developing a vaccine product—or any other life-science drug or medical device for that matter—has become significantly more complex. Since the 1950s, it has taken an average of 10 years longer to complete the value chain and costs more than twice as much as it had previously (Dimasi, 2010; Ratti & Trist, 2001). As a matter of fact, increasing development times demand even more resources, including financial investment. Estimations of the cost involved for one pharmaceutical product completing the value chain easily surpasses U.S. $1billion (Dimasi & Grabowski, 2007). This statistic also compensates for the investment in discontinued projects, yet such calculations do not usually distinguish between new chemical entities and vaccine products. Several explanations for the extended value chain are listed below (Califf, 2006):

1. International harmonization efforts, the process intended to streamline the value chain at a country-to-country level.
2. The generation of rules that aim to prevent medical incidents.

3. The generation of rules that aim to prevent fraud.
4. A raising of consciousness regarding the realization that vaccine products administered to humans require both ethical regulation as well as adequate business standards.
5. Technological resources and theoretical knowledge on the immune system increases experimental complexity.

On the one hand, there are necessary and legitimate reasons for an increase in both the duration and cost of the value chain. On the other, the value chain has to be flexible enough to allow for quick product development and distribution during the event of an epidemic or pandemic. Developing a vaccine product targeting a viral infectious disease is an unmet medical need within an international political setting. With current modes of transportation, a disease can spread to other continents in a few hours (for example, recent outbreaks of SARS and H1N1). Governments, medical facilities, and industries all over the world are affected and have to respond with appropriate strategies. At the project-level, there are two elements that play an important role: the cost of investment and the statistical chance of a product completing the value chain (see figure 17.1). Developing a vaccine is a lengthy and costly endeavor involving a risk of termination due to unforeseen circumstances (Kola & Landis, 2004). Terminating a project is not an easy decision and represents a burden at the individual and societal level for several reasons. First, the patient population does not receive appropriate treatment. In the case of an infectious disease, human-to-human spread of the pathogen can occur at an uncontrollable rate, posing a public health risk. Second, resources invested in the project are lost. So where does the money come from? A project is financed from several sources including governmental subsidies and venture capitalists, for example. In view of the fact that government subsidies are generated from national taxes, discontinuing a project also affects society at an economic level.

If we regard the value chain as being segmented into various phases, the option of milestone payments for every step are useful as this spreads the risk (see figure 17.1, right). Nearer the ending of a phase, safety and efficacy data is collected in order to decide whether to continue on to the subsequent development stage. One may believe that after the completion of a phase, when more supportive medical evidence is available, the decision to proceed will become easier. Conversely, there is actually more at stake; it is evident that when dealing with an investment of this magnitude, this inherently raises the pressure to succeed the further along the value chain it is. Risk is usually calculated as a product transition percentage (at market level), indicating the amount of products that make the transition from one phase to the next, with the ultimate goal of reaching the market (see figure 17.1, left). These types of calculation are usually retrospective analyses based on historical accounts and are descriptive.

It is believed that the value chain starts with 5,000 to 330,000 candidate molecules during the R&D stage, from which only one molecule attains

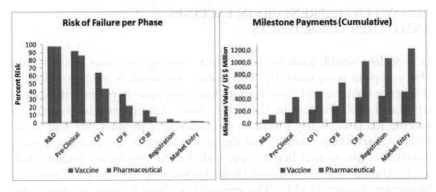

*Figure 17.1* Relationship between project success rate and cumulative milestone investments.

market approval. By combining both the financial investment and transition rates of a product, we attain microlevel context information in the form of a risk profile (see figure 17.2). This information is highly valuable when making decisions on whether to invest in later phases and whether to continue with the project. As seen in figure 17.2, the further along the value chain, the risk correlates negatively with the investment. However, there is no such thing as 100% certainty at any moment, and a project can be terminated for any number of reasons (Kola & Landis, 2004). From the financial perspective, it is crucial to discontinue a project as early as possible. Risk is always relative to something; hence, the figure depicts the risk profile for pharmaceutical products as well. In short, vaccines require a lower investment when compared to biopharmaceuticals. Moreover, it has been estimated that for every vaccine candidate that initiates the value chain at preclinical phase, 22% enter the market as commercial products. This percentage is higher for biopharmaceutical products (Struck, 1996).

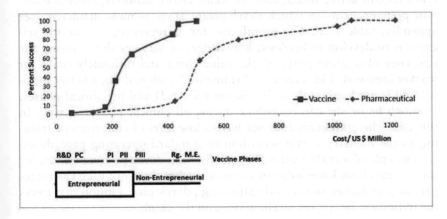

*Figure 17.2* Relationship between project cost and success rate.

## TODAY'S ENTREPRENEURS IN VACCINES
## AND OTHER LIFE SCIENCES

In a perfect world, each initial product entering the value chain would also complete it successfully. Fortunately for small biotech companies, this is not the case and there is room for entrepreneurs to enter the industry and find a position in the value chain. Entrepreneurial activity in vaccine R&D is closely linked to the concept of productivity and innovation. A standard measure for the productivity of the pharmaceutical industry is the annual license approvals by the regulatory bodies, such as the United States Food and Drug Authority (FDA) or the European Medicines Agency (EMA). The approval of these licenses is critical for market entry and is the ultimate goal when starting a project. Since the 1970s, the biopharmaceutical industry has been haunted by a so-called 'productivity gap,' an increasing amount of resources directed at R&D departments with a seemingly limited number of products entering the market (Carney, 2005). Contrary to popular belief, when looking at the graph published in literature (Schmid & Smith, 2005), a positive trend historically has been reported in terms of the productivity of the industry. The data is collected for U.S. pharmaceutical product performance only, however, it is assumed that a similar trend can be observed for any therapeutic category within the global pharmaceutical industry, including vaccines. Nevertheless, it remains a fact that the proportion invested in the value chain compared to the quantity of product approvals is unbalanced. Entrepreneurs can contribute in multiple ways to vaccine development as the various phases of the value chain require different entrepreneurial strategies and skills.

As previously mentioned, Smith and Miner (1983) and Miner, Smith, and Bracker (1992) argue that there are several types of entrepreneur, each with specific managerial motivations and who will establish different firms. Within each stage of the pharmaceutical value chain, all three types remain active throughout the value chain; however, there are certain preferences as to which development stage is most attractive (see appendix, table 17.1). The overall aim for entrepreneurs in the life sciences is to develop technology, knowledge, or services that increase the efficiency of (certain parts of) the value chain and ultimately strive for market approval. The 'craftsman' is involved with making a better product and is predominantly active during the R&D and preclinical phases, although he or she can contribute during all clinical phases as well. In this case, the craftsman does not have a low level of education or training as the industry is run according to standard operating procedures. An example of a craftsman is the scientist who develops compounds; he/she has excellent knowledge of the product but does not take the target patient population into consideration (e.g., developing a lotion that treats the indication but leaves a yellow stain on the skin).

The opportunistic entrepreneur concerned with building the business is most active within the emergence phase of the industry. Although the risk is high, it is within this time frame that the financial benefit accelerates most steeply, and there is ample opportunity to increase efficiency of the value chain and prevent project termination while doing so. From clinical phase III onward, the value chain is less attractive to entrepreneurs; this phase usually has a set outcome and requires approximately 33% of the total value chain budget (PhRMA, 2010). Only under rare circumstances is a project discontinued during a clinical phase III trial. Moreover, a small- to medium-sized firm does not have the financial resources or physical capacity necessary to complete a phase II or phase III trial and aims to be acquired, via a merger or acquisition deal, by the pharmaceutical industry as an exit strategy. From this point onward, entrepreneurship continues in the form of 'intrapreneurship' within the larger pharmaceutical company.

The inventor-entrepreneur, known to 'live for inventing,' also benefits from the window of opportunity during the industry's early stages. He or she is not only able to recognize an opportunity but will also create more efficiency in the process. An example of a current initiative from an inventor-entrepreneur is the Artemis Wildlife Health Institute (ArtemisWildlifeHealth, 2011). If considering epidemiology, it has been estimated that approximately 70% of pathogens descend directly from wildlife or domestic animals (Jones et al., 2008). With this information, entrepreneurs can unify veterinarian and wildlife centers with existing human R&D research units, for example. By developing this type of multidisciplinary interaction, infectious pathogens can be studied and strategies can be designed to identify pathogen transmission more efficiently and rapidly. More specifically, animal-to-human and subsequent human-to-human transmission can be identified using knowledge about the pathogen's underlying genetic changes as well as the predisposing factors that cause or facilitate these events. In this way, emerging epidemic or pandemic threats to public and animal health can be identified more effectively, allowing for intervention strategies to be implemented in a more timely manner.

## CONCLUSION

The objective of this chapter was to explore the distinctive contributions made by the academic inventor and the innovative entrepreneur toward the development of vaccine drugs. The complex phenomenon of science-based venturing describes the relationship between scientific knowledge creation, and its effective commercial and societal exploitation by public and private sector. The historical accounts of Pasteur and Hoffmann indicate two different approaches to science-based venturing: The former was invention driven, whereas the latter was more commercially driven. In the pharmaceutical and biotechnological industry, vaccines are considered a

226 Esther Pronker, Ab Osterhaus, Eric Claassen, and Willem Hulsink

fundamental innovation. Historically, on a global scale, vaccination has contributed greatly to decreasing human mortality rates as a result of infectious diseases and maintaining public health, for example, through the eradication of polio. With an annual compound growth rate of 23% since 2004 (Datamonitor, 2010), this therapeutic intervention will remain an essential part of preserving our health in the future.

The main themes of this chapter address the organization of the value chain during drug development and the roles scientists and entrepreneurs play in it. First of all, as a result of certain medical incidents in the past, the necessary rules and legislation governing the vaccine value chain have shaped it into its current lengthy, costly, and rigid format. Nevertheless, in the case of a pandemic threat, governments, industry, and regulators have to react quickly, requiring the value chain to respond with a certain degree of flexibility. This represents a delicate balance, taking into account the fact that vaccines are administered to healthy individuals and high-risk groups and there is a zero-tolerance attitude toward side-effects. Another theme involves the entrepreneur and the risk profile for vaccine development. Entrepreneurs endeavor to increase the efficiency, innovation, and success of vaccine development during the initial phases of the value chain. Here, entry cost is relatively low and the return on investment is potentially higher, even though there is a high failure rate. Project discontinuation not only represents a social loss (without immunization the spread of infectious diseases cannot be easily controlled) but also societal loss expressed in financial terms. Entrepreneurs are more commonly active during the early stages of the vaccine value chains as this phase offers the main window of opportunity to enter the industry. The fact remains, however, that the investment and productivity trends are not in proportion to one another. Additionally, the value chain is a holistic procedure that requires input from various disciplines and actors. The ultimate goal in life-science venturing is the development of knowledge, technology, and products while abiding by international ethical, safety, and efficacy standards.

## REFERENCES

Andre, F. (2001). Short survey: The future of vaccines, immunization concepts and practices. *Vaccine, 19*, 2206–2209.
Andre, F. (2002). How the research-based industry approaches vaccine development and establishes priorities. *Developmental Biology, 110* (2002), 25–29.
ArtemisWildLifeHealth (2011). http://www.artemiswildlifehealth.eu (retrieved on August 15, 2011)
Califf, R. (2006). Clinical trials bureaucracy: Unintended consequences of well-intentioned policy. *Society for Clinical Trials, 3*, 496–502.
Carney, S. (2005). How can we avoid the productivity gap? *Drug Discovery Today, 10*(15), 1011–1013.
Datamonitor. (2010). Infectious diseases vaccine market overview: Key companies and strategies. Datamonitor Business Intelligence Report No. HC00004–001.

Dimasi, J. Feldman, L. Seckler, A. Wilson, A. (2010). Trends and risks associated with new drug development: success rates for investigational drugs. *Nature Clinical Pharmacology, 2*, 1-6.

Dimasi, J., & Grabowski, H. (2007). The cost of biopharmaceutical R&D: Is biotech different? *Managerial and Decisions Economics, 28*, 469–479.

Dimasi, J., Hansen, R., & Grabowski, H. (2003). The price of innovation: New estimates of drug development costs. *Journal of Health Economics, 22*(151), 185.

Geison, G. L. (1995). *The private science of Louis Pasteur.* Princeton, NJ: Princeton University Press.

Hargadon, A. (2003). *How breakthroughs happen; the surprising truth about how companies innovate.* Harvard: Harvard Business School Press.

Jones, K., Patel, N., Levy, M., Storeygard, A., Balk, D., Gittleman, J., & Daszak, P. (2008). Global trends in emerging infectious diseases. *Nature, 451*, 990–993.

Keech, M., & Beardsworth, P. (2008). The impact of influenza on working days lost: A review of the literature. *PharmacoEconomics, 11*(26), 911–924.

Kola, I., & Landis, J. (2004). Can the pharmaceutical industry reduce attrition rates? *Nature Reviews Drug Discovery, 3*, 711–715.

Lagacé-Wiens, P., Rubinstein, E., & Gumel, A. (2010). Influenza epidemiology—Past, present and future. *Critical Care Medicine, 38*, e1-e9 (Suppl. 4).

Latour, B. (1983). Give me a laboratory and I will raise the world. In K. D. Knorr-Cetina & M. Mulkay (Eds.), *Science observed: Perspectives on the social study of science* (pp. 141–170). London: Sage.

Latour, B. (1988). *The pasteurization of France.* Cambridge, MA: Harvard University Press.

Miner, J. B., Smith, N. R., & J. S. Bracker. (1992). Defining the inventor-entrepreneur in the context of established typologies. *Journal of Business Venturing, 7*, 103–113.

Pharmaceutical Research and Manufacturers of America. (2008). *Profile pharmaceutical industry 2008.* Washington, DC: Author.

PhRMA. (2010). *Pharmaceutical industry profile 2010.* Washington, DC: Author.

Postlewait, A., Parker, D. D., & Zilberman, D. (1993). The advent of biotechnology and technology transfer in agriculture. *Technological Forecasting and Social Change, 43*, 271–287.

Ratti, E., & Trist, D. (2001). The continuing evolution of the drug discovery process in the pharmaceutical industry. *Farmaco, 56*(1–2), 13–19.

Robbins, L. (2001). *Louis Pasteur and the hidden world of microbes.* Oxford: Oxford University Press.

Schmid, E., & Smith, D. (2005). Is declining innovation in the pharmaceutical industry a myth? *Drug Discovery Today, 10*(15), 1021–1029.

Smith, N. R., & Miner, J. B. (1983). Type of entrepreneur, type of firm and managerial motivation: Implications for life cycle theory. *Strategic Management Journal, 4*, 325–340.

Stokes, D. E. (1997). *Pateur's quadrant: Basic science and technological innovation.* Washington, DC: Brookings.

Struck, M. (1996). Vaccine R&D success rates and development times. *Nature Biotechnology, 14*, 591–593.

Wanner, G. A. (1968). Fritz Hoffmann-La Roche, 1868–1920. Basel: Zur hundertsten Wiederkehr seines Geburttages.

# APPENDIX

Table 17.1  Individual-Level and Organizational-Level Involvement During Each Phase of the Value Chain

| Value chain phase | Description | Average length of phase/year | Who is involved: Project level | Who is involved: Organizational level | Funding source [a] | Type of entrepreneur at project level and organizational level | Institutional level |
|---|---|---|---|---|---|---|---|
| Lead discovery, selection, and optimization (R&D) | A process also known as research and development (R&D). Usually occurs *in silico* (computer simulations), *in vitro* (actual experiments in cells), and *in vivo* (animal models). | N/A | Scientist, PhD, professor | Academia, governmental, private biotech laboratory, or in-house | IP fund, pre-seed fund, venture capital | Craftsman, inventor-entrepreneur, opportunistic-entrepreneur | TTO, governmental institution |
| Preclinical phase | Including various subphases *in vivo* (experiments in disease animal models) to determine preliminary quality, toxicity, pharmacodynamics, and dosage profiles. | 1.5 | Scientist, PhD, professor | Academia, governmental, private biotech laboratory, or in-house | Proof-of-concept fund, seed fund, venture capital | Craftsman, inventor-entrepreneur, opportunistic-entrepreneur | TTO, governmental institution |
| Clinical development | Introducing the drug in healthy human volunteers and patients to establish safety, efficacy, and dosage profiles. This step is split up into three phases: I (healthy volunteers), II (small group of target individuals), and III (larger group of target individuals). | Clinical phase I 2.5 | Physician, scientist, CRA | Bioventure, CRO, in-house | Valorization grant, venture capital | Inventor-entrepreneur, opportunistic-entrepreneur | TTO, governmental institution |
| | | Clinical phase II 2.8 | Physician, scientist, CRA | Bioventure, CRO, hospital, in-house | Biotech firm, venture capital | Opportunistic-entrepreneur | |
| | | Clinical phase III 2.6 | Physician, scientist, CRA | CRO, hospital, in-house | Biotech firm, venture capital | Large established firms, corporate entrepreneurs (intrapreneurs) | Pharmaceutical industry |

| | | | | | |
|---|---|---|---|---|---|
| Approval phase | The application for a license has to be submitted by the biotechnology companies to competent authorities. Only after approval can the product enter the market. In America the FDA and in Europe the EMA decide on market entry. | 2 | Marketing and legal | Pharmaceutical industry | Pharmaceutical industry |
| Marketing life-cycle | The process that allows the product to be distributed to the target population. | N/A * | Marketing and legal | Pharmaceutical industry | Pharmaceutical industry |
| Postmarketing approval | Even after the product has entered the market, the product is watched closely for any extremely rare side-effects. | N/A * | Physician, scientist, marketing and legal | CRO, hospital, in-house | Pharmaceutical industry |

CRA Clinical research associate, also known as monitor
CRO Contract research organization, outsourced for completing (parts of) clinical trials
TTO Technology transfer office
N/A Not applicable/not available
* For as long as the vaccine product remains in the market.
a Applies to the Netherlands. This column also includes credits and special tax breaks.

# Contributors

**Marco van Gelderen** is a business psychologist specializing in entrepreneurship. He is currently a senior lecturer at Massey University, Auckland, New Zealand. His lasting affinity with entrepreneurship stems from the fact that it can be related to nearly anything of interest in human life and society. In recent years, Marco started to focus his research as well as his teaching activities on individual-level enterprising competences, such as generating ideas for opportunities, taking action, perseverance, networking and persuasion. He has developed several formats to study and further develop these competences.

**Enno Masurel** (1959) is Professor in Sustainable Entrepreneurship and the director of the Amsterdam Center for Entrepeneurship at VU (ACE@VU). His main research focus is Entrepreneurship and Small and Medium-Sized Enterprises (SMEs), with special reference to innovation. He has attended many international seminars and published in a number of international journals. In an analysis by Technovation (2006) concerning publications in the field of entrepreneurship he ended up in the Dutch Top 3 and in the World Top 8. He teaches entrepreneurship both at bachelor level and master level. He is also supervisor of PhDs in the field of entrepreneurship.

**Frits Schipper** studied physics and philosophy. After his PhD he became lecturer in the philosophy of science. Currently, he coordinates a Masters Program in the philosophy of management and organization (M&O) at VU University Amsterdam. Being a member of two research groups (dep. of philosophy and dep. of economics VU), his research is on philosophical issues in connection with M&O. Areas of interest are creativity and rationality, (corporate) governance, epistemology and knowledge management, philosophy and practice. He is a member of the Executive Editorial Board of the journal Philosophy of Management and chairman of the Vanwoodman Society.

**Karen Verduyn** originally studied Business Administration at the Rotterdam School of Management. After having spent several years in the corporate world, she returned to academia to write her PhD thesis (Tales of

Entrepreneurship, 2007). She remained with VU University and set up a master's degree in Entrepreneurship. She is interested in understanding the complexities of entrepreneurial everyday life. She has published in such journals as the International Journal of Entrepreneurship Education (2003, 2005), the International Review of Entrepreneurship (2009) and the Journal of Enterprising Communities (2010). She is a board member of the International Journal of Entrepreneurship and Small Business.

**A.M.C. Eveline Stam-Hulsink** is a PhD-candidate and lecturer at the department of Organization Sciences, Faculty of Social Sciences, Vrije Universiteit Amsterdam. She equally lectures at the Vrije Universiteit Amsterdam Centre for Entrepreneurship. Her research focuses on strategic embeddedness of entrepreneurial network ties, entrepreneurial social networking behavior and organizational legitimacy generation in the context of Dutch healthcare.

**Dr. Willem Hulsink** lectures in entrepreneurship at the Rotterdam School of Management Erasmus University (The Netherlands) and director of its Centre for Entrepreneurship. His research interests include new venture creation, entrepreneurial networking and strategic management in infrastructural and/or regulated sectors. He has published in among others Small Business Economics, Organization Studies, Technology Analysis & Strategic Management, and International Journal of Technology Management. His book publications include: Privatisation and Liberalisation in European Telecommunications (1999, Routledge); On creating competition and strategic restructuring (with Emiel Wubben, 2003, Edward Elgar); and Pathways to Research Triangles and High-tech Valleys (with Hans Dons, 2008, Kluwer/Springer).

**Bart Bossink** is professor of technology and innovation at the faculty of economic sciences and business administration and the faculty of sciences of VU University Amsterdam. His research primarily concentrates on the management of sustainable technology and innovation and his work intends to serve both science and practice. More than 60 of his papers were published as an article in various scientific and professional journals. One of his books was nominated for best management book of the year in Belgium. An article of his hand received the outstanding paper award from the Emerald Literati Network.

**Gerry Kouwenhoven** was born into a family of entrepreneurs. She obtained a degree in business administration education, and has work experience both in financial institutions, in education and research. As a project manager at INHolland, University of Applied Sciences, and project manager by the research center "Integrated Food and Production Chains" she does research in the areas of entrepreneurship, sustainability, food wastage and value supply chains.

**Sergej Bulterman** (1971) is an economic geographer with 15 years of experience in research and consultancy on spatial-economic topics. He began his career in 1997 as a researcher at the Faculty of Spatial Sciences at Utrecht University. After that he worked for 10 years as a senior economist, and later as a team manager at the Economic Research department of Rabobank Netherlands. At Rabobank he executed dozens of research projects on various topics within the working field of spatial and regional economics. In 2008 Sergej started his own research and consultancy firm called Bureon. From 2008 to 2010 Sergej was also associated with university INHolland where he worked as associate-professor in the readership of "Entrepreneurship in SMEs".

**Dr. Vijayender Reddy** started an entrepreneurial initiative (www.rvjservices.nl) to orchestrate the food value chains between Europe and Asia. He also has a profound interest in value chain orchestration and has recently written a discussion paper on food value chain orchestration a draft of which can be downloaded from the above website. He holds a doctorate in "Value chain management" from the Nyenrode University in the Netherlands. He has extensive (more than 7 years) of research and training experience in the field of value chain management.

**Dr. Caroline Essers** is an Associate Professor Entrepreneurship at VU University Amsterdam. She also works as an Assistant Professor Strategic Human Resource Management at the Radboud University Nijmegen, Faculty of Management. Caroline's research focuses at the social dynamics of entrepreneurship, such as the identity constructions of (female migrant) entrepreneurs and their networking. She uses diverse perspectives in her research on entrepreneurship, such as postcolonial feminist theory and social constructivist approaches like the narrative/life-story approach. Other topics include diversity management and expatriate management. Her work has been published in the Organization Studies, Organization, Human Relations, Gender, Work and Organization, and the European Journal of HRM.

**Yvonne Benschop** is Professor of Organizational Behavior at the Nijmegen School of Management, affiliated with the Institute for Gender Studies at the Radboud University of Nijmegen, The Netherlands. Her current research interests include the role of power and resistance in organizational change, diversity management and gender mainstreaming as organization change and gender practices in networking and impression management. She is an associate editor of Organization and of Gender, Work and Organization. She is a regular speaker on gender and diversity at work at business conferences, and provides policy advice and contract research for government departments and private organizations.

**Dr. Peter Peverelli** is working at the Faculty of Economics & Business Administration at VU University Amsterdam. He studied Chinese Language & Culture at Leiden University. He received a PhD in Arts at Leiden University and a PhD in Business Administration at Erasmus University Rotterdam. He has spent most of his occupational life as a consultant, specializing in cooperation between Western and Chinese enterprises, and has been combining this with academic work since 2001. His leading publication is Chinese Corporate Identity (Routledge 2006).

**Lynda Jiwen Song** is an Associate Professor in Management at the Department of Organization and Human Resources, Business School, Renmin University of China. She earned her Ph.D. at the Hong Kong University of Science and Technology. Her research interests include organizational culture, leadership, employment relationships, creativity, entrepreneurship, emotional intelligence, and cross-cultural studies. Her research has appeared in the Journal of Applied Psychology, Human Resource Management, Journal of Management, Journal of International Business Studies, and Management and Organization Review.

**Karel Davids** (1952) is Professor of Economic and Social History at the VU University Amsterdam. Among his publications are The Rise and Decline of Dutch Technological Leadership. Technology, Economy and Culture in the Netherlands, 1350–1800 (Brill, Leiden 2008), A Miracle Mirrored. The Dutch Republic in European Perspective (Cambridge UP 1995), and numerous articles in international and Dutch refereed journals.

**Dr. Juliette Koning** is senior lecturer at the Faculty of Business, Oxford Brookes University, United Kingdom. She holds a Ph.D. in social anthropology from the University of Amsterdam, The Netherlands. Her current research focuses on business, leadership, identity, ethnicity and religion in Southeast Asia and Indonesia in particular. Books and (co)edited volumes include Generations of Change (UGM Press, 2004), Rope Walking and Safety Nets (Brill, 2006) and Chinese Indonesians and Regime Change (Brill, 2010). Recent publications are contributions to East Asia; An International Quarterly, Inside Indonesia, Copenhagen Journal of Asian Studies and an edited volume on Christianity in Asia (Routledge, 2009).

**Prof. Dr. Heidi Dahles** is full professor in organizational anthropology and director of Graduate School of Social Sciences at the Vrije Universiteit Amsterdam. Her research interest is in transnational communities of ethnic Chinese entrepreneurs. She published in peer-reviewed journals such as the Journal of Enterprising Communities, Culture & Organization, Asian Ethnicity and Journal of Developmental Entrepreneurship. Among her recent books are "Capital and Knowledge. Changing Power relations in Asia" (co-edited with Otto van den Muijzenberg, London: Francis & Taylor, 2003) and "Multicultural Organizations in Asia" (co-edited with Loh Wei Leng; London: Routledge, 2006).

**Carel Roessingh** (1951) studied cultural anthropology and received his Ph.D. at the University of Utrecht. His Ph.D. research was on the Belizean Garifuna. His central research topic now is religious entrepreneurs, focusing on the organizational activities of the Mennonites in Belize and Central America. He works as Associate Professor at the Free University of Amsterdam, Faculty of Social Sciences, Department of Organization Sciences. His publications appeared amongst others in journals as Journal of Mennonite Studies, Journal of Developmental Entrepreneurship, International Journal of Entrepreneurship & Small Business, International Journal of Business and Globalisation, Belizean Studies and he is co-editor of the book Between Horse & buggy and Four-Wheel Drive: Change and Diversity among Mennonite Settlements in Belize, Central America.

**Roy Thurik** is Professor of Economics and Entrepreneurship at Erasmus University Rotterdam and at the Free University of Amsterdam. He is Scientific Advisor at EIM Business and Policy Research (A Panteia company) in Zoetermeer, the Netherlands and visiting professor at GSCM Montpellier Business School in France. He is a Research Fellow at the Tinbergen Institute for Economic Sciences and the Erasmus Research Institute for Management.

**Marcus Dejardin** is Assistant Professor at Université Catholique de Louvain and FUNDP-University of Namur. He is a member of the Centre for Research in Regional Economics and Economic Policy (CERPE), FUNDP-University of Namur, and of the Interdisciplinary Research Centre 'Travail, État et Société' (CIRTES), Université Catholique de Louvain. Marcus Dejardin's research explores the interrelationships between entrepreneurship and regional economic development. He has developed expertise in entrepreneurship, industrial organization—market structures, macroeconomics, and in spatial and regional economics.

**Karima Kourtit** is a researcher and PhD candidate at the department of Spatial Economics at the VU University Amsterdam. In 2007 she received her MBA and MSc in teaching Economics and Business Administration. Her research interests lie in the fields of Creative Industries (CIs), Entrepreneurship, Migration, and Regional and Urban economics.

**Peter Nijkamp** is Honorary Professor in regional and urban economics and in economic geography at the VU University, Amsterdam. He has a broad expertise in the area of public policy, services planning, infrastructure management and environmental protection. In 1996, he was awarded the most prestigious scientific prize in the Netherlands, the Spinoza award.

**Sentini Grunberg MSc** is a medical biologist specialized in management and entrepreneurship in health and life sciences. At the age of 14 she started dancing semi-professionally. Later on her passion for teaching dance became evident. In 2008 she founded dance company InMovement, which is an intermediary between freelance dance teachers and organizations such as schools and enterprises. Because she is also passionate about medical biology she is involved in creating awareness about the importance of health and vitality in order for people to reach their highest potential. Her goal is to add value to society through entrepreneurial solutions.

**Esther Pronker, MSc.** Currently a PhD candidate with international experience and passion for strategic problem solving. Esther graduated with high Honours completing a Bachelor of Science in Immunology and Biochemistry at University College Utrecht in 2007 and two years later she attained her MSc. degree in Management, Policy Analysis and Entrepreneurship in Health and Life Sciences at the Free University of Amsterdam. Esther has completed several (internship) projects successfully, including the topic of Clinical Data Management at the CHDR in Leiden, Health Technology Cost-Effective analyses at Hoffman-La Roche in Basel, Switzerland, and evaluating internal management processes at Johnson & Johnson in Leiden.

**Dr. Eric Claassen** is 10% academic and 90% entrepreneur. He is the winner of the 2009 Dutch 1 million Euro NGI Valorisation Award for 'Excellent deal making with Industry". Furthermore he is active as: President of the Supervisory Board of AM-Pharma BV, Dynomics BV, EC3MA BV, and DC4U BV. CEO/Statutory director of ViroNovative BV Coronovative BV, Viroclinics BV and ML Consultancy BV. He is a member of the SAB of ABN-AMRO life science venture fund FORBION. Among various memberships of committees he is an elected member of the Netherlands Academy of Technology and Innovation (AcTI.nl) and the Dutch Health Council.

**Professor Dr. A.D.M.E. (Ab) Osterhaus** works at Erasmus MC in Rotterdam as Head of the Department of Virology. He is also a professor of Wildlife virology and virus discovery at the University of Utrecht. His research includes studies on virus reservoirs in wildlife, mechanisms of transmission and pathogenesis of viruses. In addition, innovative fundamental research on the natural and vaccine-induced immune response and on antiviral drugs is performed to combat the threat posed by (zoonotic) virus infections. As part of his active interest in public health, he has acted as PhD mentor for ~50 students; (co-)authored over 880 academic articles, created biotech companies and held several editorial positions.

# Index

For Product Safety Concerns and Information please contact our
EU representative GPSR@taylorandfrancis.com Taylor & Francis
Verlag GmbH, Kaufingerstraße 24, 80331 München, Germany